GUITAR INSTRUCTION • TABLATURE

KIRK HAMMETT'S
GUITAR LESSONS
THE SOUND + THE FURY

Recording credit:
Nick Bowcott, Guitar

Cover photo by Scott Uchida
Other photos by Matt Masciandaro and Scott Uchida

PLAYBACK+
Speed • Pitch • Balance • Loop

To access audio visit:
www.halleonard.com/mylibrary

Enter Code
1755-1488-9723-6751

ISBN 978-1-5400-6916-0

Copyright © 2011 Cherry Lane Music Company
International Copyright Secured   All Rights Reserved

No part of this publication may be reproduced in any form or by
any means without the prior written permission of the Publisher.

Visit Hal Leonard Online at
www.halleonard.com

Contact us:
Hal Leonard
7777 West Bluemound Road
Milwaukee, WI 53213
Email: info@halleonard.com

In Europe, contact:
Hal Leonard Europe Limited
42 Wigmore Street
Marylebone, London, W1U 2RN
Email: info@halleonardeurope.com

In Australia, contact:
Hal Leonard Australia Pty. Ltd.
4 Lentara Court
Cheltenham, Victoria, 3192 Australia
Email: info@halleonard.com.au

CONTENTS

Foreword: King Kirk—The People's Champion
What This Book Is About and Why It Was Written 3

Dedication 5

Chapter 1: Indisposable Heroes
Metallica—The Story So Far 6

Chapter 2: Hammett's History
His Story So Far 13

Chapter 3: Under the Influence
The Guitarists and Musicians Who've Inspired Kirk over the Years 16

Chapter 4: Getting into Gear
A Look at the Axes, Amps, and Pedals Kirk's (Ab)Used Throughout His Career 20

Chapter 5: Start Me Up!
Warming up to Get Hot 27

Chapter 6: Harvester of Solos
Lead-Playing Tips and Techniques 36

Chapter 7: Master of Rhythm
The All-Important Art of Rhythm Guitar 70

Chapter 8: Comfort Zone Busters
Getting out of Those Darned Ruts 93

Chapter 9: . . . And Answers for All
Readers Asked, Kirk Answered 99

Epilogue: I Disappear
"Everything You Know Is Wrong" by Kirk Hammett 118

Appendices
Appendix I: Metallica Discography 120

Appendix II: The Usual Stuff About Kirk's Co-Author,
plus the Obligatory "Special Thanks" List 124

Guitar Notation Legend 126

FOREWORD
KING KIRK—THE PEOPLE'S CHAMPION
What This Book Is About and Why It Was Written

In the darkened domain of metal lead guitar, Kirk Hammett is the people's undisputed king. For the past two decades, the guy has dominated "Best Metal Soloist" readership polls in magazines all over the globe. Furthermore, he wins the vast majority of them by a veritable landslide, leaving his peers choking on his vapor trail. How many such polls has Kirk won? Let's just put it this way: It would be far, far easier to list the ones he hasn't won . . . because there really aren't any. In fact, because his stranglehold on such polls is so strong, certain publications have been forced to take him out of the running in order to give others a chance! Let's take the world-renowned monthly *Guitar Player,* for example: After Kirk won their "Best Metal Guitarist" category in 1989, 1991, 1992, 1993, and 1994, they "promoted" him to their "Gallery of Greats," thus making him ineligible in the future.

Further irrefutable proof of Kirk's profound public popularity is this: In 2002, he became the first ever inductee into the *Guitar World* "Hall of Fame"—beating out his own heroes such as Jimi Hendrix, Eric Clapton, and Michael Schenker in the final ballot count. And, as *Guitar World* is the biggest selling publication of its ilk on this planet, when its readership speaks, it does so with an incredibly loud and authoritative voice. Kirk's reaction to such amazing accolades has been typical of his endearing, self-effacing modesty: "I'm flattered, shocked, and dumbfounded. Why me?"

Another great example of our subject's humbleness was his reaction to yet another *Guitar World* Readers' Poll win in 2001. "I just learned that I was voted 'Most Valuable Player' (MVP) in the *Guitar World* '2001 Readers Poll.'" Kirk gushed. "I'd like to say a big and sincere 'thank you' to all of you who voted for me. I've got to tell you, it never ceases to amaze me how much all of you have supported my playing and the band in general . . . and you keep on doing it year after year after year. I guess I've got to keep practicing and working on my playing in case I run into someone and they say, 'Okay Kirk, play something most valuable!'"

Like many metal maniacs, I got first got sucked into Metallica's unique "Damage, Inc." approach to the genre they helped create by their powerful 1983 debut, *Kill 'Em All*. A year later, the band released their sophomore album, *Ride the Lightning*, which not only proved that the promise of *Kill 'Em All* wasn't a fluke, but also served as a firm indication that the quartet weren't even close to fulfilling their potential. As a result, I became a fully-fledged fan—and then 1986's groundbreaking masterpiece *Master of Puppets* morphed me into a full-blown Metallica addict!

Since then I've had the good fortune to interview Kirk for various magazines more times than probably either of us cares to remember—including several *Guitar World* cover stories. The first time we talked was during the English leg of Metallica's breakthrough *Master of Puppets* tour, and I was immediately struck by three things about Mr. Hammett.

1. His genuine respect for the band's fans—an admirable trait shared by the rest of Metallica, I hasten to add.

2. His overwhelming modesty.

3. His infectious enthusiasm for the guitar.

"I practice as much as I possibly can," he told me during that first interview. "Not only because I love playing but because there's always room for improvement. In fact, the more I learn about music, the more I realize just how little I know!"

I'm delighted to report that, after more than 20 years, countless sold-out stadiums all over the globe, and many millions of album sales, absolutely nothing has changed. Kirk is still the same affable guitar nut he's always been and is still 110% dedicated to trying to satisfy his insatiable appetite for more musical knowledge. In fact, such is his dedication that when the band took a well-deserved, short hiatus in the mid 1990s, he enrolled in the City College of San Francisco to study jazz!

In early 1993, Brad Tolinski, the editor of *Guitar World*, had a brilliant brainstorm: "Let's get three of the hottest players out there to write six columns each for the magazine." The trio chosen was Eric Johnson, Dimebag Darrell of Pantera (R.I.P.), and the lead guitarist in the biggest metal band on the planet, Kirk Hammett of Metallica. To a lot of players—let alone one with a touring schedule as hectic as Kirk's—the thought of writing six columns for such a high-profile magazine is both daunting and difficult. Not so for our subject, who graciously accepted the invitation. In the April 1993 issue of *Guitar World*, his *The Sound & the Fury* column made its debut.

By the time those first six columns had run, it was crystal clear to all that both Kirk's and Dime's columns were not only hugely popular, but they also had legs. As a result, Kirk was asked if he wouldn't mind carrying on as a columnist. His answer was an instant "yes!" and *The Sound & the Fury* not only continued, but it developed a life of its own! The first run of Kirk's column ended after 35 installments, in July 1996, when Metallica embarked on another one of their mammoth world tours. But wait, there's more!

Inspired by the large number of fans who had told him how much they liked *The Sound & the Fury* and how much they'd learned from it, Kirk resumed his column in 1999, churning out another 34 quality pieces over the course of the next three years. That brought the total number of columns to a staggering and unparalleled 69—a far cry from the half-dozen initially planned! With Metallica's latest album, *Death Magnetic*, reminding the world just how great a lead player he is, we're keeping our fingers crossed that Kirk will return for a record-breaking third run of his wildly-popular column. Here's hoping.

His fame aside, the thing that truly made Kirk's column resonate with so many *Guitar World* readers was the simple fact that instead of merely using *The Sound & the Fury* as a "here's how to play my riffs and solos" platform, he actually used it to teach—what a concept! Sure, Metallica's riffs and his licks weren't uncommon visitors to his column, but they were *always* used to illustrate a particular technique or playing idea.

Another cool thing Kirk did in his column was answer some of the multitude of questions that readers sent in to him. As a result, no fewer than eight installments—aptly titled " . . . And Answers for All"—were dedicated to answering snail-mail and e-mail questions.

After Kirk's initial six columns had run, I was deeply honored to be asked by the *Guitar World* big-wigs if I wanted to work with Kirk on his column, as they liked what I'd been doing with Dimebag on his. Of course I said "Yes"—actually, "Hell, yeah!" As I've already mentioned, I'd been fortunate enough to know Kirk for a few years, and I knew that this opportunity would be an absolute blast—which, of course, it was. I learned a lot, too, and I got paid to have Kirk show me how he plays his stuff. It was a tough gig, but someone had to do it!

Now, at this point, I must point out one extremely crucial thing. Just as with Dime, my role in Kirk's column was similar to that of a recording engineer in a studio—to merely capture his thoughts and playing on tape, transcribe them, and then make sure he liked the result. Kirk was the artist—the writer and performer. I was merely hitting "record" and then doing some splicing and mixing where necessary.

To this end, once a column's topic was decided, Kirk would talk to me about it at least twice in addition to showing me the examples he wanted to use. Armed with that information, I'd go away, transcribe everything, "mix" the best "takes" from each session into a piece that would fit the page, and then send it back to Kirk for further scrutiny. And, being the pro he is, Kirk would proceed to dot every "i" and cross every "t," often coming back with more suggestions that made the column under construction even better. He did this for each and every installment of *The Sound & the Fury*, which is why he ended up with such an incredibly popular column—and why this book exists.

In the pages that follow, what you will find is the wisdom and advice Kirk shared with us in his 69 installments of *The Sound & the Fury*. This book is the result of a massive exercise in the sacred art of cutting and pasting. Instead of merely reprinting the columns, I've dissected Kirk's impressive body of work and put it into chapters. Also, wherever appropriate, I've used stuff from the many interviews and *Guitar World* "Private Lessons" I've done with Kirk over the years to add even more meat and bones to the subjects covered. Also, as I know you'll be pleased to learn, I've kept as much of it in Kirk's voice as possible—hell, it's his book, not mine!

To further make the book a little better rounded and complete, I've also included a discography plus a brief "The Story So Far" section on both Metallica and Kirk. Although putting this together took a lot of time, thanks to the sheer quality of the material, it never seemed like "work"—in fact, it was a blast! This project also reminded me on a daily basis just how cool Kirk's column was. Anyway, to quote Marty DiBergi, the legendary producer of the classic *Spinal Tap* movie, "Enough of my yapping!" Here's hoping that you have half as much fun reading what follows as I had putting it all together.

Track 1 contains tuning pitches:
1. Standard tuning
2. Standard tuning, down one half step
3. Drop-D tuning, down one half step
4. Standard tuning, down one and a half steps

A Note on the Audio

All examples are performed at a moderate tempo so you can hear the exact phrasing of the riffs, licks, and exercises. Master each one slowly and then build up speed sensibly. As the saying goes, "You can't run before you can walk, and you sure as hell can't walk until you can crawl!" Slow and steady will win this race, and if you want to hear any of the included riffs at speed, it's simple: Listen to Metallica playing them! Enjoy.

DEDICATION

This book is respectfully dedicated to the loving memory of my mother and father, Margaret and John Bowcott. If it weren't for the faith, support, and trust they put behind everything I pursued with passion (regardless of what they thought), none of this would've been possible, let alone happened. Thank you both so much for those priceless gifts. I just hope I can be half the parent you fine folk were. Your memory lives on fondly in my heart and always will. Rest in peace.

CHAPTER 1
Indisposable Heroes
Metallica—The Story So Far

As promised at the very start of this tome—I'm gonna keep this as brief as I can. Why? Well, with over 25 years already under this band's bullet belt, Metallica's story is a vast one that could easily fill a book five times the size of this bad boy and then some. After all, Metallica is more than just a successful band—it's a legendary institution that's capable of selling out enormous stadiums in just about any country with electricity. In fact, the band is not only a household name with its own *Guitar Hero* game, it's also one of the biggest selling acts of all time—the seventh biggest in US history, to be exact. And, as the six acts who've sold more are either extinct or have put out only the rare album, the chances are that by the time you read this, Metallica's stock will be even higher. After all, 2008's *Death Magnetic* passed the million-units mark in the US within the first month of its release, and the band's total album sales worldwide are reported to be in excess of a staggering 100 million.

If you're interested in delving into real detail, the band's story has been well documented in various books, both authorized and unauthorized. Numerous music magazines have also tackled this subject in depth over the years and will no doubt continue to do so, as the Metallica story is hopefully far from over. Also, if you really want to learn more about Metallica, look no further than the band's splendid website, *www.metallica.com*. The "Timeline" section alone is simply staggering!

Just so we're all on the same page, I'm going to take you on a short chronological journey of the main events. I'll also dig a little deeper into the first few years, since that section of the story is a little blurry, thanks to some less-than-stellar articles that have somehow made it to print over the years. Make sense? Good—here we go.

1980-1982

In 1980, a 16-year-old Dane named Lars Ulrich moved from Denmark to Los Angeles. Obsessed with the NWOBHM (New Wave of British Heavy Metal), Lars decided to quit a promising tennis career and replace his racket with a pair of drumsticks.

That summer, Lars put an ad in a local magazine called *The Recycler*, looking for fellow NWOBHM fanatics to jam with. Said ad was eventually seen by a guitarist named James Hetfield. The two met for the first time in mid-1981, but James was underwhelmed by the Dane's playing prowess. "He really wasn't a good drummer," the guitarist told *Playboy* many years later.

Despite this less-than-ideal introduction, later on that year Lars managed to persuade James to join forces with him by promising that he'd secured a spot on a compilation album for his band—even though he didn't have a group at the time! James jumped at the chance, and so Metallica was born.

Where did the band's moniker come from? Lars "stole" it from a local DJ friend, Ron LaQuintana! Ron was looking for a name for a metal fanzine he wanted to put out, and *Metallica* was one of the options. As legend has it, Lars managed to convince Ron that another name on the list was far more suitable for his publication, and the rest is now history.

Here are a few other pivotal Metallica moments from 1980 to 1982.

Metal Massacre

This infamous mid-1982 compilation album featured the first ever Metallica recording, "Hit the Lights." It was put together by one of Lars' first U.S. friends and the mastermind behind Metal Blade Records, Brian Slagel. Ironically, the sleeve notes of *Metal Massacre* had the band's name spelled "Mettallica." The band was listed on the album as James Hetfield on vocals, Dave Mustaine on guitar, Ron McGovney on bass, Lars Ulrich on drums, and Lloyd Grant on guitar. The snarling lead guitarist, Dave Mustaine, was the last member to join the fledgling group. As for Lloyd Grant, he was a local guitar teacher friend who was recruited purely to play lead on the track prior to Mustaine being recruited; one of the two solos recorded was his.

No Life 'Til Leather

A re-recorded "Hit the Lights" along with six other songs—including "Metal Militia," "Seek & Destroy," and "Jump in the Fire"—was put out in 1982 on a demo tape entitled *No Life 'Til Leather*. This time around, though, the band's name was spelled correctly, and the line-up included Ulrich, Hetfield, Mustaine, and McGovney. At the time, underground tape–trading was a huge deal in metal circles (remember—shock and horror—that there was no internet back then!), and the demo made some serious waves, as did a live tape recorded at a San Francisco show in late '82 that was humorously and aptly entitled *Metal up Your Ass*.

Cliff Burton

While looking for a replacement bassist for McGovney, Lars and James saw a monstrously talented and visually captivating bassist, Cliff Burton, perform in LA in late '82. They immediately asked him to join. Cliff said he would, but only if they relocated to his native San Francisco.

1983

With LA being overrun with hair-metal bands and Lars', James', and Dave's keen desire to have Cliff Burton in the band, they relocated to San Francisco and snagged Cliff. At the same time, an East Coast record store owner and metal concert promoter named Johnny Zazula (a.k.a. Johnny Z) heard *No Life 'Til Leather* and flipped out. He tracked the band down, asked to be their manager, and got the quartet to pile into a rented truck and head over to the East Coast to play some shows.

For reasons that have been documented and discussed *ad nauseum*, in early April 1983, Metallica fired Dave Mustaine and handed him a Greyhound Bus ticket back to L.A. Mustaine, of course, went on to form and front the highly successful and influential Megadeth, and remains a much-respected figure in the metal kingdom.

Dave's replacement was a young San Francisco–based axeman who played lead in the fast-rising thrash band Exodus. His name? Kirk Hammett, of course. He flew into New York and, as you know, fit in perfectly. (More details surrounding Kirk's pre-Metallica history and also the full story behind his joining the band can be found in the next chapter of this book.)

With 20-year-old Kirk on lead guitar, Metallica recorded their debut album, *Kill 'Em All* in May 1983; it was released on Johnny Z's recently founded Megaforce Records on July 25th of that year. They then toured the U.S.A. with English label-mates Raven, and did an East Coast run with their good friends, Anthrax.

What were Metallica's live shows like in those early days? I'm going to leave the answer to the late, great, and much-missed Dimebag Darrell of Pantera and Damage Plan fame. *Guitar World* gave me an assignment to ask a bunch of prominent metal guitarists, "What's the best live show you ever saw?" Dime's immediate answer spoke volumes: "The winner on this one would have to be Metallica in Tyler, Texas, in the early '80s on the *Kill 'Em All* tour. It changed my life, dude."

1984–2009

As already stated, from '84 forward the story has been accurately told many times in many places, so the rest of the saga will be covered in a very abbreviated form.

In early '84, the band recorded their second album, *Ride the Lightning*, in Demark. The album proved the band had huge potential, and they were quickly picked up by a major management company, Q-Prime, and a major label, Elektra. After playing in front of 70,000 people at the Monsters of Rock Festival at Castle Donnington, England, in August of 1985, Metallica started to record album number three, *Master of Puppets*.

Master of Puppets was released in February 1986 to great critical acclaim; a lengthy U.S. tour opening for the legendary Ozzy Osbourne followed. The short- and long-term impact *Master of Puppets* had on both redefining the metal scene and influencing a whole new generation of artists is so colossal that it is difficult to quantify. Simply put, the album raised the bar—hugely—and over 20 years later, *Master of Puppets* is still rightly heralded as a pivotal, all-time classic. A good indication of its immeasurable inspiration can be found in the words of one of mod-ern metal's leading lights, Mark Morton of Lamb of God: "*Master of Puppets* was the pinnacle metal record to me. Every song is so ambitious and so epic, even down to the intros. *Master of Puppets* is still an inspiration to me as an artist. That a band so new, young, and relatively inexperienced strived for—and actually achieved—something so huge is pure genius."

Another powerful indication as to the true depth of the influence that *Master of Puppets* had was the fact that in 2006, *Kerrang!* magazine—an English publication regarded by many as the heavy metal bible—did a 20th-anniversary tribute version of the album with well-known bands covering each and every track. Among the acts that took part were Machine Head ("Battery"), Bullet for My Valentine ("Welcome Home (Sanitarium)"), Mastodon ("Orion"), and Trivium ("Master of Puppets"). Matt Heafy, Trivium's frontman, stated that "*Master of Puppets* is one of the most influential albums ever made. . . . Metallica are the main reason why we're here today." This is a sentiment echoed by all artists involved. Diversion over—back to the main story.

On September 27th, 1986, during their highly successful Damage, Inc. tour of Europe, tragedy struck when bassist Cliff Burton was killed after their tour bus skidded and flipped over in Sweden. Shattered, the band returned to the U.S. Knowing that Cliff would want them to continue, after a brief period of mourning, James, Lars, and Kirk started auditioning for a new bassist. Flotsam & Jetsam's Jason Newsted was chosen, and touring commenced almost immediately.

An E.P. of cover tunes was recorded in Lars' garage and released in August '87 with the apt title of *The $5.98 E.P.: Garage Days Revisited*. In January 1988, with Jason as a fully-fledged member of the band, Metallica started recording their long-awaited fourth album, *. . . And Justice for All*. This lengthy, progressive, and technically challenging album was released in August of that year and, despite being completely un-commercial and radio-unfriendly, sales exploded. The band were added to the bill of the Monsters of Rock US tour and blew away every other act on the bill, including Dokken, the Scorpions, and even the headliners, the almighty Van Halen.

In late '88, the band filmed their first-ever music video for the brooding epic "One." Due to sheer public demand, MTV were forced to air it, and sales of *Justice* continued to soar, with the album selling over 1,000,000 in the US alone. "One" was nominated for the first ever "Best Hard Rock/Metal Performance" Grammy category, and the band performed it at the televised Grammy Awards ceremony in February of 1989. To the total disgust and disbelief of the vast majority, the "Best Hard Rock/Metal Performance" Grammy went to Jethro Tull! Go figure. In typical Metallica fashion, all subsequent copies of *. . . and Justice for All* featured a sticker stating "Grammy Award Losers"!

After touring for the better part of two years, Metallica started recording their fifth album in October 1990 with producer Bob Rock—a guy with a radio-friendly reputation, having previously worked with the likes of Mötley Crüe, the Cult, and Bon Jovi. In August 1991, the resulting album, *Metallica* (a.k.a. *The Black Album*) was released, and the first single, "Enter Sandman," became a hit the world over. The band then hit the road hard and stayed there for nearly three (yes, three!) years.

Despite the predictable cries of "sellout" by certain hardcore followers who were expecting . . . *And Justice for All: Volume II*, mainstream metal fans embraced the band's new, stripped-down, and slightly more radio-friendly approach. To date, *Metallica* has sold in excess of 18 million copies worldwide. It also deservedly garnered the band a bunch of awards, including a Grammy, thus righting a past injustice. As if to close the chapter on this truly remarkable period of the band's existence, in late '93 Metallica released a must-have box set, aptly titled, *Live Shit: Binge & Purge*, which featured both audio and video.

After a well-earned break, most of 1994 was spent writing and demoing new material. This process continued until May of 1995 when the band went back into the studio to start recording in earnest. In June '96, the fruits of these labors surfaced in the form of a 79-minute, 14-song album titled *Load*. *Load* also marked a first for the Metallica recording process. In the past, all studio albums represented a division of labor, with Kirk concentrating solely on his solos and James recording all the rhythm work. On *Load* however, the two shared rhythm duties equally. This trend would continue for the next four studio albums. Kirk revealed the following in his November 1999 *The Sound & the Fury*.

> I find it hilarious when people come up to me and say, "Hey Kirk, it's great that you're playing rhythm guitar *and* lead nowadays." The truth is, I've *always* played rhythm—I just never got to record my parts until we made *Load*.
>
> James and I used to be very defined in what we each did in the studio—he'd play all the rhythm parts and I'd play all the leads. Now we've both loosened up and so, instead of effectively being a power trio in the studio with me spewing leads all over the place, we record more like an actual band! And, in addition to me playing more rhythm guitar, James is playing more lead.
>
> Another thing that's changed is this: In the pre-*Load* days, the vast majority of the rhythm parts were one part that was doubled. That's definitely no longer the case. On both *Load* and *ReLoad*, I rarely play the exact same thing James does—instead I try really hard to come up with a part that is completely different than his, but that complements it. For example, when James is doing something like a heavy chug, I'll try to find a different, much lighter part which will help emphasize the heaviness of what he's doing."

As soon as *Load* hit the stores, the band immediately hit the road with a vengeance, continuing way into '97 on a truly spectacular tour featuring stuntmen, two stages, and a two-hour set. Then, midway through that year, the band returned to the studio to put the finishing touches on a glut of material left over from the *Load* writing and recording sessions. This was released as—wait for it—*ReLoad* in November '97. As is their M.O., the band hit the road once again, selling out venues all over the globe with consummate ease.

A faction of old-school Metallica fans consider both *Load* and *ReLoad* to be too mainstream and "safe," and the band also received a considerable backlash due to what was effectively a 180-degree image change: haircuts and an almost glam vibe in certain photos exuded by both Lars and Kirk. That stated, both *Load* and *ReLoad* were critically acclaimed by the press, sold like hot cakes, and won Metallica a whole new generation of fans.

In my opinion, while definitely different, this brace of albums contains some truly classic Metallica cuts such as "King Nothing," "Cure," "2x4," "Fuel," and "Devil's Dance." As already mentioned, the supporting tours were colossal successes visually, sonically, and in terms of sales. The live *Cunning Stunts* video/DVD, filmed at a two-night stand in Fort Worth, Texas, in May '97 and released in late '98 is proof positive of the tremendous live show the band put on during this period.

In true "Workaholica" tradition, instead of taking a break after two back-to-back albums and extensive touring, in late '98 Metallica decided to re-package all of the covers they'd recorded thus far (many for B-sides of singles—remember those?) and also record another 11 of their favorite songs by other artists. The result? The double album *Garage Inc.* released in November 1998.

"Making *Garage Inc.* was a really fun thing for us to do," Kirk stated in his April 1999 column, "It was very recreational and it kinda cleared our heads a bit, too. It was really liberating for us to be able to go into the studio and work on recording stuff that wasn't our own—we could have our way with it and have fun at the same time. The only tough thing about making the album was picking the "new" songs we covered because there were just so many great ones for us to choose from. *Garage Inc.* is gonna be a great springboard for us to leap from when we go in to record our next album because it definitely helped us wipe the slate clean."

With Metallica still clearly driven and eager to work, their next move was not only quick, it was an even bolder one: a collaboration with the San Francisco Symphony Orchestra and renowned composer/conductor, Michael Kamen. Two new songs ("No Leaf Clover" and "–Human") and a batch of classic material including "Master of Puppets," "The Call of Ktulu," and "Of Wolf and Man" were subjected to this unique marriage of two world-class, musical opposites—Metallica and an orchestra. Two shows were performed in April of '98, which were recorded and filmed. Both were released as *S&M* (Symphony & Metallica—get it?) in late 1998 to deserved critical acclaim.

> When the idea was first presented to us by conductor Michael Kamen, we jumped at it because it was something fresh and different. We love exploring new musical avenues, and playing with a symphony orchestra was definitely a challenge. So we sat down and carefully picked out the songs we felt were most suited for a symphonic approach—I mean, you can't take a track like "Whiplash," throw in an orchestra, and expect it to work!
>
> Playing with the orchestra turned out to be one of the most amazing musical experiences I've ever had. It made the songs we played into things they weren't before by bringing a certain beauty to them. We weren't exactly sure how the audience was going to react, but at the end of both nights we got a standing ovation, which told us it was a cool thing for both the band and the audience. Michael scored the whole thing, too, so if we want to, we have the option of taking the music to any orchestra in the world and doing it again.

After the hugely successful Summer Sanitarium stadium tour in 2000, 2001 turned a little dark and stormy for the band. First, bassist Jason Newsted left under a cloud of discontent, and then James Hetfield decided that the time had come for him to enter rehab, take a break, and totally refocus. Kirk dedicated much of his June 2001 *The Sound & the Fury* to answering the slew of "What's going on with Jason leaving?" letters sent in by concerned readers. The column was aptly titled "– Human," and here's what Mr. Hammett had to say on the subject.

> As expected, letters and e-mails have been coming in from all angles regarding the news of our bassist Jason Newsted's decision to leave the band. So, I guess I should speak on this subject a little, as I'm sure many of you are curious. I'm going to do so by answering the following question, which is pretty typical of what's been flooding in.
>
> *Dear Kirk,*
>
> *I'm a huge Metallica fan and look forward to reading your column every month. I was initially going to ask you if the three most recent new Metallica songs, "No Leaf Clover" (S&M), "–Human" (S&M), and "I Disappear" (Mission: Impossible 2 soundtrack), are a good indication of what your next album is going to sound like. Then, just as I was about to submit that question, I heard the crushing news that Jason had quit Metallica. I'm sure this is a difficult time for you guys right now, but I know countless fans like me want to know what's going on.*
>
> *Ken Bruno*
> *Denver, Colorado*
>
> Right off the bat, I can tell you that we are all deeply upset by Jason's decision to leave the band because, as well as being a great bassist, he's like a brother to us. But at the same time, he's doing what he feels is

right for both himself and the band, so I totally respect his choice and wish him well. I can also tell you that we haven't even thought about looking for a new bass player yet—so please stop bombarding us with letters, calls, and tapes! At the moment we're more interested in maintaining our relationship with Jason and making sure everything is cool. And it is. In fact, believe it or not, as strange as it may sound, if anything, we're actually even closer to him than we were when he was in the band!

I don't know if you've read the interview with us that appeared in *Playboy* recently. If you have, even though it's a really good read, I'd like to say that all of us, Jason included, are miles away from where we were when we did that interview. We did that back in September of last year, and we were four completely different guys back then. We're not like that anymore; we've worked through all our shit, we're a lot closer, and it's a really good time to be in Metallica right now. In fact, it feels better to be in this band now than it did in the '90s.

Another thing I can tell you is that now it's just the three of us—James, Lars, and myself. We're more enthusiastic about making our next album than we ever have been before. I feel like we're re-energized now that the situation is different and we've gone through a major catastrophe, which is Jason leaving. Whenever something like this happens, it's always a good opportunity to take a left turn because you're not necessarily carrying the same baggage as you were before. What's occurred has definitely brought the three of us really close. Metallica feels like a brotherhood right now, and it's really strong. In fact, in a weird way it almost feels like the '80s again—like it's us against the world once more, but even more so than ever. It felt like that when we were first starting out, and it started feeling like that a couple of years ago, too, when we cut our hair and started pissing-off people all over again!

As for what we're going to do next: Well, we're just about to start work on the writing stages of the next album, and we're just going to do it as a three-piece. Then, once we've got it all together and we feel like we need a bass player, that's when we'll start looking. We're probably not going to record in a studio this time around either. We're tired of working in studios and that's the bottom line. We're tired of the atmosphere and all the traffic, and we're tired of the traditional approach. So we're going to spend some time researching doing it differently. We want to find an approach we're all comfortable with and can work in without distractions. And, when we find it, I think it'll definitely change the way the new album's going to sound.

Don't worry, though . . . whatever we do will involve the three of us working together. We're not going to be recording separately on our home computers, which seems to be a very popular way to work these days. Our emphasis is definitely going to be on spontaneity and doing things together. Our aim is to use technology to bring us closer together than ever before, rather than have it separate us, which, if you think about it, is what a lot of modern advances seem to be doing to people right across the board now. I mean, cell phones and e-mail are great, and they seem to be bringing us closer together, but in a strange way they're really pushing us further away from each other because no one seems to actually talk face-to-face anymore.

As Kirk's well-written words predicted, Jason's departure and James's self-imposed leave-of-absence, while being serious setbacks, instead of breaking the band, eventually served to make Metallica even stronger.

In early 2002, with James back in the fold, the band began working on their next studio project, *St. Anger*, with longtime producer Bob Rock handling bass duties. In February 2003, after a period of closed auditions, Metallica recruited ex–Suicidal Tendencies/Ozzy Osbourne bassist Robert Trujillo. *St. Anger* was released in early Summer 2003. The exact opposite of radio-friendly, *St. Anger* entered the US charts at #1 but was greeted by an incredibly mixed reaction from both the public and the press. Some critics hailed it as a true classic while others stated the exact opposite due to its primal rawness and complex, almost chaotic nature. Indeed, the metal masses were so divided over it that *St. Anger* had the unique "honor" of being voted both "Best Album of the Year" and "Worst Album of the Year" in several readers' polls in prominent magazines.

To most fans, myself included, the hardest thing to grasp about *St. Anger* was the fact that it was totally devoid of guitar solos. To the vast throng of Kirk Hammett worshipers, this was a bitter pill swallow. Needless to say, regardless of whether you loved or hated *St. Anger* or the soul-bearing *Some Kind of Monster* 2004 film that showed the band at their lowest ebb, it netted them yet another Grammy and the resulting 18-month tour was a colossal global success. Plus they got to be on an episode of the classic cartoon TV series, *The Simpsons!*

With the exception of some scattered live shows and festival appearances, the next couple of years were relatively quiet by Metallica standards. In 2007, they started working on their ninth studio album. When Kirk announced in the press that it will sound like a cross between *. . . And Justice for All* and *Metallica* and will feature solos, needless to say, public anticipation was sky-high. The release of *Death Magnetic* in September 2008 did not disappoint. With James back to recording all of the rhythm tracks, Kirk was left to work on solos. The result? *Death Magnetic* is bursting with Hammett solos and chockablock with old-school Metallica riffing and arrangements. Both the press and the public were united in their reaction, proclaiming it a truly classic Metallica album. "We needed to reboot, we needed to reset everything," Kirk concluded. Amen.

On April 6th, 2009, Metallica was deservedly inducted into the hallowed Rock and Roll Hall of Fame. The fact that the band's performance at the ceremony included Jason Newsted as a guest on "Master of Puppets" and "Enter Sandman" was a truly magnanimous and touching gesture. "Dream big and dare to fail, because this is living proof that it is possible to make a dream come true," said Hetfield in his emotional acceptance speech.

2009 also saw the band get another four Grammy nominations, and they won in two categories—"Best Rock Instrumental Performance" for "Suicide and Redemption" and "Best Rock Album" for *Death Magnetic*. This pair brought Metallica's Grammy Awards total to an impressive nine.

As I finish this project in the beginning of 2010, Kirk, James, Lars, and Robert have spent much of the year doing what they do best—touring the world—and both old and new Metallica fans couldn't be happier. Summer 2009 also saw the band dominate Europe's busy festival calendar with their own series of sold-out, multiple-band, one- and two-day events under the moniker of Sonisphere.

And, if that's not enough, in December 2009, a truly historic Sonisphere announcement was made. In June 2010, the legendary "big four"—the quartet of bands responsible for spawning the thrash metal genre—will play together for the first time in history. Those four bands are, of course, Slayer, Anthrax, Megadeth, and Metallica. At the time of penning this tome, only two dates have been announced, in Poland and the Czech Republic. Here's hoping that this historic occurrence will hit other countries, too. As Scott Ian, Anthrax's rhythm ace, stated, "People have been talking about these four bands playing together since 1984. That's 26 years of expectation! I believe not only will we live up to the expectations, we will shatter them! No other four bands as influential as the four of us have ever done this. Imagine if the Beatles, the Stones, the Who, and Zeppelin had done shows? Or Sabbath, Priest, Maiden, and Motorhead? Well, I may be getting into some rarified air here, but as a fan, that's how big I feel this is."

Whatever does or doesn't happen with the Big Four tour, here's hoping that Metallica will continue to kick ass, innovate, and reign over the metal kingdom for many years to come.

CHAPTER 2
HAMMETT'S HISTORY
His Story So Far . . .

Kirk was born on November 18, 1962, in San Francisco, and grew up in the East Bay town of El Sobrante. The middle child of three, Kirk first got interested in rock music thanks to his older brother Rick and his vast record collection. "I used to hang out with him and his college friends and also listen to a lot of the same music he did back then: Jimi Hendrix, Led Zeppelin, Cream, Jethro Tull, Black Sabbath, Deep Purple, and Santana," Kirk recalls. "Rick also had a guitar, a red Gibson SG. When I was about nine years old, I remember picking it up one time when he wasn't around, plugging it in and banging around on it. I didn't touch the guitar again for another six years after that, though."

Kirk continues, "When I got into buying albums, I started playing air guitar. Then I decided to do the real thing. I got my first guitar from a friend of mine when I was 15. I traded him a copy of the *Dressed to Kill* KISS album and $10 for a piece-of-shit Montgomery Ward catalog special." The first song he learned how to play? "'Calling Doctor Love' by KISS, then 'Purple Haze.'" Kirk replies. "My real triumph was 'Whipping Post' by the Allman Brothers, which took about six months to learn! I was listening to all the popular stuff at the time—Hendrix, Thin Lizzy, and Aerosmith. Then, when I heard UFO, I was totally blown away. *Obsession* had just come out and it inspired me to go out and buy all their albums—I spent the next two years trying to play Michael Schenker solos!"

Another thing that was a huge factor in Kirk picking up the guitar was seeing bands perform live in concert. "I started going to shows when I was 14," he recalls. "One of the very first bands I got to see was Thin Lizzy on their *Live & Dangerous* tour. I saw them at Winterland in San Francisco, and they were just incredible." Other live acts that left a lasting impression on the young Hammett included Lynyrd Skynyrd, Peter Frampton, Santana, and the British legend, Robin Trower.

Not being one to hang around, once he started playing, Kirk began collaborating with other musicians almost immediately. The following story concerning his first band is one he relayed to me for a multiple-artist story that appeared in the September 2000 issue of *Guitar World*. The piece was aptly entitled "Garage Days Revisited: A bevy of modern and classic rockers take a look back at their first bands—when amps were 10 watt, P.A. systems were scarce, and gigs even scarcer." Here's Kirk's amusing tale in his own inimitable words.

> I started playing in a group pretty much as soon as I got my first guitar. After I'd been playing it for all of about two weeks, I figured it was time to get in a band, which I did with some friends of mine. We called ourselves Strombringer. The only trouble was I didn't have an amp, the bass player didn't have one either, and the singer didn't have a mic, let alone a P.A. So we went to the band room at school and asked if we could borrow their Univox bass amp and a microphone. They said okay, so we took this huge orange and blue amp back to my friend's garage. It had four inputs, so we all plugged into it and started jamming on the only two songs we knew: "Wild Thing" and "Purple Haze." And after 15 minutes or so, the amp blew up!
>
> So we quietly took it back to school, put it in the back room, and then snuck away. The great thing was that the bass player on the school jazz band at the time was a guy—named Les Claypool, incidentally!—who played standup bass. So, he didn't need an amp, and the school didn't even notice the amp was broken! After a few months, I got kicked out of the band because I wasn't good enough. I wonder whatever happened to those guys?

> As a kid I'd solo over anything. I'd spend hours noodling away to whatever was on the radio and that habit carried on pretty much throughout the '80s. I was one of the biggest nerds in high school. Myself and John Marshall (one-time Metallica roadie who went on to play guitar in Metal Church) were outcasts because we had long hair and didn't conform. I only had a few friends and I never went to any football games, a prom, or anything. Me and John basically went straight to my house after school each day to play guitar.

Despite the "piece of shit" quality of his first instrument, Kirk stuck with it and got his first "real" guitar a few years later, which was a blonde '78 or '79 Fender Strat. "My Mom was making payments on it, and we couldn't afford a case so I used to carry it around wrapped in a black garbage bag!" Kirk laughs. After experimenting with the Strat for a while, thanks largely to his already-admitted obsession (bad pun not intended!) with Michael Schenker, Kirk fell in love with a black 1974 Gibson Flying V. "I got it from Leo's Music in Oakland," Kirk recalls. "I got myself a job washing dishes at a country club to pay for it. It took me eight months to save up enough money to buy the V." As soon as the 15-year-old could afford his dream guitar, he promptly bought it. With his mission accomplished, Kirk also promptly gave up his dishwashing job.

As far as getting a good amp was concerned, Kirk took a job at Burger King in order to buy his first Marshall. "As soon as I'd saved enough money up, though, I quit" he confesses. While doing his Burger King stint, Kirk formed a band called Exodus with a singer named Paul Baloff (R.I.P.). These thrashers caused quite a stir on the Bay Area metal circuit and played with Metallica a few of times in the early '80s.

On April 1, 1983, Kirk got a call from Metallica asking him if he'd like to audition for the band, as they were on the verge of firing Dave Mustaine. Kirk agreed, bought a plane ticket, and headed for New York. The audition obviously went well. "I played my first gig with them a week later." Kirk states. "Actually, they never officially told me I was in the band. I didn't actually figure I was until we were in the studio making the album! I only had four or five days to do my leads and I remember thinking, 'that means two solos a day.' Because of that, I didn't have much time to think about it. I'd just throw down a lead and then move on."

As already revealed in these pages, Kirk is totally dedicated to his instrument and is always looking for ways to improve. In addition to studying classical guitar in high school, as soon as the *Kill 'Em All* tour was completed, he started taking lessons from a local San Francisco teacher who you may well have heard of—a guy named Joe Satriani. "I've known Joe since '83. I used to bring him guitar solos, and we'd go through them and tear them apart. I took about 20 lessons on and off over the course of about five years. I would've taken more, but I never had enough time because I was always touring. Eventually, I stopped bringing him stuff to show me and we just concentrated on theory. Joe showed me how to use modes and what scales to play over what chords. I learned a lot of finger exercises from him as well."

As already mentioned in the introduction to this book, in the mid '90s Kirk attended college to study jazz, and in more recent times he has taken lessons from a local jazz teacher named Scott Foster to help fine-tune his jazz chops.

> The whole concept of playing guitar is amazing to me because there's just so much to learn out there. One of the greatest things about music in general is that there's just so much great stuff to learn out there. Every single time I think I've learned something that's really cool and is the be-all-and-end-all of everything, it doesn't take me long to realize that it's only just the very tip of the iceberg and there's a whole lot more to learn. It definitely gives me a goal to shoot for, because I always feel I could do better. I'm the kind of guy who believes there's something to learn from every guitar player, because every player approaches his instrument differently. I guess I'll be playing forever . . . in fact, I'll probably be buried in a guitar-shaped coffin!

In addition to his self-confessed, six-string addiction that forces him to play guitar "at least 361 days a year," Kirk is also an avid horror comic and movie buff. In fact, his San Francisco abode boasts an impressive array of

Hollywood memorabilia. "I collect vintage horror comics, artwork, toys, and movie posters," he once told me. "My collection is enormous and it defines part of who I am. In fact, if I was never in this band, I would probably be running a comic store that sells horror and monster stuff! I guess I've always had a pretty morbid fascination, and it manifests itself in some strange ways. For example, I love dark furniture, old houses, and antiques. Plus, I invariably wear black 24 hours a day."

Kirk's dark leanings are also reflected in the artwork on some of his favorite custom ESP guitars—particularly "The Mummy" and "Ouija." And speaking of guitars, who are some of the key players who initially inspired Kirk to pick up the instrument, and who are those who continue to make him do so? Read on.

CHAPTER 3
UNDER THE INFLUENCE
The Guitarists and Musicians Who've Inspired Kirk over the Years

Many, many moons ago I remember reading an interview with one of my first guitar heroes—Ritchie Blackmore of Deep Purple and Rainbow fame. In it, he said something I thought was so profound that it has stuck with me ever since. It went something like this: "If you really like a particular guy's playing, then don't study what he does; find out who his influences are and then study them." Research the players who influenced your influences? Wow, what a concept!

To this end, let's do the same with Kirk. As already revealed in the previous chapter, some of his earliest influences included Jimi Hendrix, Aerosmith, Cream, KISS, Led Zeppelin, and Thin Lizzy, plus Michael Schenker of UFO and MSG fame. Let's drill a little deeper into what makes Kirk pick by looking at a column he penned, aptly titled "Under the Influence." This revealing expose appeared in the July 2001 issue of *Guitar World* and spilled over into the August 2001 installment of *The Sound & the Fury*.

> When I first started playing guitar I was around 15, and I don't mind admitting that a lot of my initial influences came courtesy of my older brother's album collection. He'd listen to stuff by Hendrix, Zeppelin, Aerosmith, ZZ Top, and the Rolling Stones all the time and being exposed like that definitely had an impact on me. One of the records I always looked forward to him putting on was the *Bluesbreakers (John Mayall with Eric Clapton)* album, especially the song "Hideaway." Clapton's ability to say something with just one note made him a big early influence of mine. Funnily enough though, having said this, as amazing as Clapton's version of "Hideaway" is, I actually prefer Freddie King's original (on the *King of the Blues* CD). Man, I love that song, it's really uplifting.
>
> Like pretty much every rock guitarist in my generation, Ace Frehley of KISS definitely had an impact on me in my early days. In fact, the first song I ever learned was "Calling Doctor Love" [*Love Gun*] by KISS! Jimmy Page, Jimi Hendrix, Jeff Beck, and the Allman Brothers were also big early influences—you know, the usual suspects! I also improvised a lot. Back then, I would try and solo over literally anything and I'd spend hours noodling away to albums and whatever was on the radio. I had a couple of friends who were learning to play, too, and every day after school we'd go home, put on the latest UFO, Pat Travers, ZZ Top, or Scorpions album, and just play along with them. We'd jam for ages, learning whatever we could from what we were listening to and from each other. It probably sounded like crap, but we didn't care because we were having a blast!
>
> As well as playing along to records, going to concerts used to inspire the hell out of me, and it still does to this very day. The first band I ever got to see play live was Thin Lizzy on their *Live & Dangerous* tour, and it was amazing. The band's two guitarists, Brian Robertson and Scott Gorham, blew me away. As I've said many times, I just love the way Brian Roberson uses the wah pedal. In fact, I don't mind admitting that my solo in "Enter Sandman" *(Metallica)* is basically me trying to be him! My goal was to capture the same kind of wah intensity that he played with, and there's even a couple of his licks in there which no one has ever seemed to pick up on . . . until now of course!
>
> Another gig I remember going to that had a huge impact on me was the 1978 "Day on the Green" festival in Oakland when AC/DC, Van Halen, Pat Travers, and Aerosmith were all on the bill. There I was, a young kid, barely able to play a barre chord, and all these bad-assed guitarists were appearing together under one roof—Joe Perry, Brad Whitford, Angus Young, Pat Travers, and Eddie Van Halen! As you can imagine, it was one of the most influential shows I've ever seen.

I've already called-out a lot of great guitarists, but if I had to pick just four rock players who were major influences—not counting Jimi Hendrix, Stevie Ray Vaughan, and Brian Robertson, of course—I'd probably have to say Billy Gibbons, Ulrich Roth, Carlos Santana, and Michael Schenker. Here's why.

Billy Gibbons

Looking back, this guy has been a much bigger influence than I actually thought he ever was! As far as having great tone and just playing with a lot of soul goes, Billy just has *it*. He's the perfect example of a guitar player who's playing for the song and not playing for his own ego. He's the master of understatement who makes you realize that it's all about the feel and how you actually hit the notes, rather than how many notes you actually play.

Ulrich Roth

The first time I ever heard him with the Scorpions, I was totally floored. His clarity, dynamics, tone, and technique were all flawless, and his use of arpeggios, modes, and harmonic minor scales were way ahead of their time. Ulrich's playing inspired me to learn new scales/modes and study theory, too. He also got me into learning three-octave scales. I used to wish I could play some of his solos note for note, and I still do! His lead in "Sails of Charon" [*Taken by Force*] is totally amazing and is a wonderful example of how to use the harmonic minor scale to maximum effect.

Carlos Santana

I just love him to death! He's been a massive overall influence on me—not just as a guitar player, but as an overall musician. He preaches the gospel of Miles Davis and Jimi Hendrix and Bob Marley, and I'm delighted that he's finally gotten the recognition he's deserved all along. He's done it on his own terms, too, which is another thing that I respect about him. He's always done what he's wanted to do and has always followed his gut rather than his wallet.

Michael Schenker

This guy influenced me so completely that it will always be with me. I studied his playing for the longest time . . . seven or eight years straight. I mean, even by the time *Master of Puppets* came out, I was still trying to learn some of his guitar solos! I still listen to him today, actually. In fact, myself and John Marshall were just listening to a song on UFO's *Obsession* L.P. called "Born to Lose" that has an incredible guitar solo. Even after all these years, Michael Schenker still has the ability to inspire us by just reaching out and saying, "This is the way it should be done, boys!"

I learned a lot about phrasing and sense of melody by listening to Michael. He knew how to play with incredible economy and taste, and when he wanted to play real fast he did so with a level of expression that not a whole lot of guitar players are capable of. Whenever he blazed, it was never just a flurry of notes—it was always incredibly melodic and expressive, and full of little sections you could single out and hum because they would stick in your mind. When I finally got to meet him in 1998, I immediately told him how I learned everything he did when he was in UFO and MSG and how I tried to get his sound by buying a Flying V, Marshalls, and wah pedals. In a weird way it was like meeting Santa Claus, as far as I was concerned—that's how much influence he had on me!

In addition to being a great soloist, Michael Schenker is also responsible for one of the greatest rock riffs ever written: "Rock Bottom" [*Phenomenon*, studio version; *Strangers in the Night*, live]. I just love the sheer energy, feel, and heaviness it exudes—it's definitely a seminal riff for me. If you've never heard this guy play, do yourself a favor and check out the live UFO album, *Strangers in the Night*. His solo on "Rock Bottom" alone is worth the price of the CD!

Now that's what I call "drilling deep." And speaking of that, in 1996, *Guitar World* gave me an assignment to ask several leading rock guitarists what their favorite albums were. One of the guys I spoke to was Kirk, and his choices were eclectic and often unexpected. Here's his list and the rationale behind each of them.

Jimi Hendrix: *Electric Ladyland* and *Band of Gypsys*

These are both genuine classics—especially *Electric Ladyland*. There hasn't been enough said about this album but, at the same time, there's been too much said! *Electric Ladyland* is akin to a musical encyclopedia, and I find it incredibly inspirational. I love *Band of Gypsys* for the total over-the-top spontaneity and moodiness that runs throughout the whole damn thing.

UFO: Every Single Album with Michael Schenker on it!

Michael has a very European-sounding style in that it is blues based, touches on a lot of modal ideas, and also has a classical bent to it. His amazing phrasing is brilliant, and he always manages to be very articulate with a whole lot of notes—he never resorts to wanking.

Christopher Parkening: *Christopher Parkening: Guitar*

This is a classical guitar album and contains some of the greatest playing I've ever heard. He plays a lot of classic pieces from different periods and style. Some of the material has never been interpreted on guitar before.

John Coltrane: *Ballads, Giant Steps,* and *A Love Supreme*

I've mentioned three albums by Coltrane because his playing is very similar to a guitar player's. The first time I heard *Giant Steps,* it blew me away. It sounded like Eddie Van Halen on steroids. *Ballads* stands out the most for me because it's just so lyrical, atmospheric, and romantic. I love playing along with it.

King Crimson: *Thrax*

I always thought that King Crimson was a "math rock" band, but I never really listened to any of their stuff until I got *Thrax*. The first song on it was so heavy and aggressive I literally freaked out. The concept on the album is two "power trios" playing together, and the result is amazingly powerful. The songs are great, too, and the interplay between Robert Fripp and Adrian Belew is just nuts!

Stevie Ray Vaughan: *Texas Flood*

For all the obvious reasons—great tone, great phrasing, great attitude, great songs, and great playing. He's an endless source of inspiration.

Carlos Santana and John McLaughlin: *Love, Devotion, Surrender*

The collaboration between these two great guitarists on this album is very inspiring. They do two John Coltrane songs, and the way they weave Coltrane licks with their own is amazing—they're pushing each others' limits.

Robert Johnson: *The Complete Recordings*

You can tell where it all came from by listening to him. He's just the granddaddy of them all. His only pal was his guitar, and he sang about the devil, drinking, and womanizing years before it was "cool"—sounds like my kinda guy!

David Bowie: The "Eno Trilogy" of Albums: *Low, Heroes,* and *Lodger*

On these albums the collaboration between Bowie and Eno is so strong, the guitar is out of the limelight. As a result, the guitarists, including Robert Fripp, have to play with a lot more space and come up with different textures that work with all the electric stuff. I guess I also have to throw in *Scary Monsters* for good measure, too, because Fripp's playing on it is totally amazing. He was doing burning arpeggios way before cats like Yngwie. I'm a huge Fripp fan nowadays—his whole approach to guitar is like a mad scientist's.

Uli Roth: *Electric Sun, Fire Wind*, plus *Virgin Killer* and *Taken by Force* by the Scorpions

Uli Roth has the whole thing down: his technique, his tone, the Hendrixisms mixed with that Euro-classical style of modal playing. He wrote some incredible stuff, too, and did some amazing whammy bar work that was way ahead of its time. I think he influenced a lot more people than he's given credit for.

To close this section, here's Kirk's answer to a couple of reader's questions that were inspired by this very topic.

Dear Kirk,

The "Under the Influence" stuff you did in the July 2001 and August 2001 issues was incredible! Based on your enthusiastic words I recently added Thin Lizzy's Live & Dangerous *and UFO's* Strangers in the Night *live CDs to my collection—they're both awesome albums and Michael Schenker is fast becoming one of my all-time favorite axemen. Are there any current guitarists you like, too? I'd really love to know and I'm sure I'm not alone.*

Bobby "Red" McFadden,
Long Island, NY

Dear Red,

I'm delighted to read that my "Under the Influence" column got you into Michael Schenker—what a phenomenal (bad pun not intended!) player he is! In case you're interested in exploring his playing more, when he left UFO he formed his own band called MSG (the Michael Schenker Group) and did some pretty amazing stuff in that, too. There's a compilation CD out called *Essential Michael Schenker Group* that contains a lot of killer Schenker playing, including his instrumental tracks "Into the Arena" and "Captain Nemo." The MSG live album, *One Night at Budokan,* is well worth checking out, too.

As for your "Are there any current guitarists you like?" question, the answer is a definite "Yes." As I'm sure I've already pointed out in this column, I really, really like Tom Morello and his weird guitar sound thing—he's definitely raised the pole a little higher for everyone! To my mind he's the modern-day equivalent of Eddie Van Halen in terms of breaking new ground. Even though the last Rage Against the Machine album, *The Battle of Los Angeles,* is a couple of years old now, I still can't enough of it—I just love it.

I really like the rhythm work Dino [Cazares] does in Fear Factory a lot; he's just a monster. And talking of monsters, Dimebag Darrell from Pantera is a killer guitarist and is one of the few newer guys out there that still plays lead! I also like the guy in Perfect Circle, Billy Howerdel—he's not so much a great lead player as he is a great rhythm player. The way he orchestrates modern sounds on the album *Mer de Noms* is something he does really well.

Another newer guy whose playing I respect a lot is Kenny Wayne Shepherd. He has a great sound and a great feel—he's got that whole "heavy strings, high action, big frets, and percussive attack" thing happening. I've heard some people put him down by saying that there's no way he can possibly play the blues because he's too young. Well, as far as I'm concerned, that whole "too young to play the blues" attitude is nonsense—age has nothing to do with it. Playing the blues is all about tapping into emotions that we're all born with, and that's exactly what Kenny's doing.

CHAPTER 4
GETTING INTO GEAR
A Look at the Axes, Amps, and Pedals Kirk's (Ab)Used Throughout His Career

Like the vast majority of electric guitarists, regardless of genre, Kirk is on that seemingly never-ending quest for the perfect tone . . . or tones! And, after clocking in more than a quarter of a century with Metallica, as you can imagine, he's been through a staggering amount of guitars, amps, and pedals—both on stage and in the studio. Not surprisingly, to go through each and every axe, amp, and pedal he's (ab)used in that time would make for a sizeable, stand-alone book, and that's just not possible or practical here. That said, here are some of the pivotal gear essentials that have aided and abetted Kirk during his journey on that endless road to tonal perfection, presented chronologically, album by album.

Note: Although it's already been stated elsewhere in this tome, it is once again worth reminding you that on all of Metallica's studio albums aside from *Load*, *ReLoad*, *Garage Inc.*, and *St. Anger*, Kirk didn't record any rhythm tracks. James "Captain Crunch" Hetfield covered that ground, leaving Kirk to concentrate 100% on his lead work.

Kill 'Em All (1983)

"I used 'James's magical, mythical Marshall' head on that one. It had been hot-rodded by Jose Arrendondo, the same LA guy who modded Eddie Van Halen's Marshalls, and we considered it to be *the* Marshall at the time. It had a really incredible sound, and I refer to it as 'James's magical, mythical Marshall' because it got stolen after we did some shows in Boston, so it's not around anymore. When it came time to do my leads, I just plugged into that with my trusty old Ibanez Tube Screamer, wah pedal, and my 1974 black Gibson Flying V." Kirk's V had an old '57 humbucker in the bridge position, and he also used a Boss distortion pedal on certain leads.

Ride the Lightning (1984)

"Once again we were using Marshall amps," Kirk states. "If I remember correctly, I tracked the whole album with Marshalls and my Gibson Flying V." He also used his Boss distortion pedal and a T.C. Electronics EQ.

Master of Puppets (1986)

"This one was tracked with a combination of a Mesa/Boogie amp Mark II-C head and Marshalls. I used my Gibson Flying V, my black Jackson Randy Rhoads Custom Shark Fin [loaded with EMG 81 pickups], and also a black mongrel Strat with a Fernandes body, EMGs [an 81 humbucker in the bridge and two single coils], a Floyd Rose, Gotoh tuners, and an old Charvel neck. I was going to put a Fernandez sticker on it, but then I decided to rename the guitar 'Edna'—our name for groupies back in the day," Kirk grins. "I also used an Aria Knight Warrior that I tuned down to C# to play 'The Thing That Should Not Be.'" If you've never seen "Edna," check out the cover of the next release.

Garage Days Re-Revisited (1987)

By this time, Kirk had begun his longstanding relationship with ESP guitars that's still going strong to this very day. Although he now has a great many ESPs in his arsenal, his first one was a 1987 black Custom with EMG 81 pickups in both lead (bridge) and rhythm (neck) positions, sporting a Floyd Rose locking system and skull-and-crossbones fretboard inlays on its reverse headstock neck—an axe often fondly referred to as "Skully" for this very reason. It also sports a "Caution" sticker on it. "That E.P. was recorded when I first started using ESP guitars, and all my lead parts came together really quickly," he recalls. "'Skully' has been my mainstay ever since then."

. . . And Justice for All (1988)

"I used a Mesa/Boogie power-amp, an ADA preamp, and an Aphex Parametric EQ on the album," Kirk told *Guitar World* in the early '90s. As per his usual MO, in addition to his growing arsenal of ESP axes, Kirk also stomped on an Ibanez Tube Screamer from time to time, plus a Dunlop wah pedal or five!

Metallica (1991)

Kirk's main guitars for this one were his custom ESPs. That stated, he did use a few other makes of axe for different tones and textures, including several Gibson Les Pauls—an "off-the-rack" '89 black Custom and producer, Bob Rock's '71 blonde model for the solo in "Sad but True." He also used a '61 Fender Strat into a Fender Deluxe combo for his clean sound.

When it came to distortion on *Metallica*, Kirk blended amps to create his tone—a Bradshaw preamp into a VHT power amp driving a Marshall 4x12 for his mids and lows, plus a couple of modified vintage Marshall heads for the highs. For once, he didn't use an Ibanez Tube Screamer, and he used an old Vox wah as opposed to his usual Dunlop Cry Baby.

Load (1996) and *ReLoad* (1997)

"I was experimenting so much with tone on those albums that I had to keep journals on what equipment I was using on each track," Kirk grins. "We literally dragged out tons of guitars, amps, and effects." As a result, even though, once again, his 1987 ESP Custom was a principal guitar on *Load*, Kirk used a lot of other axes, including a '58 Gibson Flying V, a '63 seafoam green Fender Strat, a '60s Les Paul Junior, a Parker Fly, and a '58 Les Paul Standard loaded with PAF pickups. "PAFs have a warmth and clarity that you just can't get from anything else," Kirk reports. He also plugged a Roland VG-8 into a Roland Super JV synth module plugged into his Marshalls for texture in places, and used a '63 Gibson ES-335 for some slide work.

The collection of amps Kirk plugged into to record *Load* was equally large, and included a Matchless Spitfire, a Vox AC30, Fender Twin Reverb, a Dumble, and several vintage Marshalls. That said, "70% of my overall amp sound was Boogie stuff," Kirk reveals. The "Boogie stuff" in question? A Triaxis preamp, plus MarkIIC and Triple Rectifier heads.

As far as effects pedals and rack units go, name one and it was probably used during the *Load* and *ReLoad* sessions! From gnarly, vintage stompboxes to cutting-edge digital technology—often blending the two worlds to create new tones. "We would do anything to get an interesting sound," Kirk admits. "We did a lot of blending of old stompboxes with new technology—like a new Eventide effect with some distortion pedal that was only made for six months in 1967. Looking back, we used so many stomp boxes on *Load* and *ReLoad* that I can't even remember the names of half of them. In fact, the real question should be: What pedals *didn't* we use on those two albums?!"

A Digitech whammy pedal also made its way into Kirk's arsenal during the *Load* and *ReLoad* recording sessions. "Even though that pedal's been around for quite a while, I've only just discovered it," he stated in his June 1999 *The Sound & the Fury*. "In my opinion, the whammy pedal is one of the most important new guitar effects to hit the market since the wah-wah. You can get microtones out of it and five-step bends, too—it's amazing! I abused one pretty heavily on 'Devil's Dance' *[ReLoad]*, and it really helped me get the hellish lead sound I wanted to match the mood of the song."

Kirk continues, "'Devil's Dance' happened to be one of the very last songs I did on *ReLoad*. Bob Rock said, 'Hey Kirk, you've gotta do something a little bit different here.' So, I got the whammy pedal out and just went for it. I don't mind telling you that for the first hour or so it didn't really sound like anything, especially when I set the pedal to go up two octaves. Jeez, did that sound horrible! Then, all of a sudden the solo started to come together . . . I set the pedal to go up an octave, grabbed my whammy bar, and used both whammy devices at the same time. That's the standout moment for me on that album; it's definitely my favorite solo."

Garage Inc. (1998)

Kirk dedicated much of his May and June '99 columns to the gear used on this splendid double-disc set of cover songs that pays homage to Metallica's influences. So, I'll hand off to the man for this one.

> We literally started rehearsing for the album the day after our [1998] summer tour was over. Our crew loaded our live rigs into my basement and off we went. And that's exactly how we approached the recording; our tonal starting point was our live shit.
>
> To be perfectly honest, I didn't expect my live stuff to work out that well in the studio—but it did. When you're playing live, your sound is totally in your face. It's loud, you're feeling the wind being pushed by the speakers, you're totally feeding off the vibe of the audience, and it's a very gutsy, almost organic thing. The trouble is, as we've learned from past experience, that same exact setup doesn't always work that well in the studio environment. You put your live rig in a nice little "live" room with state-of-the-art, $15,000 mics all over the place and suddenly you get to scrutinize your live sound a little better. You soon discover that your live tone is not quite as good as you thought it was. It's too dirty, there's too much of one frequency but not enough of another, etc.
>
> Judging from past experiences, I was expecting to have to do a whole lot of tonal tweaking once we'd miked up my rig in the studio. Instead, I was pleasantly surprised at just how good my live rack sounded. Bob [Rock] and I listened to it and decided there wasn't really that much we had to do. Perhaps that could be due to the fact that my taste in tone has definitely changed over the past few years. I don't use as much distortion these days, I've got more mid-range happening, and my overall sound is much crisper than it used to be. So we just fine-tuned my tone ever so slightly and we were ready to roll.
>
> Ninety percent of what you hear on *Garage Inc.* is Boogie stuff because that's what's in my live rack. Trouble is, I've been using the same rig for so long that I forget what's in it! I can tell you, however, that I use Boogie Dual-Rectifier heads and a Tri-Axis preamp for that extra bit of kick. My 4x12 cabinets are Boogies as well, and they're all loaded with Celestion "Vintage 30" speakers. James' rack is pretty much all Boogie, too.
>
> In addition to our Boogie shit, we also used a bunch of other amps in the studio to spice up our main sounds. By doing this, it doesn't sound like we were each just using one tone all the way through the album. One of the amps I used in this way was a Trainwreck [a small, "boutique" amp company] combo, which is pretty amazing sounding. It's super clean and super loud—a lot like a Vox AC30, actually. It's also like a killer Fender Tweed amp, too, because it is so clear and bell-like.
>
> Another amp I used to blend in with my main sound was a really trippy one made by a fairly new company called Line 6. Basically it's one of those new, digital modeling [Flextone] heads with a bunch of effects built-in. You can dial in a bunch of different sounds on it. It's great.
>
> Speaking of using different amps to create interesting tones, a lot of people have asked me how I got the unusual sound at the very start of our cover of Killing Joke's "The Wait." Here's what I did: Using my old ADA preamp, I took out all the bass and all the mid-range while cranking up the treble and distortion to the max. I did this because the band Killing Joke used a keyboard for that intro on their original version of the song and that's kinda what it sounded like!

When it came to the guitars I used on *Garage Inc.*, as always, it was mostly ESPs . . . man, I just love my signature ESPs! They play great, sound great, and look great, too. They also stand up real well to all the abuse they endure on lengthy Metallica world tours, and that's a pretty important quality for my guitars to have, especially when you're on the road as much as we are. One of my all-time favorite ESPs is one that has a picture of the Mummy on it. It also happens to be one of the best-sounding guitars in my collection.

As far as strings go, I'm still using Dean Markley .010s [.010 -.046] on all my guitars. In the early days, I used to use .009s [.009 - .042], but I switched to .010s in '91 or '92 and I've stuck with them ever since. As for pickups, all my ESPs are loaded with EMG 81 humbuckers, which I've been using forever. They give me a great lead tone and are chunky and full for rhythm. I get great low end out of them, too; they're definitely an integral part of my sound.

St. Anger (2003)

As already touched on, this is the album that shocked the lead-loving metal-masses by not featuring a single solo from the genre's most popular lead player! In order to get the ear-frying, in-your-face tones you hear on *St. Anger*, Kirk relied largely on his live rig, which has a Mesa Boogie Dual Rectifier (the older, two-channel version) as its sonic heart.

"We used our road rigs in the studio to record with so we'd have maximum reproduction of our studio tone live," he reveals. "The bulk of my tone came from there, and then, whenever needed, I embellished that sound with other amps, mainly Marshalls—I used an old 100-Watt Super Lead that sounds incredible, a 100-Watt DSL100, a red head from '68 or '69, my modified Master Volume JMP from the '80s that has the 240V sticker on the front, and a rare Kitchen-Marshall head that's so loud and clean it sounds like a harp . . . literally! I also used some Randall amps plus a Fender Twin Reverb from '59. The Twin has two rectifiers in it and it is creamy sounding and loud; it's one of my favorite amps."

In the studio, Kirk relied on two 4x12 cabinets: a "Mesa Boogie 4x12" loaded with Celestion Vintage 30s and "an old Marshall cab from the '60s with a cool pinstripe grille," loaded with Celestion "Greenback" speakers.

"For guitars I obviously used my ESPs," Kirk continues. "I also played a 1959 Les Paul loaded with stock PAF pickups, and they tonally complimented James's EMGs really well. The PAFs sound really warm and have a spongy distortion, whereas EMGs are the exact opposite; it was a good combination. I used a '63 foam-green Strat, too, and my '59 blonde Tele Toploader, which is all over the album—I love that thing to death. I also broke out a Tom Anderson, which I haven't used since . . . *And Justice for All* because I wanted a Strat-kinda sound but with a humbucker. I put a spare PAF I had lying around in the Anderson and it sounded amazing—that was pretty much it, guitar-wise."

Last but not least, we come to Kirk's *St. Anger* effects that, shockingly enough, didn't include his most beloved effect: wah. "I used a lot of [Digitech] whammy pedal, but I locked up my wah pedals for this album," Kirk told me just before *St. Anger* was released. "People always comment on my wah playing—good and bad—and I didn't want it becoming an albatross. I didn't want to feel like I had to use it, so I locked it up. Of course, I still have my fleet of wah pedals at my house and I still use them all the time."

The other pedals he stomped on a lot were the four Line 6 Modeler pedals. "I love Line 6 stuff because it's so over the top," Kirk enthused. "Pretty much everything they do is right on, but those pedals in particular are just great. If you have them, the sky's the limit, and I try to get all four running at the same time!!"

Kirk's *St. Anger* Tour Rig

Even though Kirk didn't play lead on *St. Anger*, he sure as hell did on the lengthy world tour that followed in its wake. I was fortunate enough to get a guided tour of our subject's live setup on that trek by his guitar tech extraordinaire, Justin Crew. Here's the skinny.

Guitars

1. "Skully," his beloved 1987 ESP Custom KH-2.

2. "The Mummy," a Custom ESP KH-2 with the "Mummy" graphic.

3. "Ouija," another Custom KH-2, this time with—wait for it—a Ouija board graphic.

4. A Gibson Les Paul Standard, loaded with EMG 81s and the same strings as above but with a .052 low E string. This guitar was tuned to drop-D, down a whole step (low to high: C–G–C–F–A–D) and used for songs on *St. Anger*.

The first three axes all boast EMG 81 pickups, a Floyd Rose whammy system, and were tuned down a half step (low to high: E♭–A♭–D♭–G♭–B♭–E♭) and strung with Ernie Ball "Power Slinky" strings (.011, .014, .018, .028, .038, .048)

Wireless

Sony UHF Synthesized Diversity WRR-840.

Effects

All in a Digital Music Corp GCX Guitar Audio Switcher system, controlled by a Ground Control Pro MIDI Controller: a Dunlop DCR-15 Rack Wah, an Ibanez Tube Screamer, a Digitech WH-1 Whammy, a Line 6 DL-4 Delay Modeler, a Line 6 MM-4 Modulation Modeler, a TC Electronics G Major, and a DBX 1074 Quad Gate.

Amps

A Mesa Dual Rectifier, a Mesa/Boogie Triaxis, and two Mesa/Boogie Strategy 400 Stereo Power Amps.

Cabs

Five Mesa Standard Recto 4x12 straight-front cabs loaded with Celestion Vintage 30 speakers. Kirk had four of these cabs on stage and one in a custom-made isolation box under the stage.

Death Magnetic (2008)

"For this one I pretty much used what I always use," Kirk states, "My standard touring rack, which is filled with my usual Boogie stuff, an old Marshall I've had forever, plus my new Randall Signature head that I helped design." He also used an "incredible" Ampeg guitar head made in the early '90s for a short time. "It has a great, warm, clean sound that blended well with my other amps," he reveals.

With his recording role on *Death Magnetic* totally dedicated to lead work, Kirk's "workhorse" guitar was "The Mummy," his infamous Custom ESP featuring a stunning graphic of Boris Karloff in arguably his best role. "It just sounded the best," Kirk explains. He also used "Skully," his '59 Gibson Les Paul Standard, and an old Fender

Telecaster for some of his clean tones. And, as you'd expect, as per Kirk's usual lead playing M.O., he stepped on his trusty Dunlop wah quite a few times and also his faithful Ibanez Tube Screamer. "My Tube Screamer has been such a part of my lead sound for years and years," he admits. "Whenever I do a solo, it's always there. It's my secret weapon. I like the body and warmth it brings to just about any sound or setup. Give me a Fender Twin and a Tube Screamer and I'm in heaven!"

Phew! Like I said, that's one hell of a lot of gear. And, if truth be told, there's a lot more, too, like the Marshall JMP-1 MIDI preamp that was an integral part of his live rig for quite a few years in the '90s, and a veritable laundry list of weird and wonderful vintage and boutique pedals. This all said, to summarize . . .

Kirk Hammett Setup Essentials

As mentioned at the very onset of this section, over an incredibly long career that spans more than 25 years, Kirk has experimented, recorded, and performed live with a vast array of gear. That said, if one had to come up with an abbreviated but essential Kirk Hammett setup, here's my list.

Guitar

ESP KH-2 with EMG 81 pickups and a Floyd Rose.

Pedals

His Signature Dunlop KH95 wah and an Ibanez Tube Screamer for leads.

Amp

A Mesa Dual Rectifier ("for some reason I like the Double Rectifier more than the Triple"), or one of his Signature Randall heads, the RM100KH.

Cab

A straight-fronted Mesa or Marshall 4x12 loaded with Celestion Vintage 30s, or one of his new signature Randall 4x12 RS412KHs.

Two Important Kirk Gear P.S. Notes

Kirk on the Whammy Bar!

As the vast majority of Kirk's axes all boast a locking Floyd Rose whammy system, it would be remiss not to touch on Kirk's use of this groundbreaking device. We're going to do so via Kirk's answer to a reader's question way back in May 1995.

> *Hey Kirk,*
>
> *Your column rules! I was lucky enough to see Metallica twice last summer and I loved the wild whammy bar work you were doing. Why don't you do that sort of stuff on your albums?*
>
> *Garrett Dawson,*
> *Kent, WA*

I'm a self-confessed musical masturbator when it comes to (ab)using the whammy bar! That's one vice I have—I love my Floyd Rose and I use it all to hell on stage. I did make huge, bulging, farting effects and basically any sort of weird noise. I think my favorite whammy effect is when you depress it so low that the strings are just flopping against the pickups and shaking. That lower-than-low stuff sounds so heavy to me—it's just like the Melvins!

Having said that, I pretty much restrict all that sort of stuff to my live playing because nobody in the band wants to waste expensive studio tape on my wild whammy bar excursions. But on the live album, *Live Shit: Binge & Purge*, there are a few spots where I'm pretty much just doing push-ups on the damned thing!

With regards to how Kirk has his Floyd bridges set up, read on: "I set it so it's floating because I like to pull up on the bar as well as push it down. In fact, these days I pull up on my whammy bar a lot more than I push down. I also have a Hipshot Tremsetter in there as well so it always returns to the same spot. Also, when you have a Tremsetter, if you bend your G string up one and a half steps, the bridge won't move as much."

Kirk on the Wah-Wah

As any fan of Kirk's playing knows, his solos are invariably spiced with his favorite effect of all-time . . . his beloved wah-wah! As a sizable section of Chapter 6 is dedicated to the device Kirk is addicted to, I'll merely mention it here with a quote from our teacher on how his lifelong obsession began: "The first time I ever heard a wah pedal was listening to Brian Robertson of Thin Lizzy. Of course, I was already aware of the sound it created thanks to Jimi Hendrix, but I always assumed he was doing it via some form of guitar wizardry with either his hands or his tremolo bar, not with an effect pedal! Then I heard Brian's solo in the Thin Lizzy song "Warrior" [*Jailbreak*] and I asked a friend, 'How's he doing that?' He told me it was a wah-wah pedal controlled by shaking it around with his foot. I really liked the sound, so I got one. I still remember getting my first wah pedal. It really was a true life-changing moment, and I've never looked back."

Not surprisingly, in 2009, Dunlop honored Kirk with a Signature Wah—the KH95. Housed in a sturdy, green-burst casing and boasting a skeleton foot on the rubber tread, this eye-catching beast was awarded a Platinum Award for Quality and Design in the 30th Anniversary issue of *Guitar World*. Not surprisingly, given Kirk's influences, the review also stated the following: "in half-cocked position it delivers expressive, vocal-like midrange that's a dead ringer for Michael Schenker's seventies UFO solo tone."

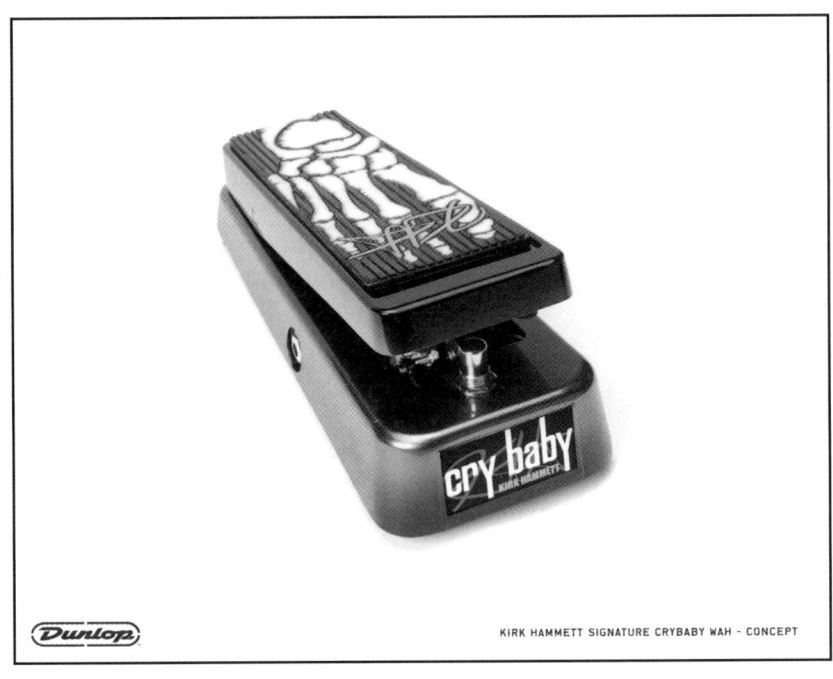

CHAPTER 5
START ME UP!
Warming up to Get Hot

There is no "right" way to warm up because everyone's approach is different. I've even met a few guitarists who don't warm up at all before they play a gig because they believe that they play better going in cold. Personally speaking, I've always found that I have to warm up in order to play my best. This is especially true if it's really cold or if we're playing outdoors—then warming up becomes a must because cold weather definitely deadens your hands. While many players are rightly concerned that they might hurt their hands if they don't warm up, I also worry about a different kind of "hurt"—the pain that comes from the embarrassment of standing in front of an audience and being unable to play what I'm supposed to play because my hands aren't ready for action. Hell, I even do a quick warm-up routine before I mess about on a guitar in a music store!

Important Warning!

At the risk of sounding melodramatic, please treat your hands and fingers with respect. Professional athletes always warm up before exerting themselves for a reason—guitarists need to do the same, especially as they get better and faster. If you don't heed this advice then serious injury could occur, and the only thing that will do is prevent you from playing for a while until you're fully recovered. So why risk it? Always take the time to warm up before going for that break-neck thrash riff or warp-speed inducing lick . . . your precious digits will thank you!

There are things you can do instead of practicing guitar from the moment you wake up to the moment you go to bed to keep your hands in good shape. I don't know why, but when I'm away from the guitar for even a short while my hands seem to lose strength, flexibility, and dexterity. That's why I often use one of those finger exercisers for guitarists [e.g., the Gripmaster] that you can pick up at a music store. I realize that I probably look like a complete geek using one, but they do work for me so I don't really give a damn! Some guitar players won't touch them with a ten-foot pole, but I find mine really useful because it helps keep my hands in shape when I'm not able to pick up the guitar as often as I'd like too. That said, let's look at a few warm-up exercises that involve playing.

Look, Ma—One Hand!

A great way of zoning in on your picking technique is to simply alternate-pick (down, up, down, up, etc.) continuous 16th notes (Music 1) or sextuplets (Music 2) on the low E string. These exercises also function as excellent warm-up exercises for your picking hand. Sure, they might seem simple, but after a few minutes you'll definitely start to feel it! Start off slowly, especially if it's cold, and then build up speed once your hand is warmed up. If you've got a metronome, use it to help develop precision—if not, tapping your foot is a good substitute.

Music 1

Track 2

Music 2

Track 2

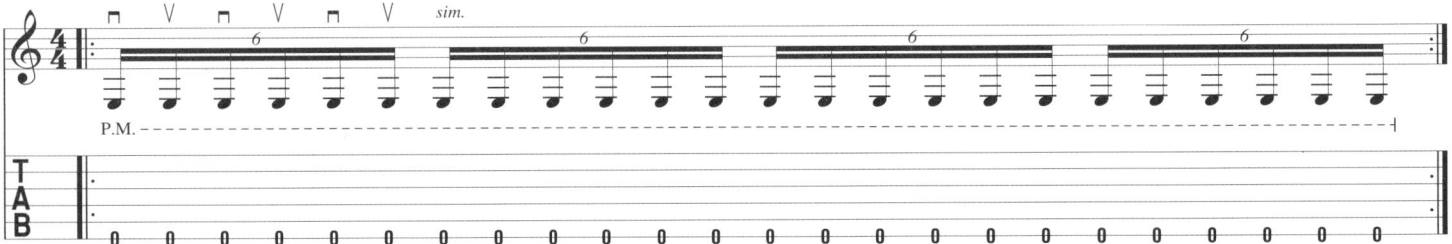

Go Down . . . and Up!

I also recommend you practice these exercises using *downstrokes only* as well because developing strength and stamina in your downpicking is essential for handling intense rhythm work like the stuff we do in Metallica. For maximum "heaviness," most of our riffs are played using downstrokes only. That said, it's important to be proficient at upstrokes, too, because they have a different attack and that can be useful sometimes. I can remember watching old Deep Purple videos carefully and noticing that Ritchie Blackmore picked upwards on a lot of his riffs. And if it's good enough for Ritchie . . . !

I also recommend practicing this one-handed idea using all six strings as shown in Music 3. Doing this will help you get accustomed to moving fluently between strings when picking at high speed.

Music 3

Track 3

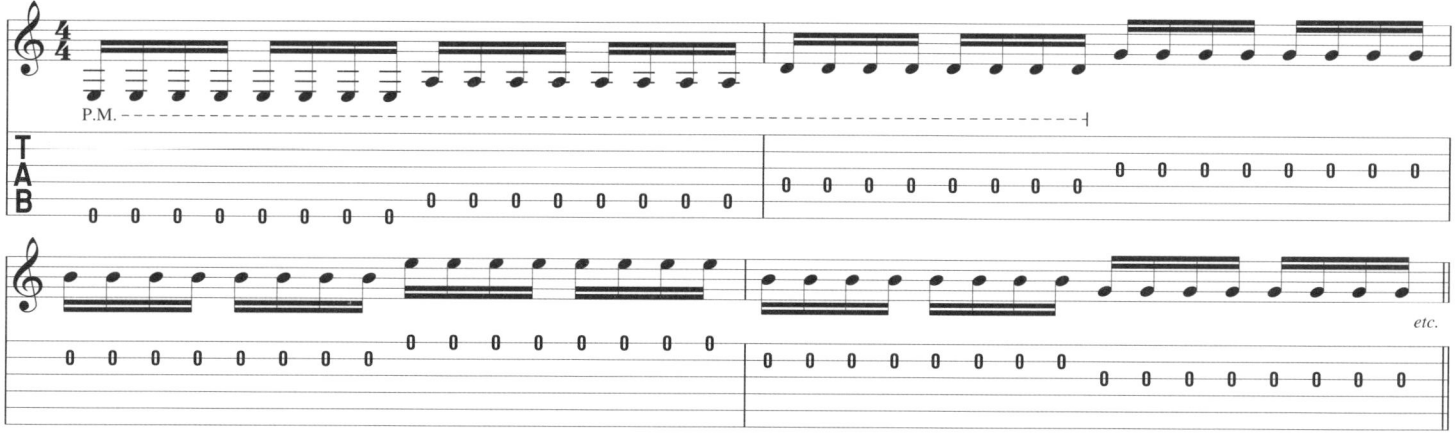

Another good way to perform this exercise is to do it using just downstrokes or upstrokes. When I warm up I usually run through Music 3 a total of four times, taking a different approach each time—once using alternate picking, once using downstrokes only, once using upstrokes only, and then back to alternate picking again.

Wrist Watch

I realize that the trio of one-handed exercises just discussed are unbelievably simple, but who cares—they work! Actually, the sheer simplicity of these exercises makes them especially useful because they enable you to really zone in on your picking technique since you aren't required to do anything with your fretting hand.

Some people tend to pick by pivoting around their elbow, but I've found that I can get a much more precise, controlled, and economical movement by pivoting around my wrist instead. So pay close attention to your right hand when doing these exercises and see if you can spot ways to improve your picking technique. Basically, the smaller and more controlled the movement, the better.

Chromatic Climber

Music 4 is an ascending exercise I learned from a friend and it's really good for developing coordination between your left and right hands. It also gets you to move diagonally around the neck, which is a cool thing to get used to.

Music 4

Track 4

29

Music 5 is the descending version of the same thing. These two exercises are both really good warm ups because they cover the whole fretboard and require you to use all four left-hand fingers of your fretboard (left) hand.

Music 5

Track 5

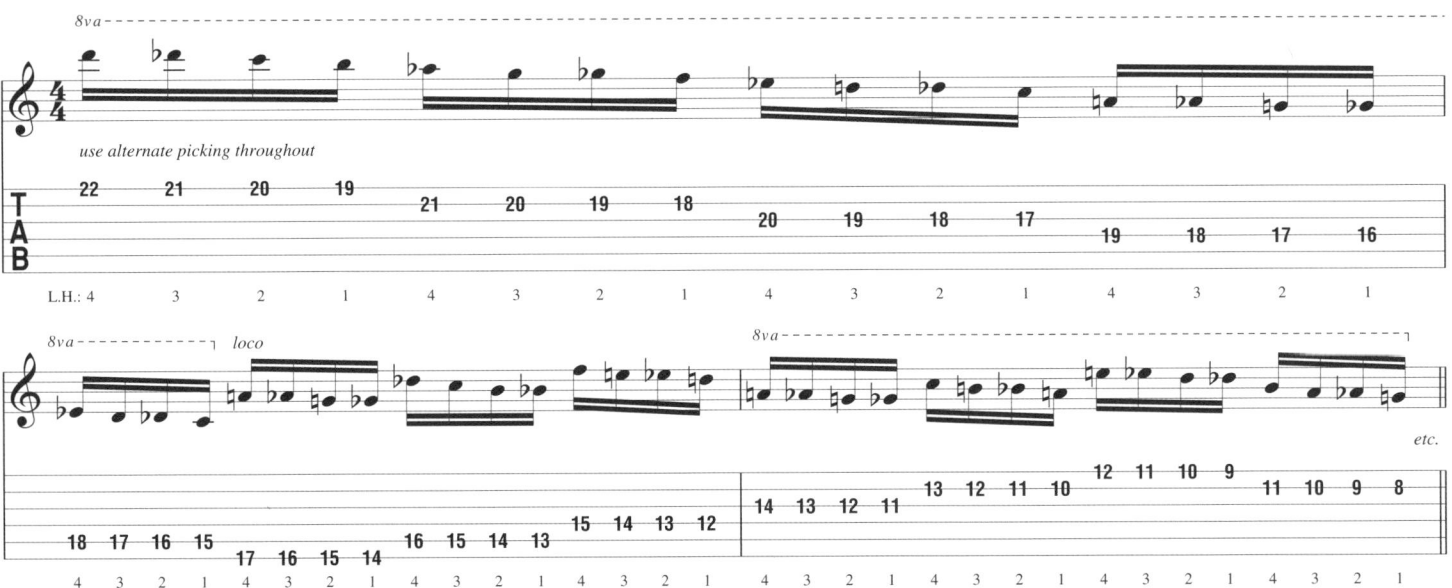

As already mentioned, when practicing it's very important that you keep the tempo of your playing constant. So keep that foot tapping or, better still, if you've got a metronome then use the sucker! You should also concentrate real hard on making sure that your pick attack remains rock-steady. Lastly, if you want to get the most out of these exercises, don't play them sloppily . . . make sure your hands are coordinated.

Guitar-playing friends of mine use these two exercises (Music 4 and 5) for the exact same reasons I do: They make you think about what you're doing because of the diagonal movement involved. They also help you get out of the "playing in a box" mindset that's so easy for a lead guitar player to fall into. Y'know, the solo's in E minor so you go to the 12th position and stay there!

Next up is Music 6, another cool alternate-picking and hand-coordination exercise that Joe Satriani taught me back when I took lessons from him. Basically, all that's happening here is I'm taking a fingering pattern and moving it across the neck as far as it can go and then back again. This particular one is pretty tough to play quickly because of the amount of string-skipping involved, but stick with it and you'll master it.

Music 6

Track 6

Slurring Time

Having zoned in on your picking hand pretty hard, it's time to look at a few exercises that'll give your fretboard hand a good workout. Music 7 is a good one for loosening up and strengthening your fretboard hand—especially your pinky (little finger). It may look like a bit of nothing, but if you repeat this pattern for 20 seconds or more, you'll definitely feel it.

Music 7

Track 7

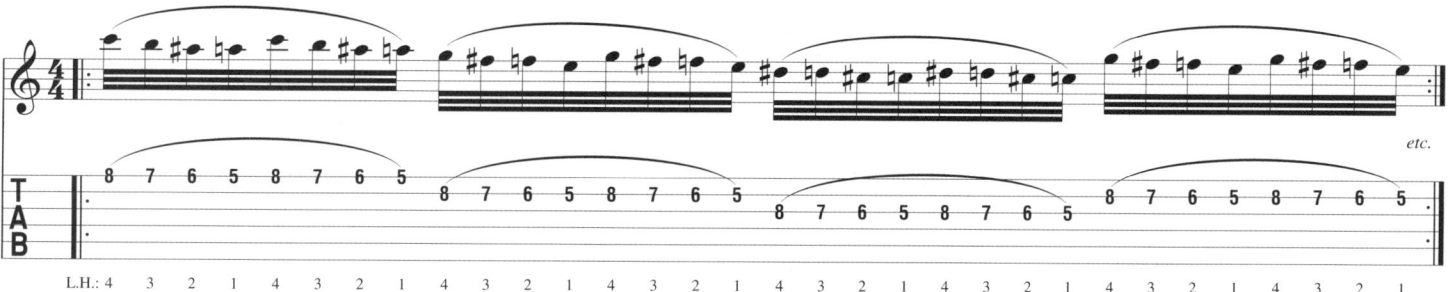

31

Reach for It

The next warm-up example, Music 8, may seem like a pretty basic hammer-on idea, but it's a great exercise because it can really help build up the strength and stamina of your fretboard hand. It also gives your hand a good stretch, too, which is always a wise thing to do whenever you're warming up. If you're not used to doing a lot of hammering-on with your little finger, then you'll probably find this exercise a real mother! I've only given you the first six bars of the pattern, but the idea is for you to continue it all the way up to the 12th position and then back down again. By the time you've done this a couple of times, it'll have done a real number on your fretting hand—especially your pinky!

Music 8

Track 8

Skip 'Em All!

Music 9 is another warm-up exercise that involves the same exact, wide-stretch, hammer-on patterns we've just used in Music 8 but also incorporates string-skipping. Once again, I've shown you the first few bars of the pattern, but to get the most out of it, take it all the way up to the 12th fret and back down again—just like you did with the previous example.

Music 9

Track 9

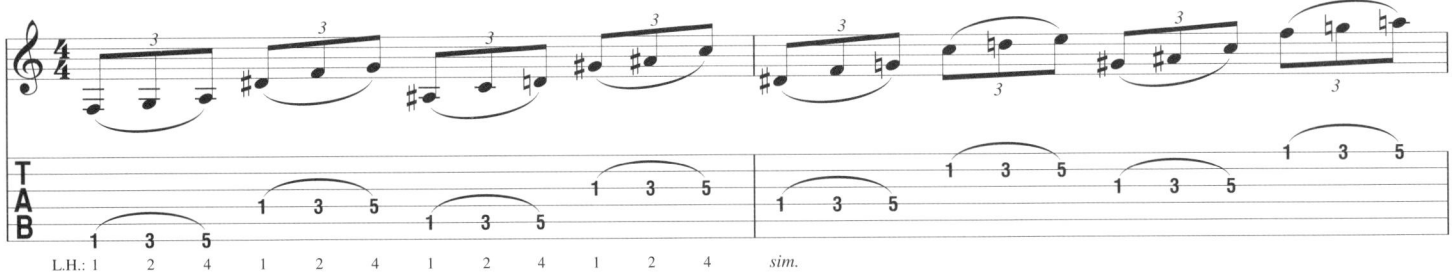

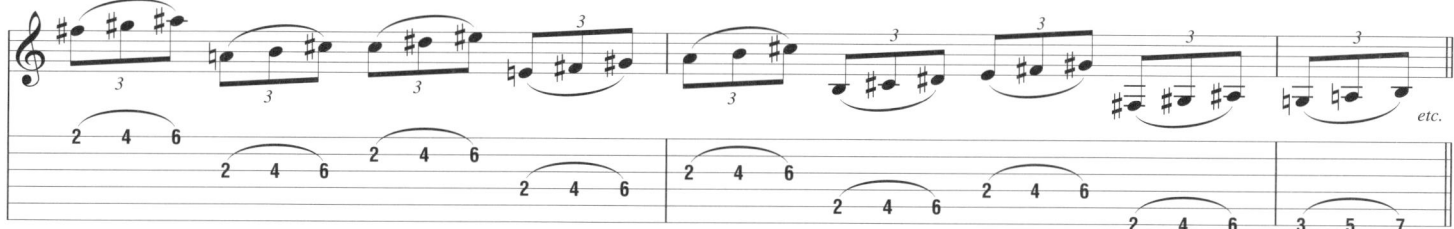

WARNING!

While you will find that the last few exercises will strengthen your fretboard hand considerably and also make wide stretches easier, please be extremely careful when playing them!! As was already mentioned, don't risk injury by overexerting yourself, and never attempt either of these until your left hand is well and truly warmed-up. Don't just take my word for it though; take Kirk's by reading on.

Warming-Up Revisited

Kirk's initial forays into the all-important aspect of warming-up that we've just covered were made way back in his 1993 and 1994 columns during the first run of *The Sound & the Fury*. I also plundered a really cool *Private Lesson* entitled "Run Like Hell" he did for the March 1992 issue of *Guitar World*, following the magazine's venerable readership voting him "Best Heavy Metal Guitarist" in the 1991 Readers' Poll.

Kirk came back to the subject in his September 2001 installment of *The Sound & the Fury*, which opened with the following statement: "This month I'm going to revisit something I've discussed in this column before—warming up. The reason I'm going to do this is because I've learned a few new things that have cut down the amount of time I have to warm up. So, I figured I'd pass them on to you. Unfortunately, the way I learned the exercises I'm about to show you is by receiving treatment for a rather painful injury."

Damage, Inc.

A while ago, I developed tendonitis in the rotator cuff of my right shoulder. This was caused by the way I was playing my acoustic guitar. Apparently, I was over extending my right shoulder out over the guitar's body and then strumming. Because of this my rotator cuff was getting rubbed, and that caused tendonitis in my right shoulder, which was pretty scary because I couldn't play for about two months. In fact, it was so bad that I couldn't even pick up the guitar because its weight would cause so much pain.

Then, to make matters worse, once I'd developed tendonitis in my right shoulder it moved over to my left shoulder as well. Apparently that tends to happen with a lot of "sports injuries"—your "good" side compensates for the other one and works extra hard as a result. And, because of this extra work, tendonitis can occur in your "good" side, too. For example, not so long ago I pulled the hamstring in my right leg and it eventually worked its way over to my left leg as well, for the reasons just mentioned.

A while back, I got hip to the fact that if you're having any pains or problems that are instrument related, you should always see a muscle therapist rather than just a straight doctor or chiropractor. This is because nine times out of ten, if it's obviously not the bone, then your problem is going to either be muscle or tendon related. So, I went to see a muscle therapist and got my tendonitis cleared up through therapy and yoga. Then, once that was done, I went back to another specialist who looked at my right hand, wrist, and arm and said, "Wow, you need a lot of work here." What had happened was I had all these calcium deposits that had built up all over my hand from bruising it constantly.

I wasn't really surprised to hear this because, looking back, I've definitely beaten the shit out of my guitar over the years and, by doing that, have beaten the shit out of my right hand, too! I'd never really thought about it before, though, because when you're caught up in the moment and you're banging your arm all over the place, you don't really feel it or care because you're having fun and you're also trying to play the guitar!

So, the therapist got hold of my hand and rubbed out all those calcium deposits, and they were literally everywhere—in the middle of my hand, on the underside, where the knuckles are and in-between my fingers. Then, after quite a few sessions with him, my right wrist popped—you know, just like your back or neck pops when you go to a chiropractor. When it popped he went, "There it goes," just like he was expecting it to. I asked, "What happened?" And he said, 'Well your wrist was slightly out of place and I've finally got it back into place—you must have had a really bad fall at onetime.

As soon as this happened my wrist felt really good for the first time in a long time. I started thinking back, trying to remember what I'd done to hurt it, and all of a sudden I realized, "Goddamn it! I got into a pretty bad skateboard accident right before the tour we did opening for Ozzy way back in '86." As a result of that fall, I jammed my wrist really badly and I couldn't play for about a week. The therapist told me that my wrist had probably been in that position ever since then . . . until he finally got it back into the right place, of course.

Start Your Engines! Some Ways to "Quick Start" Your Warm-Up

Both therapists showed me some exercises to do, and I've found that they're really good for warming up if you don't have a guitar. In fact, they're so effective I always do them before I even pick up my guitar. The great thing about them is that they're low impact, which means you're not straining any of your muscles. Here are the three things I do before I start playing.

The first thing I do is shake both hands up and down, and from side to side. Next I stretch both arms straight out to the side so they are level with my shoulders, with both palms facing the floor. Then I bend both wrists up so that my fingertips are pointing up to the sky and my hands and arms are at a 90-degree angle to each other (Photo 1). Then I do the same exact thing but the other way, so my fingertips are pointing down towards the floor (Photo 2). I alternate between pointing "up" and "down" quite a bit before moving to the third and last exercise . . .

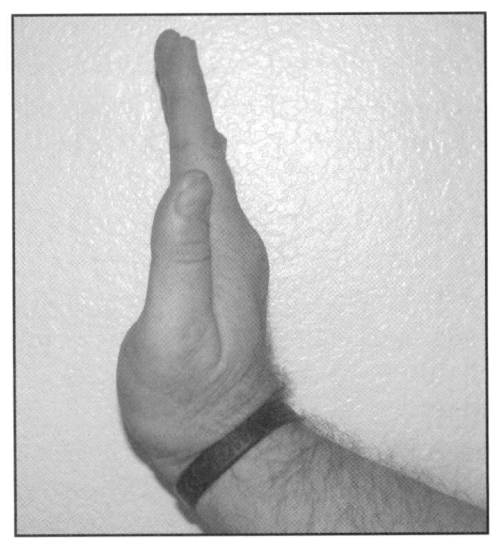
Photo 1

Photo 2

For the final exercise, you hold your hands out in front of you with the palms facing upwards—kind of like you were going to throw water on your face except that your palms are flat, not cupped. Then, spread your pinky and ring fingers as far away from each other as you can horizontally. [*Important warning: This "spreading" is NOT to be done by forcing your fingers apart with your other hand, as injury could result. You're just moving your fingers as far apart as they can go by themselves.*] Looking at your right hand, this would mean spreading your pinky all the way to the left, and your index finger all the way to the right (Photo 3). That's the stretch. It's kind of like the sort of leg stretch an athlete would do before a race or an event, and it makes sense. Then you do the same exact thing with both hands, but between your ring and index fingers (Photo 4), then between your middle and index fingers and, finally, between your index finger and thumb. I repeat these four stretches several times on both hands and then I pick up my guitar.

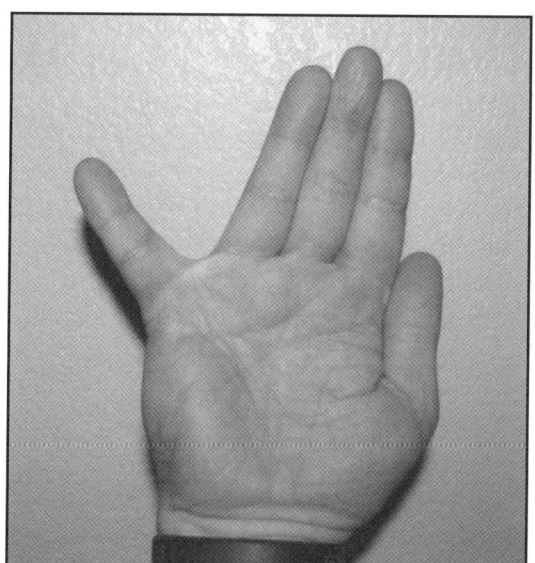

Photo 3

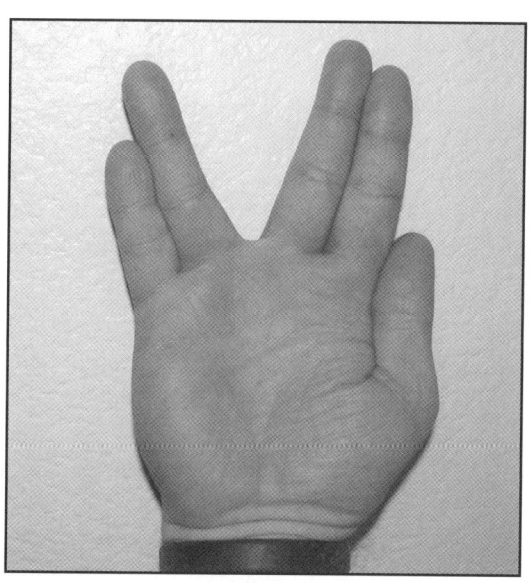

Photo 4

By doing these exercises first, by the time I get to my guitar I'm a little bit more loser than I normally would be. If you do this and make it part of your routine, eventually you'll warm up a little quicker, too. Like I said earlier, I've found that doing this cuts my warm-up time down by a lot. I hope you find these exercises useful, too.

Ouch! Kirk's tale is proof that sometimes something seemingly awful can lead to something good, and it was very cool of him to share. I've tried the "low impact" exercises he's just described and they definitely help, especially when combined with a few of the other warm-up tips he's also just shown us. As Kirk has alluded, warming-up is a vital procedure, especially when it's cold.

To quote our teacher: "You only have two hands and 10 fingers; treat them with respect." These are wise-words, my friend, and you'd be foolish not to heed them at all times. Speaking from bitter experience, developing tendonitis in your hand is a painful and debilitating injury, and the *only* cure is not playing for a considerable time. I could've avoided it by spending a few minutes warming up before going for broke but I didn't. As a result, an important recording session had to be postponed for several weeks while my hand healed. So please, please, learn from the error of my ways and, as already stated, do what every single, serious athlete and sportsman/woman always does before exerting themselves . . . spend a few minutes stretching out and warming up. It's time well spent, and it will help minimize the chances of you sidelining yourself!

Sermon over, as is this vitally important chapter. Back to Mr. Hammett.

35

CHAPTER 6
HARVESTER OF SOLOS
Lead-Playing Tips and Techniques

Now that you're thoroughly warmed up, it's time to get some invaluable playing tips from Kirk on the aspect of his playing that has made him a household name in every rock loving country with electricity: soloing. In this lengthy chapter, Kirk covers a vast array of essential and often mind-opening array of lead playing topics and ideas. To whet your appetite (for construction!) here's a listing of just some of the subjects and techniques our guest teacher will touch on—wide-stretch licks, string skipping, using open strings, tapping, string bending, vibrato, and sliding around the neck. Phew!

This chapter kicks off with some great advice on wide-stretch licks using your pinky, and yet another warm-up exercise. As you'll see, this particular topic was prompted by one of the many hundreds of reader questions inspired by *The Sound & the Fury*.

Enter Stretchman! Wide-Stretch Licks and Using Your Pinky

Dear Kirk,

Thanks a million for writing such a great column, I look forward to it every month as I've learned a bunch of great stuff from it. I recently got hold of the Live Shit: Binge & Purge *box set and also the* Cunning Stunts *video, and have been studying your lead-playing a lot. I've noticed that you use your little finger a lot and do some really cool, wide stretches with your left hand too. I've been playing for just over five years and am guilty of not using my left-hand little finger when I solo. If you could talk about how you use your pinky and give us some exercises that'll help strengthen it in one of your columns, that'd rule. Thanx in advance, Kirk, and keep up the good work!*

Doug Irving,
Detroit, MI

I've been using my left-hand pinky for as long as I can remember. Right when I was first learning to play, a friend of mine said to me, "Hey, you'd better use your little finger or it's just gonna hang out there!" I heeded his advice and have used it ever since—as indicated by many of the warm-up exercises in the previous chapter, since the vast majority of them utilize that finger.

Using my pinky definitely helps me play certain wide-stretch things that I probably couldn't reach if I was a three-fingered player. Like the pull-offs on the high E string in bar 3 of the E minor lick shown in Music 10, which is similar to something I do in my " . . . And Justice for All" solo." As well as sounding cool, messing around with wide-stretch lick ideas can often open up new doors in your playing because it can introduce you to intervals you don't normally use. Doing wide stretches can also rejuvenate and breathe new life into tired old scales and fretboard patterns.

Music 10

Track 10

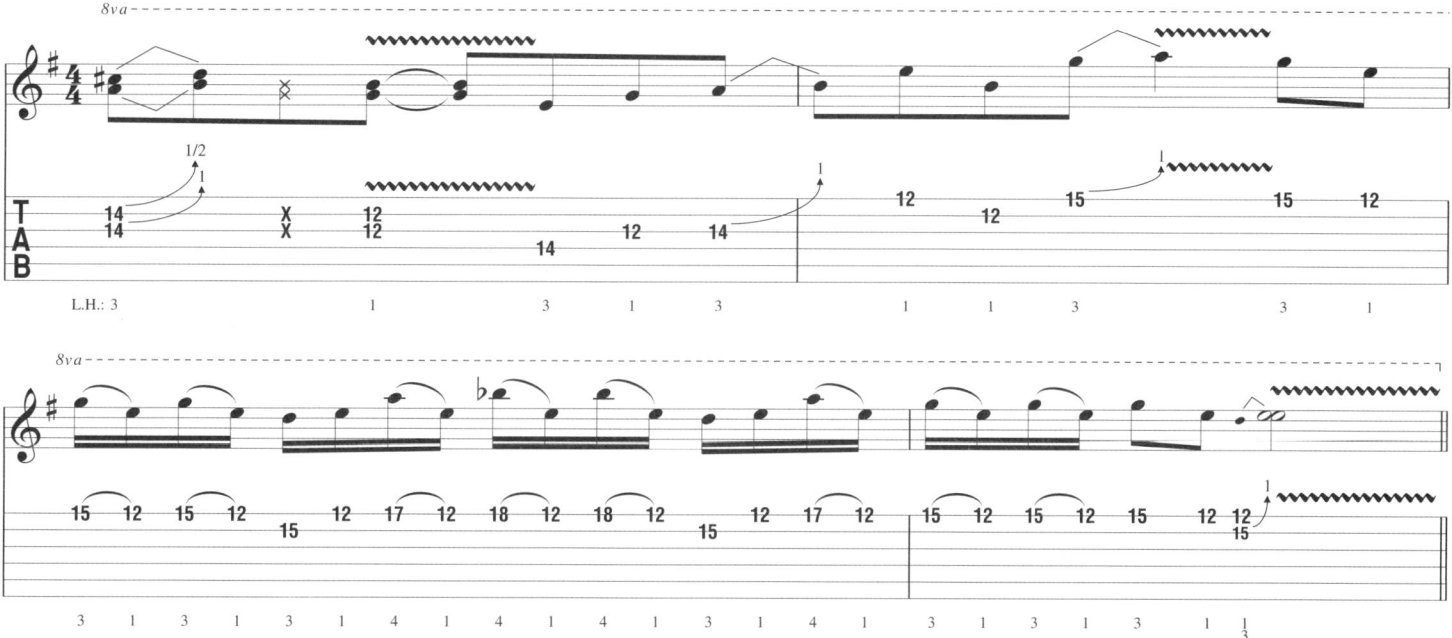

Important Warning: Just in-case you skipped over the warm-up stuff in Chapter 5, never attempt any wide-stretch playing ideas until you've warmed up your left hand thoroughly. If you go into this sort of thing cold, you could injure yourself, which would definitely suck the big one. You have only two hands and ten fingers—always treat them with respect!

Wide-Stretch Sickness from Satch!

Once you've worked on Music 10 for a few minutes, your left hand should be warmed up sufficiently to tackle Music 11, which is a brutal trilling exercise that my old guitar teacher and friend, Joe Satriani, showed me. As you're about to discover, it's a real mother! It looks extremely simple but is actually really hard because it forces you to expand your reach. By increasing the space between your fingers, it makes each trill more and more difficult. This exercise will definitely push your stretching capabilities and stamina to the max. I've only shown it on the high E and B strings, but you should practice this pattern on the other four strings as well.

Music 11

Track 11

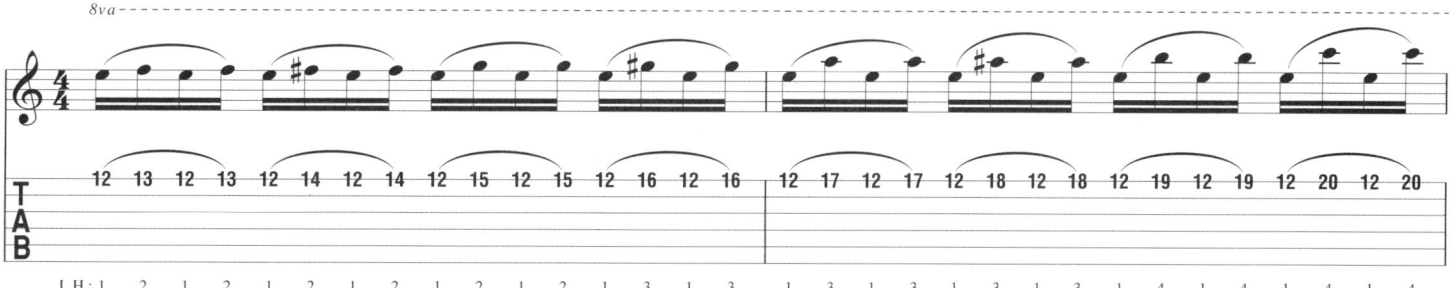

37

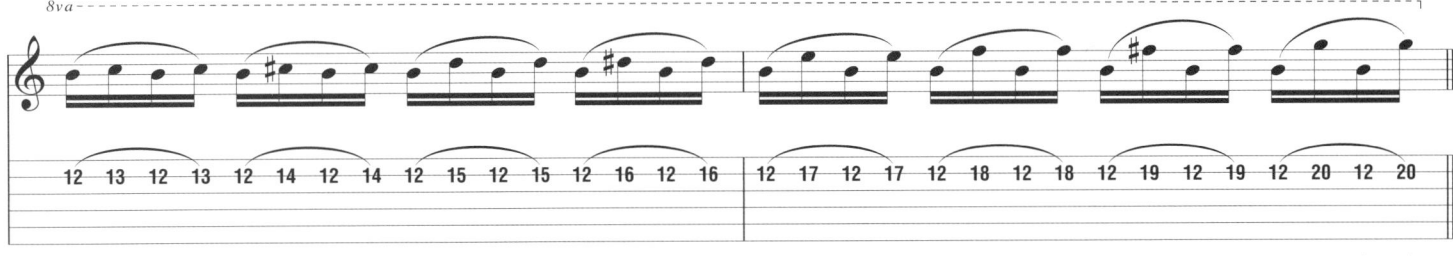

Once you've mastered Music 11, you can try moving the exercise further down the neck, which will obviously make it more difficult due to the fact that the frets get further apart as you get closer to the nut. Please be sensible when doing this, though—don't risk hurting yourself, OK? Move it towards the nut one fret at a time. I can do it as far as the 7th position comfortably. To be honest with you, I don't do this one too often because after I do it, my left hand feels like it is paralyzed!

Music 12 is a simple, wide-stretch, E minor pentatonic (E–G–A–B–D) lick that sounds cool and unusual because you end up playing the same note consecutively, but on different strings—the E note at the 12th fret of the high E string and the same note at the 17th fret on the B. Since these two E notes have slightly different sounds, they complement each other in a weird, almost dissonant way. This lick sounds really good when repeated at high speeds over a changing chord progression, and is also a great little exercise for loosening up and strengthening your left hand—especially your little finger. It might seem like a piece of nothing, but if you play it repeatedly for about a minute or so, you'll definitely feel it. In fact, this one is another excellent warm-up exercise and is well worth throwing into your routine from time to time.

Music 12

Track 12

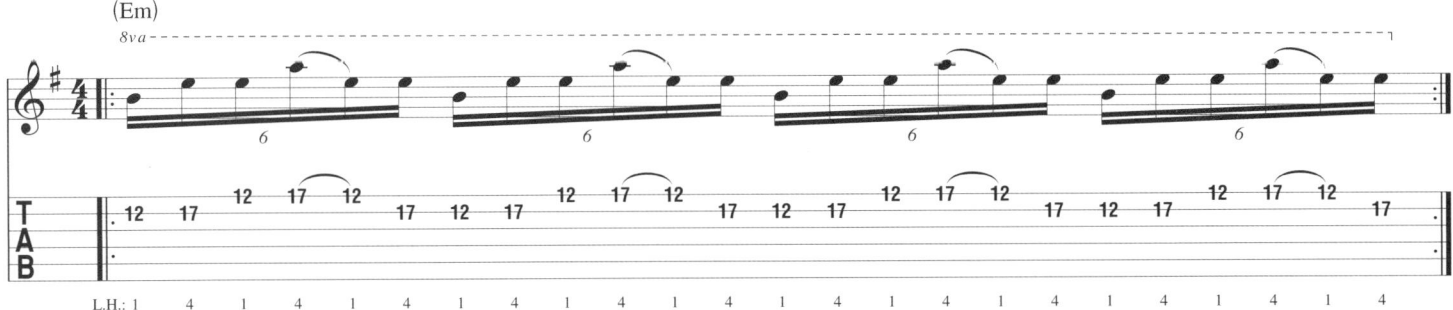

Music 13 is another E minor wide-stretch run that uses the blues scale (E–G–A–B♭–B–D), and just like Music 12 it involves consecutive repeats of the same note but played on different strings, and this time, three notes are involved in total—E, G, and D.

Music 13

Track 13

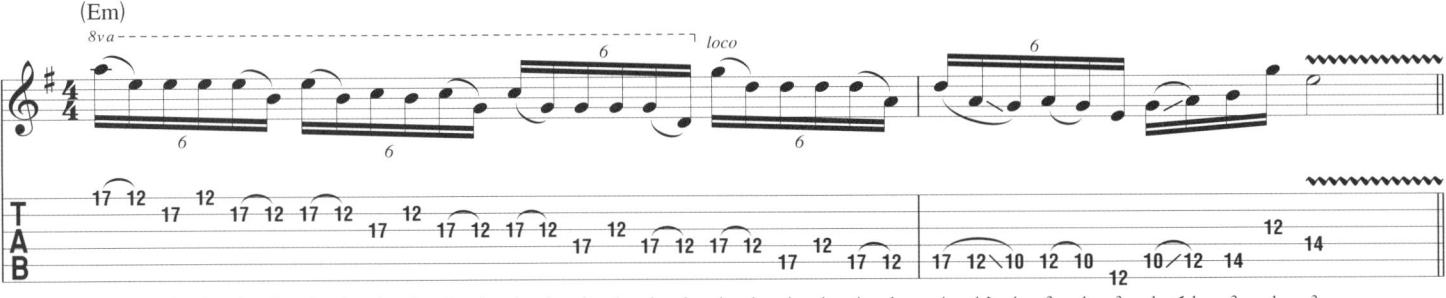

This run in Music 13 is similar to one I use in "Don't Tread on Me" [*Metallica*]. As you can see, the first bar of it merely involves you moving a six-fret, wide-stretch pattern symmetrically across the neck. A fretboard diagram of the symmetrical pattern being used is shown in Diagram 1.

Once you've mastered the examples we've just gone over, try coming up with some wide-stretch licks and runs of your own. Another idea worth exploring in your pursuit of new and different-sounding licks is combining wide stretches with string-skipping, as illustrated in Music 14. Here, all I've done is combine a five-fret stretch with a string skip, and the result is a cool sounding Am7 arpeggio (A–C–E–G) that'll work in just about any A minor context.

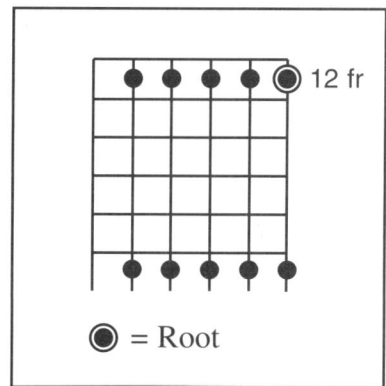

Diagram 1

Music 14

Track 14

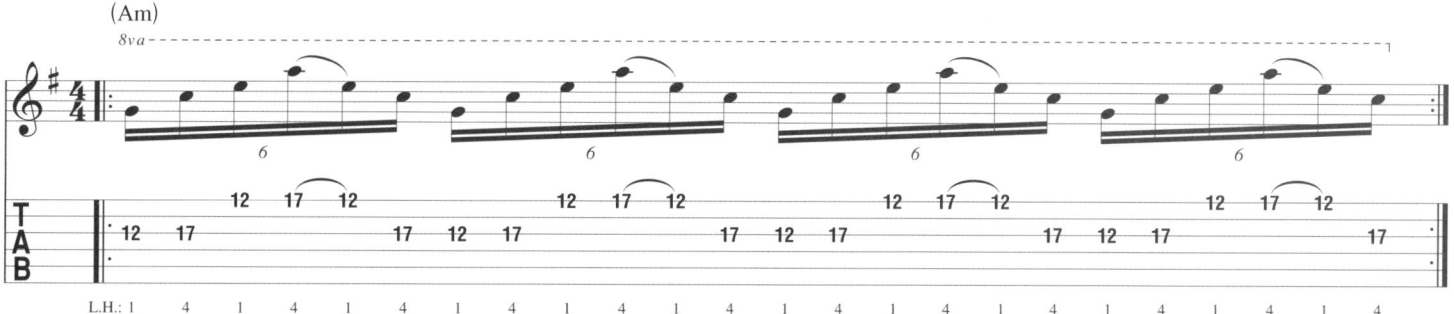

Skip 'Em All, Revisited

Kirk already touched on this in the previous chapter, hence the "revisited" tag. Here, he discusses some of the cool things that string-skipping has to offer—one of them being getting you out of your comfort zone. Read on . . .

Learning to string-skip fluently is very useful in that it instantly changes your "normal" horizontal/vertical outlook on a scale because it automatically gives you a different order of notes . . . and sometimes that's all you need to add color to a solo or run. For example, let's take a well-worn, 12th-position, E minor pentatonic scale pattern that we all know (Diagram 2) and apply a simple string-skipping pattern, similar to the one we just used in Music 9 [Chapter 5]. The resulting run, shown in Music 15, definitely makes that familiar, old scale sound new and fresh again.

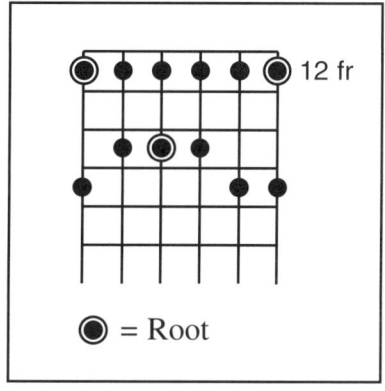

Diagram 2

Music 15

Track 15

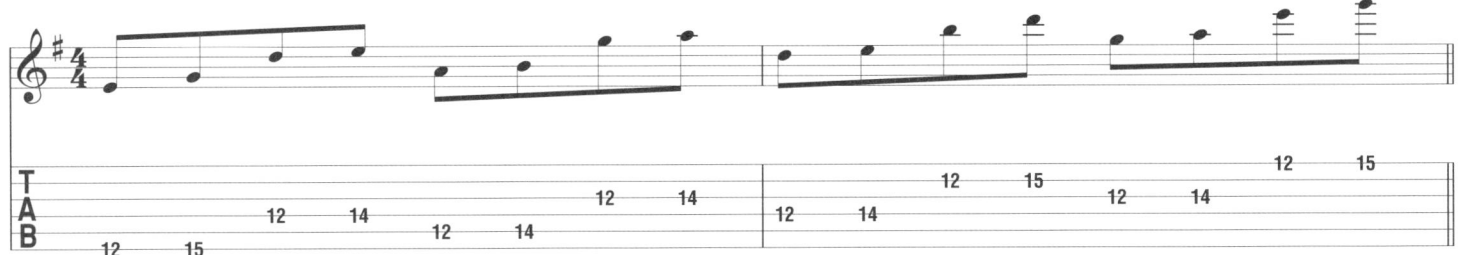

I'm not saying that string skipping is something you should do all the time, but it's a great way to break away from what I call your "comfort zone." Every guitarist has a batch of licks and runs we know will work, and we all have a natural tendency to head straight for them—especially when jamming with or trying to impress some friends! As a result, instead of being creative and fresh, we merely regurgitate our basic vocabulary of tired old but safe "hot licks." String skipping is a great way of forcing you out of that comfortable rut and into exploring new avenues and ideas. As we all hit those dreaded ruts in our playing from time-to-time, I'm going to dedicate an entire chapter to the art of "rut-busting" later on in this book.

Music 16 is an E minor string-skipping lick similar to the one that I do at the end of my "Of Wolf and Man" [*Metallica*] solo. When I play it, I always barre the G and B strings at the 12th fret with my index (first) finger and let them ring. Doing this gives the lick a fatter, more colorful sound and definitely works during an E minor solo because both notes are part of the E minor chord (E–G–B). Jimi Hendrix crafted a bunch of great-sounding, melodic licks by playing moving lines while allowing other notes to ring out—"Little Wing" is a perfect example of him doing that.

Music 16

Track 16

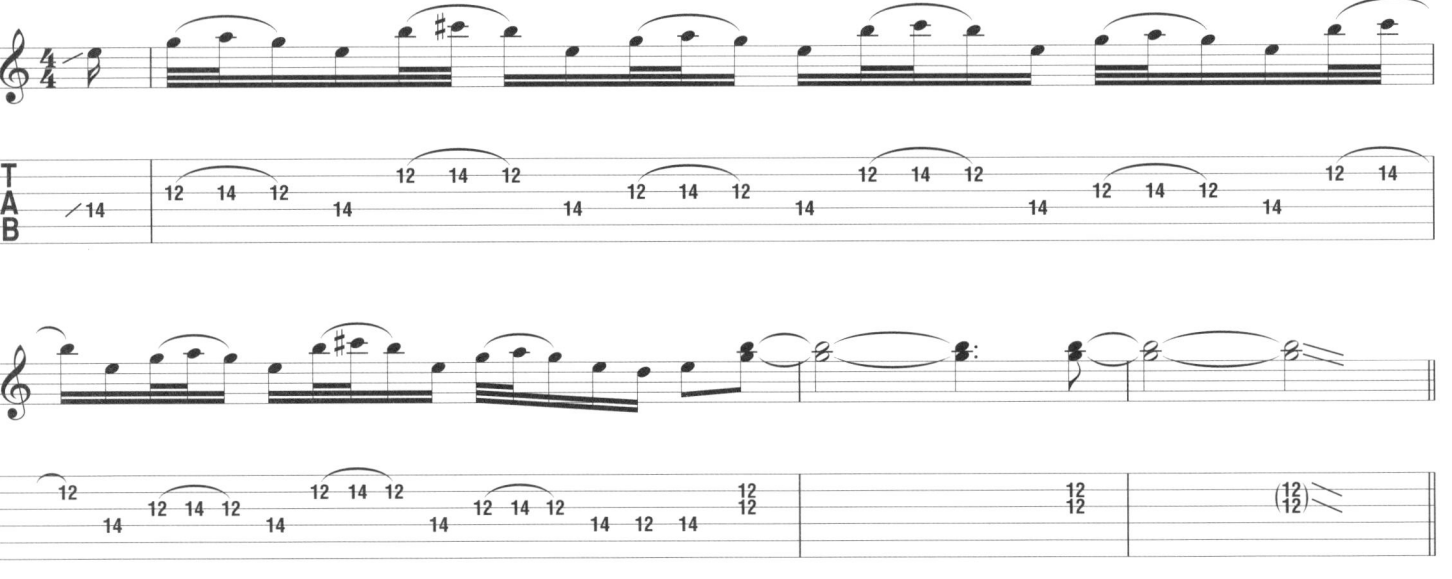

Bend Me, Shake Me! Developing String-Bending and Left-Hand Vibrato Skills

String-bending and vibrato are two techniques that are pretty important ones for lead guitar players to have down cold. Here are a few tips and suggestions that you'll hopefully find useful in both of these vital areas.

Getting the Bends

Looking back, I've had some kind of string-bending fetish for as long as I can remember. Soon after I first started playing, I saw someone bend a string for the very first time, and my eyes practically popped out of my head. I ran straight home and immediately started bending the shit out of pretty much every single note I played—and I guess I've never stopped since. As far as I'm concerned, there's no limit to how wide a string bend can be either: I mean, I've seen [blues great] Buddy Guy literally bend notes on the B and high E strings all the way up to the upper edge of his fretboard! Stevie Ray Vaughan was also a master of the big bend, as is another one of my all-time favorites, Gary Moore.

As I'm sure you know, how hard or easy a particular note is to bend not only depends on which string it's on, the gauge of that string, and how far you want to bend it—it also depends on where you are on the neck. The closer you are to the 12th fret, the easier it is to bend any string. Play the four full [one whole step] bends shown in Music 17 one after each other and you'll feel exactly what I mean.

Music 17

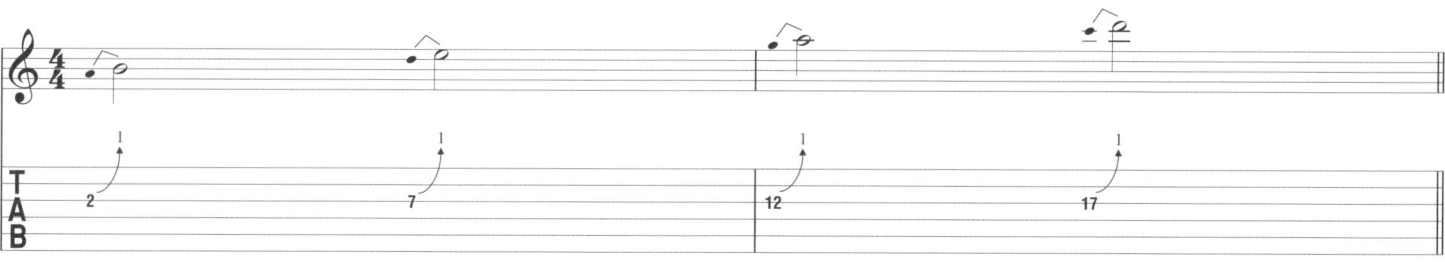

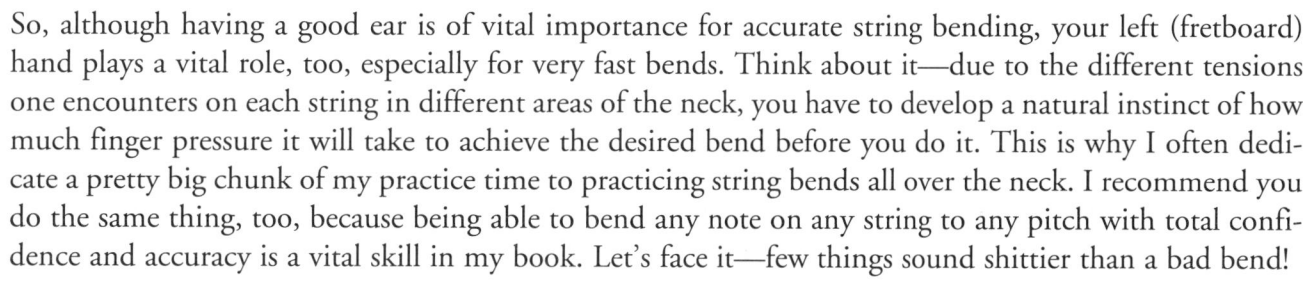

So, although having a good ear is of vital importance for accurate string bending, your left (fretboard) hand plays a vital role, too, especially for very fast bends. Think about it—due to the different tensions one encounters on each string in different areas of the neck, you have to develop a natural instinct of how much finger pressure it will take to achieve the desired bend before you do it. This is why I often dedicate a pretty big chunk of my practice time to practicing string bends all over the neck. I recommend you do the same thing, too, because being able to bend any note on any string to any pitch with total confidence and accuracy is a vital skill in my book. Let's face it—few things sound shittier than a bad bend!

Call in the Reinforcements—The Importance of Reinforced Bending

When I'm working on my bending, I don't just practice half step and whole step ("full") bends; I also like to go for really wide ones like those shown in Music 18.

Music 18

Track 18

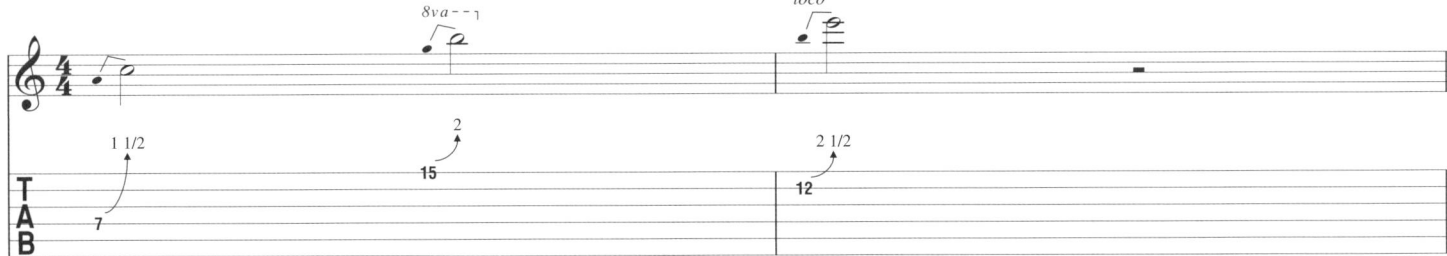

The great thing about wide bends (bends greater than a whole step) is that, provided they're done well, they can help add a "vocal" quality to a solo, especially when played in conjunction with a wah pedal. The only drawback of doing a lot of big bends is that you greatly increase your chances of breaking a string. I've always hated changing stings—especially on a guitar with a whammy bar. I guess that's a small price to pay for adding a more lyrical feel to your leads. Just like half step or whole step bends, though, wide bends have to be performed accurately.

Wide bends really test the accuracy of your string bending, so I'm going to start by giving you a few simple exercises to help you ensure you're doing them right. Before we go any further, though, for maximum strength and control, I recommend that you use a technique called *reinforced bending*, which simply means using more than one finger to do a bend. For example, if you're bending a string with your middle finger, use your index finger to help (Photo 5), and if you're bending with your ring (third) finger, use your index and middle fingers to help out with the bend (Photo 6). By doing this, you can even perform accurate, wide bends using your pinkie. Sure, the pinkie is the weakest finger, but when you *reinforce* it with one or more of the other three (Photo 7), it quickly gets strong! If you've never tried bending with your pinky before, it isn't as tough as it sounds—especially if you can assist it with one or more of the fingers behind it as just described.

Here's a tab tip: In order to, er, reinforce the idea of reinforced bending, sometimes the suggested fingering underneath the tab will include the reinforcing finger in parentheses. For example, "3(2)" under a bent note suggests that you bend with your ring finger and reinforce it with your middle finger. Likewise a "2(1)" would indicate a middle-finger bend reinforced by your index finger. Geddit?

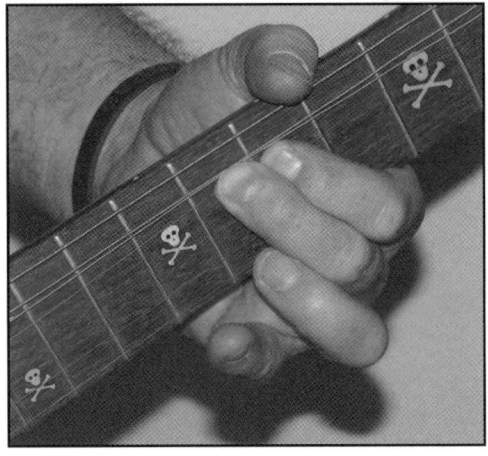
Photo 5

Photo 6

Photo 7

I work on bending with each finger, including my index finger, which is probably the weakest when it comes to string-bending because you obviously can't reinforce it with any of your other digits because it's the first in line! Bending with your index finger is a useful skill to develop, though, as it enables you to play licks like the E minor blues one shown in Music 19.

Music 19

Track 19

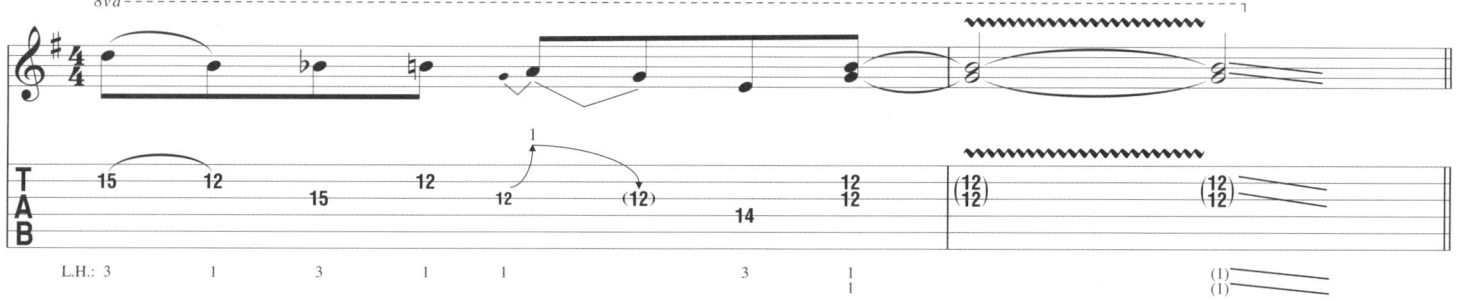

Push or Pull?

When doing the index-finger bend shown above, you'll probably find it easier to do by pulling the string down towards the floor (Photo 8) rather than pushing it up towards the ceiling—I find I have more strength/leverage by pulling down as I can "anchor" my hand with my thumb, which is hooked over the top of the neck as shown in the photo. Either way is obviously good, though—pick the one you're most comfortable with.

Talking of pushing (bending upwards) or pulling (bending downwards) when you're bending—as a rule, most players tend to bend the top three (unwound) strings upwards and the bottom (wound) strings downwards. In

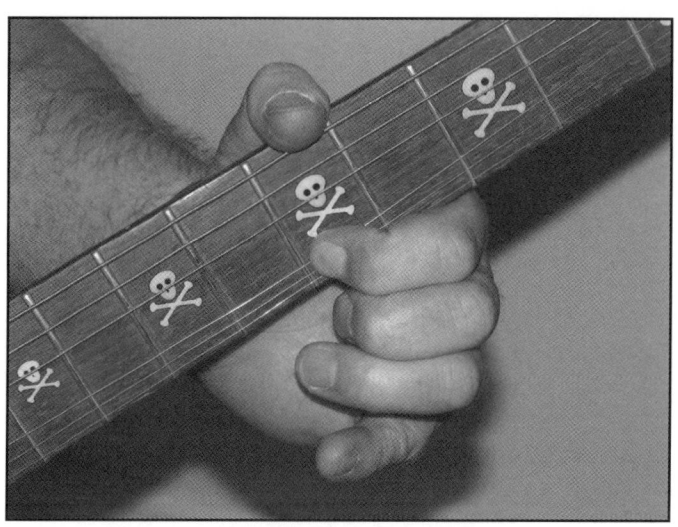

Photo 8

some cases, though, you have no choice—it's obviously not possible to bend the high E and B strings by pulling down on them as you'll literally pull the string off the fretboard. Likewise, when bending the low E and A strings you have to pull down on them, otherwise you'll push them off the top of the fretboard. Photo 9 shows a reinforced "upward bend" on the high E string, and Photo 10 shows a reinforced "downward bend" on the low E string.

Photo 9

Photo 10

Hitting Your Target—Bending Notes with Precision and Accuracy

Whenever you're doing any bend, wide or small, it's important to know what your *target pitch* is because if you overshoot or undershoot it you're gonna sound pretty stupid—unless you deliberately want to do that, of course! Music 20A, B, C, and D are four simple exercises, and each one involves three different bends in succession—one whole step, one and one half steps, and two whole steps. As you will see and hear, before each bend you play the target note to help fix it in your mind's ear.

Work on mastering each example separately first and then try and string them together. Don't get frustrated if you don't nail this right away. Like any playing technique worth learning, wide, accurate bending takes time to master.

Music 20A

Track 20
:00

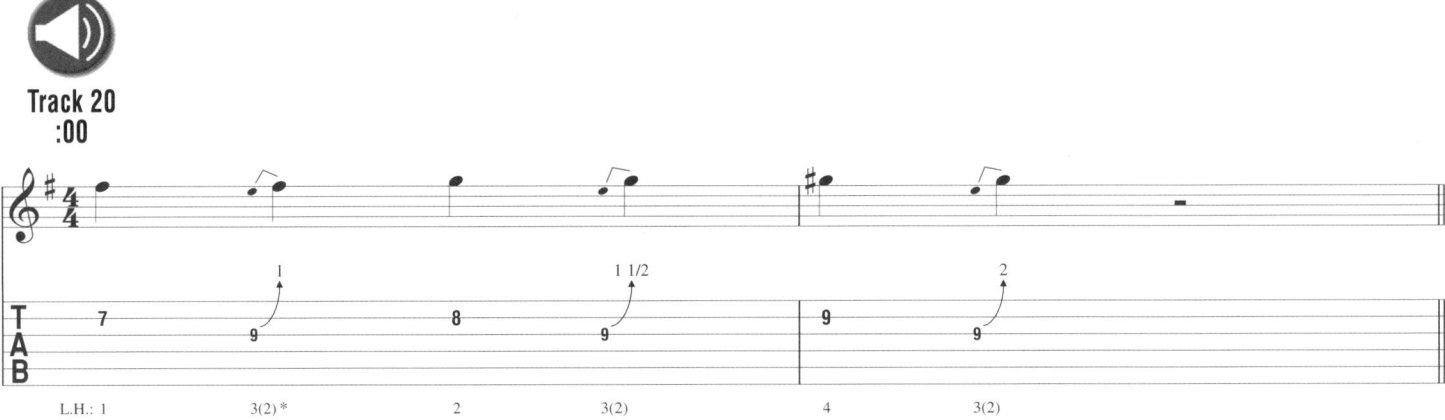

*Reinforced bend

Music 20B

Music 20C

Music 20D

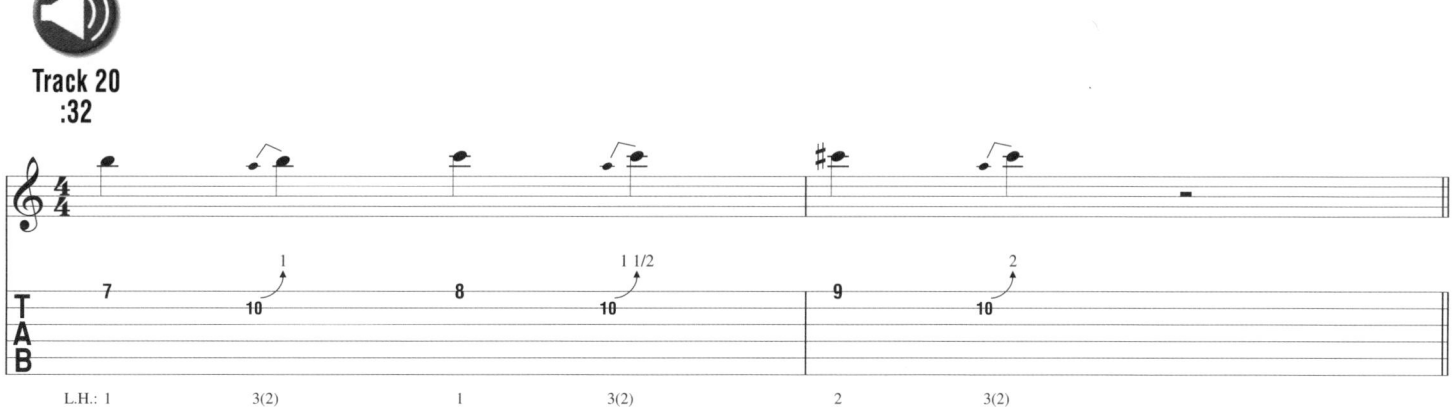

As mentioned earlier, you'll find that the closer you get to the 12th fret (the midpoint between the nut and the bridge), the easier the bends become. Once you feel you've gotten the hang of bending the G and B strings like this, try to execute similar bending exercises on the other strings. As already mentioned, you'll also quickly discover that how hard (or easy) a particular note is to bend not only depends on how far you want to bend it, but also on what string you're on and where on the neck you are. The B and G strings are usually the easiest strings to bend because of the ratio between their thickness and pitch.

When you feel comfortable doing these bend exercises and are hitting the target notes with ease, try doing them in "slow motion." Then, to make them even more challenging, add some sweet left-hand vibrato on the end of each bend, too—and don't forget to use reinforced fingering!

Shake Me—Pursuing and Perfecting the Vital Art of Left-Hand Vibrato

There are countless variations on the speed and width of left-hand vibrato you can apply to a bent or unbent note. A lot of players make the mistake of just mastering one particular type of vibrato (e.g., fast and wide) and then do it all the time, no matter what. Falling into a rut like that is easy to do, but I suggest you try and avoid it at all costs because it's a definite limitation. Slow and wide, slow and narrow, fast and narrow. . . . Like I've just said, there are numerous left-hand vibrato possibilities and they all have their place. So, use your ears, experiment, and find what works. Also . . .

Listen, Look, and Learn

Being able to shake a note in a way that compliments both the song and also the mood of the solo is a highly expressive art that's been perfected by great players such as Eric Clapton, Stevie Ray Vaughan, Ace Frehley, John Sykes, Jimi Hendrix, and Michael Schenker. Unfortunately, this technique is almost as difficult to describe as it is to do. So, to learn more about it, I recommend two courses of action.

1. Listen carefully to the guitarists I've just mentioned.

2. Watch videos or DVDs of them in action and really zone in on what each one does with their left hand . . . or, in Hendrix's case, his right hand!

You'll probably find the second suggestion particularly useful. As the saying goes, sometimes a picture is worth a thousand words, and this is definitely one such instance.

Bend Over! Compound String Bends

Next, we're gonna expand a little bit more on string-bending ideas and talk about using compound bends, which are a great way of adding fire and expression to your licks and solos.

Double Your Pleasure

So far, we've only talked about bending a note up to another note. Let's take this a step further by bending a note up to one pitch and then, without releasing the first bend, bending it up *again* to another note. This is what is known as a *compound bend* (a.k.a. *a multiple bend*). If you're not quite sure what I'm talking about here, check out bar 2 of Music 21.

Music 21

Track 21

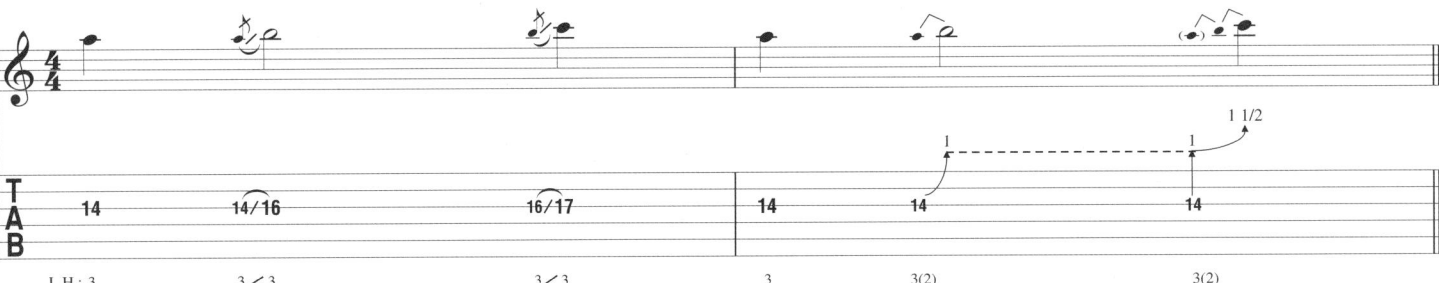

In the second bar of Music 21, we're bending the A note on the G string at the 14th fret up a whole step to B, holding it there for two beats, and then bending it up an additional half step to C. And, as you can see, the second bend is done without releasing the first one. So, what you're doing is bending an already bent note even further, for a total of one and one half steps. Geddit?

Compound bends really test the accuracy of your bending technique, which is why using *reinforced fingering* and hearing your *target pitches* are so important. Although these types of bends may look easy on paper, they're pretty hard to do accurately, so don't get mad if you don't nail this example right away. To help you get the sound of the two notes you're aiming for fixed firmly in your head, bar 1 of Music 21 "mimics" the sound of the two pitches you're aiming for using slides instead of bends.

Repeat this two-bar exercise over and over until you're nailing the compound bend in bar 2 accurately and fluently (i.e., without hesitation) every time. Then, once you've got this down, try adding some left-hand finger vibrato to the bends, as shown in Music 22. This is not an easy technique to master, but make a determined effort to learn how to do it well because the soulfulness the vibrato adds to the bends definitely makes it worth the extra effort. To achieve the desired vibrato effect on the bent notes, you'll need to repeatedly release the bend slightly and then bend back up to the target pitch in a smooth, steady rhythm.

Music 22

Track 22

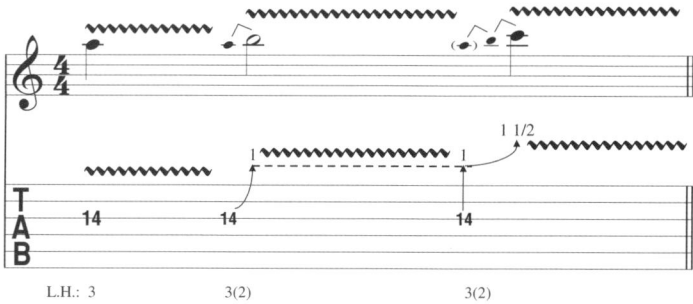

Here are a couple more examples of compound bends for you to work on. Music 23 is a half step bend that is bent up an additional whole step, while Music 24 is a whole step bend on top of another whole step bend. Once you feel you've conquered both of these examples, try adding some vibrato to each bent note, just like we did previously.

Music 23

Track 23

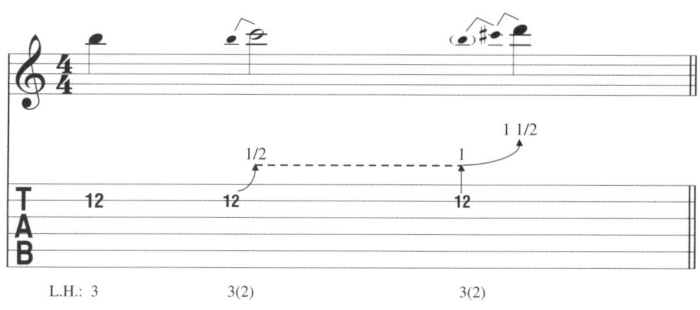

Music 24

Track 24

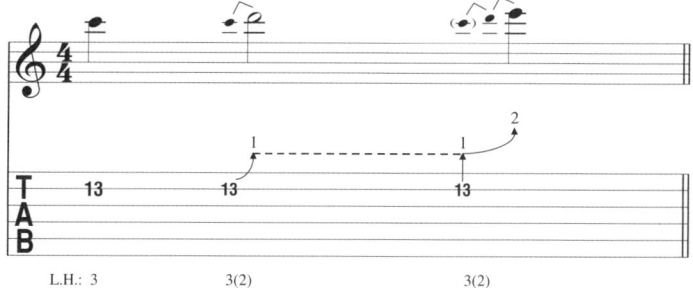

Music 25 is a three-stage compound bend that will really challenge you: a whole step bend, followed by another whole step bend, and then a half step bend on top of that. Be sure to use two or three fingers to push the string (reinforced bending) for maximum control. Once you feel you can accurately hit the "target" pitches every time, add some vibrato to the bent notes to make them "sing."

Music 25

Track 25

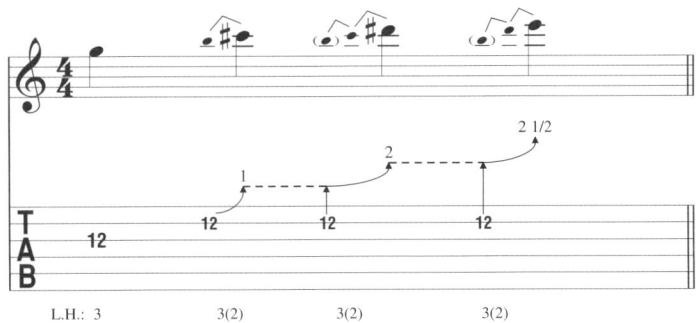

I realize that the examples we've just gone through aren't the most exciting ones on the planet, but stick with 'em, because mastering these bending techniques will definitely add an exciting new dimension to your playing, and that's what *The Sound & the Fury* is all about.

Slide It In—Using Finger Slides to Open up the Neck and Explore Uncharted Fretboard Territory

A great way of making use of the whole neck and getting around it as seamlessly as possible is by using *finger slides*. A good example of what I'm talking about here is the E minor pentatonic (E–G–A–B–D) passage shown in Music 26, which is similar to the cool run KISS guitarist Ace Frehley uses during the breakdown in the middle of "Love Gun" [*Love Gun*]. As you can see, in the space of just four bars, it covers quite a lot of fretboard area. It starts at the 10th fret on the low E string and ends up at the 22nd fret on the high E string. And, as you'll hear when you play it, the thing flows very smoothly from start to finish, without any pauses or gaps. Plus, as you'll also discover, all it took to achieve this was three simple finger-slides up the neck. They're pretty short slides, too; the first two go up just two frets, and the third one goes up three.

Music 26

Track 26

48

 You can obviously do the same kind of thing going the other way, too (descending). Music 27 shows an E minor run that uses a couple of slides going down the neck (toward the nut).

Music 27

Track 27

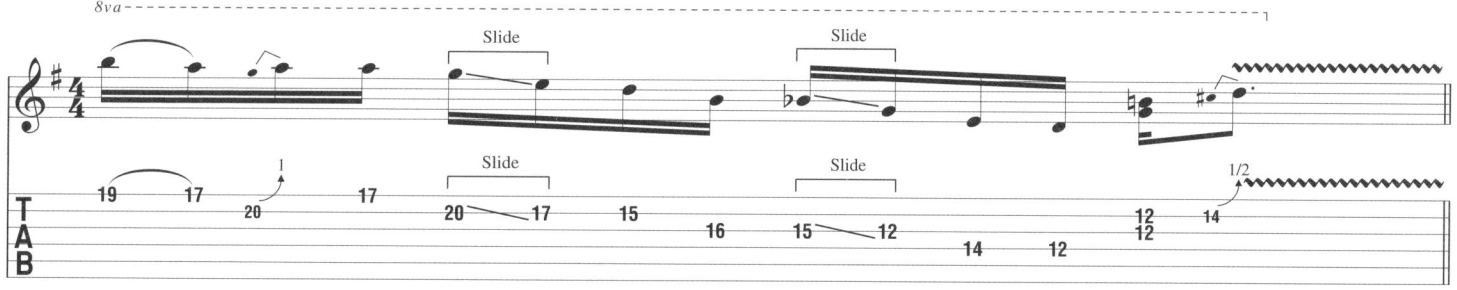

 I've heard quite a few people say that they always slide up the neck using their ring or middle fingers, and down using only their index finger. I generally avoid that kind of thinking like the plague, though, because it causes you to lock into using certain fretboard patterns all the time, and that's what we're trying to avoid here. This is why I always try to use all my fingers to slide both up and down the neck. Let me give you an example of why this is a good habit to get into.

Let's say you're playing a lead in E minor and you start out using the well-worn blues box shape we all know at the 12th position. A real common way of getting out of this box is to slide up the G string from the 14th fret to the 16th using your middle finger, just like we did near the end of the second bar of Music 26. By doing this, we go from one well-worn box shape (Diagram 3) straight into another, equally familiar one (Diagram 4).

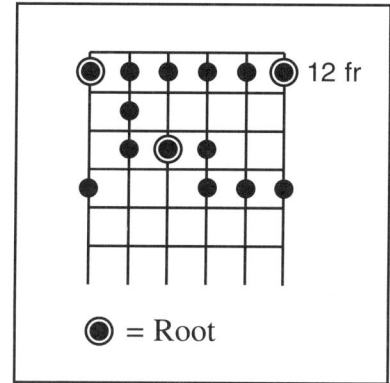 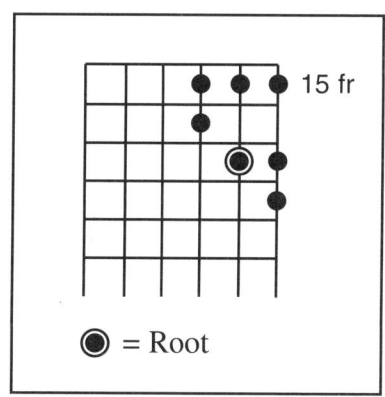

Diagram 3: The E minor 12th-position blues box Diagram 4: The E minor 15th-position blues box

All we're doing here is retreading old, familiar ground. So go ahead and try something new . . . like sliding up the G string from the 12th to the 16th fret using your 1st finger, as depicted in Music 28. By doing this, you force yourself to explore a new area of the neck.

Music 28

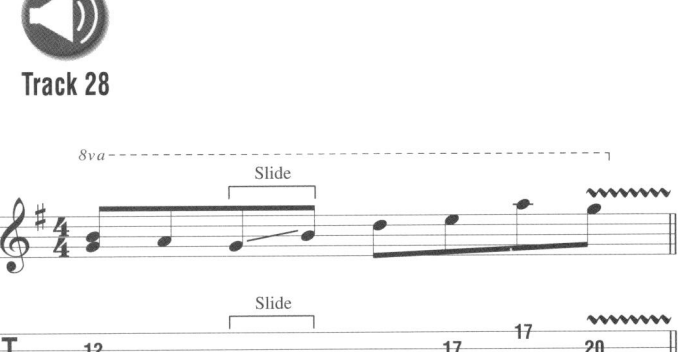

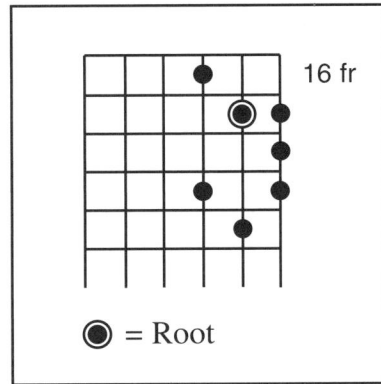

Diagram 5: The E minor 16th-position blues box

The "new" blues box this slide takes us into is illustrated in Diagram 5. And, once we've lingered there for a bit we can slide up into another minor pentatonic box in 19th position as shown in Diagram 6. Music 29 shows the run extended into this new box.

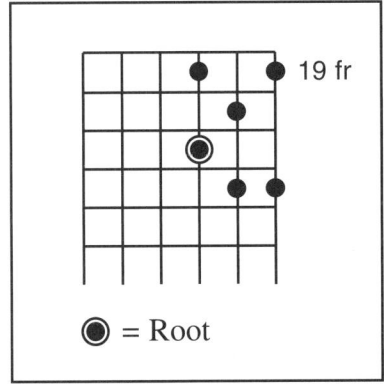

Diagram 6: The E minor 19th-position box

Music 29

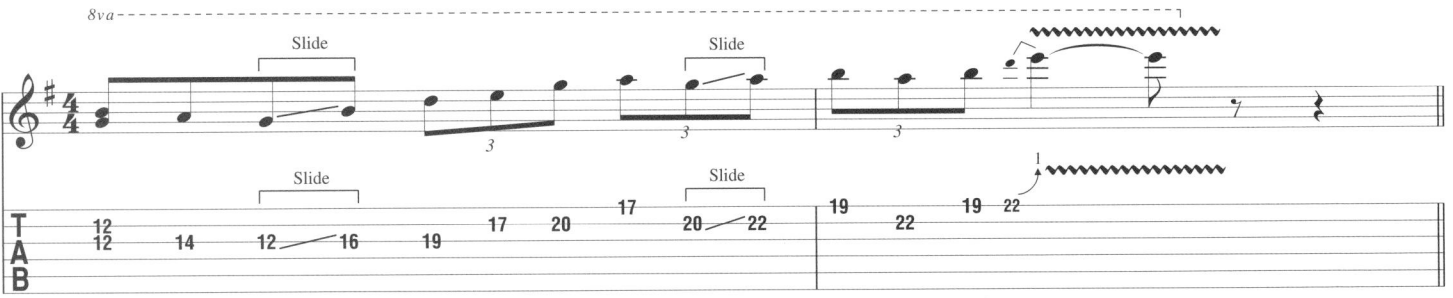

Talking about sliding around the neck with all your fingers, some players seem to avoid doing it with their pinkies at all costs. To me, that's a mistake—your little finger is there so you should use it. My friend Larry Lalonde of Primus slides with his little finger all the time; in fact, I don't think I've ever seen anyone slide around the neck with their pinkie as much as he does!

Sliding on a Single String

A real simple way you can open up the whole fretboard with finger slides is by merely sliding up and/or down the neck on a single string. For example, check out the A minor run shown in Music 30. It starts off in 5th position and, within the space of less than two bars, ends up a whole octave higher in 17th position. Furthermore, it does so without sounding disjointed or jerky—it's fluent and smooth throughout, and all we've done to achieve this is slide up the G string in a few relatively small steps.

Music 30

Track 30

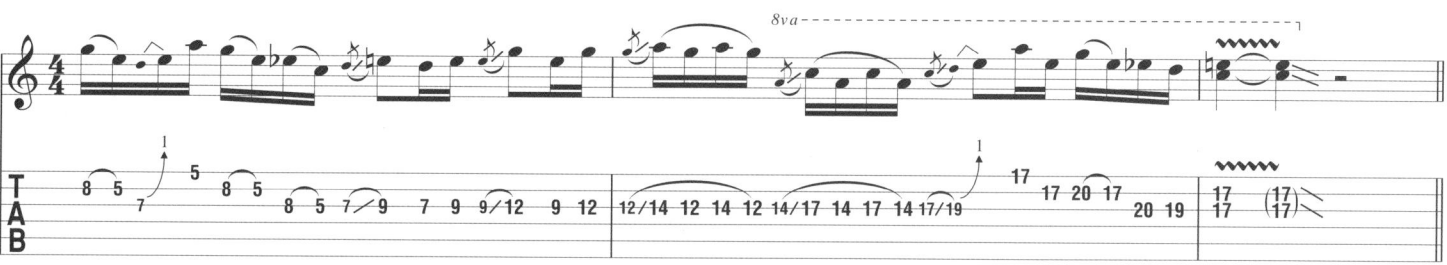

Similarly, Music 31 is a descending A minor run that does the exact opposite—it starts in 17th position and finishes in 5th. And, once again, the only string used to slide on is the G string.

Music 31

Track 31

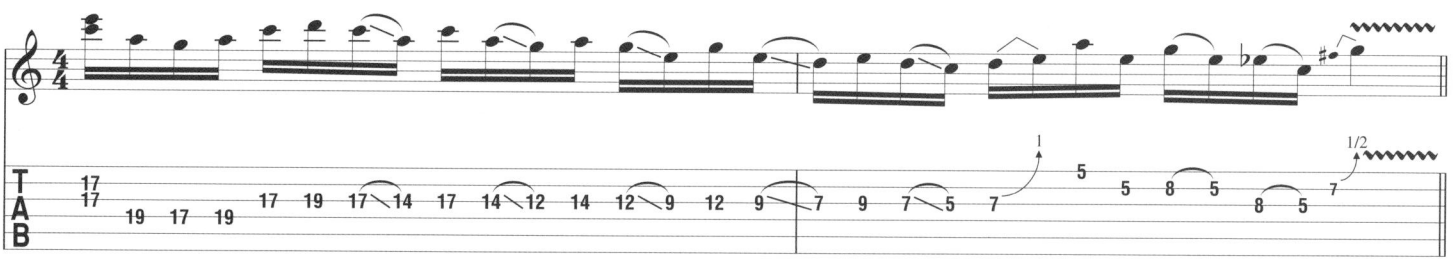

Doing this sort of thing on one string not only gets you moving around the neck, it also increases your knowledge of the fretboard. Try using other strings to do this, too, in a variety of keys. For instance, Music 32 [top of page 52] is a descending E minor lick similar to one I do about two-thirds of the way through my "The God That Failed" [*Metallica*] solo. As you can see, I cover a lot of ground, and all I'm doing is sliding on the high E string.

Music 32

Track 32

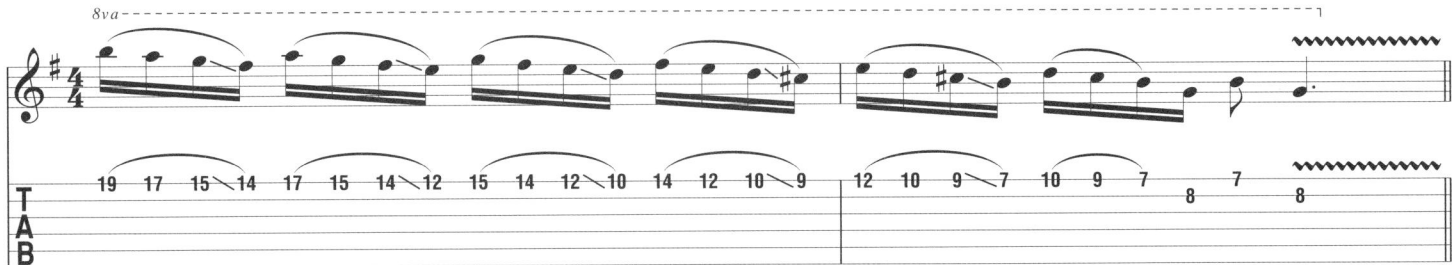

One of my favorite string-sliding tricks is using this technique to create seamless, legato trills up and down the neck. Jimi Hendrix did this kind of thing a lot—he'd pick one note and then do a really smooth-sounding run up and down that string without picking it again by combining trills (hammer-ons and pull-offs), string slides, and bends. The E minor lick in Music 33 illustrates what I'm talking about here, and using your neck (rhythm) pickup will make this lick sound even more fluid. Another great player who does this sort of thing a lot is another Strat user, Dave Murray from Iron Maiden.

Music 33

Track 33

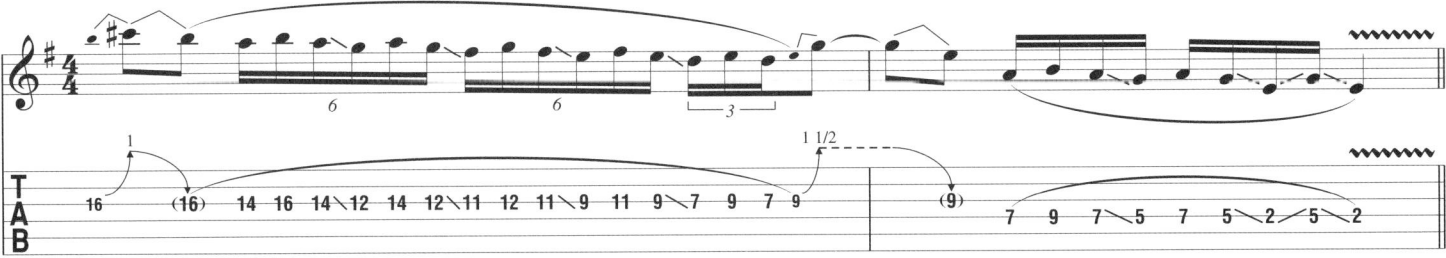

Another thing I find finger slides really useful for is playing wide intervals—like octaves and half-octaves. A great example of this is Music 34, a Michael Schenker–style run in B minor. This idea goes back to something we've talked about several times already—using wide intervals to create unexpected excitement in your playing. My old teacher and pal, Joe Satriani, does a lot of really long slides like this, and that's probably where I got it from.

Music 34

Track 34

Open Up and Say "Ah!"

Next, I'd like to touch on a simple but cool playing concept that can add life, dimension, and character to your lead breaks—the use of open string notes. And, just like the two things we've just covered, wide-stretches and string-skipping, using open-string notes is another highly effective yet incredibly easy way to introduce unexpected wide intervals into a solo.

The ironic thing about open strings is that we all use them like there's no tomorrow when we're riffing, but most of us tend to forget about them when it comes time to solo. That's a crying shame as far as I'm concerned because, in my humble opinion, using open strings during a lead break can be very effective. In addition to being easy to play, open-string notes have some very useful advantages.

- They're instantly accessible, regardless of where your fretboard hand is on the neck.

- They work well in a bunch of different keys. Think about it!

- They have a naturally bright and twangy sound that can't be matched by any of their fretted counterparts. Compare the open high E string with the exact same note at either the 5th fret on the B string, the 9th fret on the G string, or the 14th fret on the D string, and you'll hear exactly what I mean.

To illustrate just how effective open-string notes can be during a solo, I'm going to give you a few examples. Music 35 is an ascending E Phrygian mode (E–F–G–A–B–C–D) run that uses the open G-string note as a *pedal point* [a type of repeated note] while the left hand climbs the neck using a series of rapid hammer-on and pull-off combinations. In addition to sounding flashy while being relatively easy to play, Music 35 allows me to move seamlessly up the neck without missing a beat. I do a very similar run in my "Whiplash" [*Kill 'Em All*] solo.

Music 35

Track 35

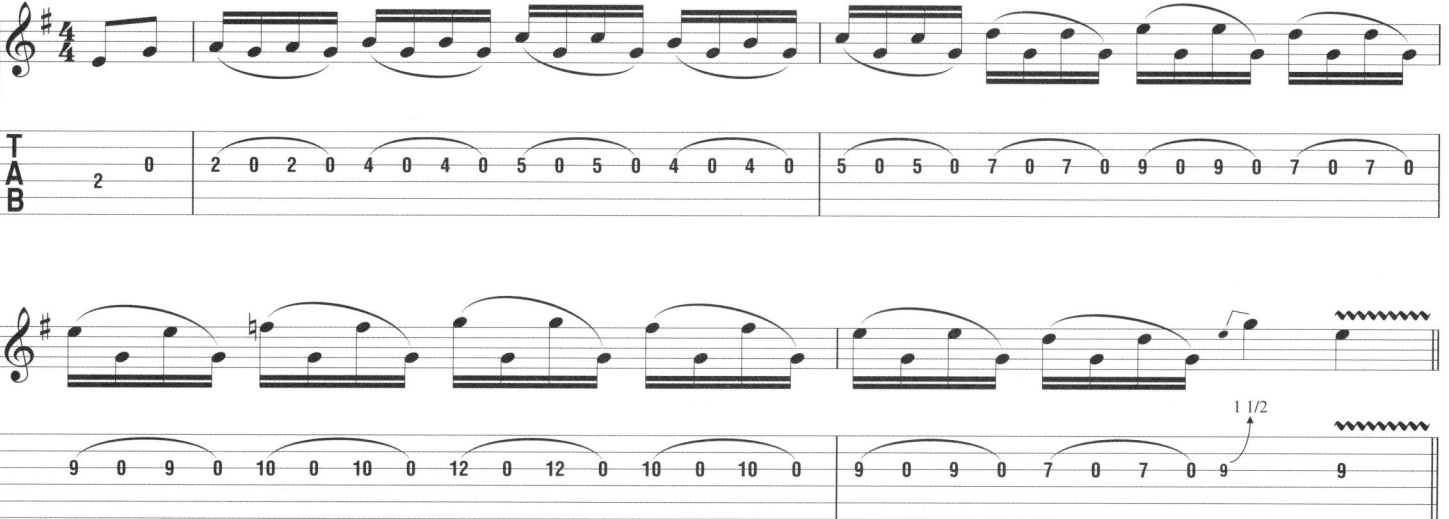

Using open-string notes can also provide you with a very simple and effective way of playing *arpeggios* [broken chords] and Music 36 is a great example of this approach in action. The arpeggios being played (B–Em–E–Am) are indicated above the tablature. As you can see, this passage makes use of the open B- and open high E-string notes, and consists of two simple hammer-on patterns—open string to 4th fret to 7th fret, and open string to 5th fret to 8th fret. You can hear me making good use of the Bm and Em arpeggios on the B string during the intro to our cover of Diamond Head's classic "Am I Evil?" [*Kill 'Em All*].

Music 36

Track 36

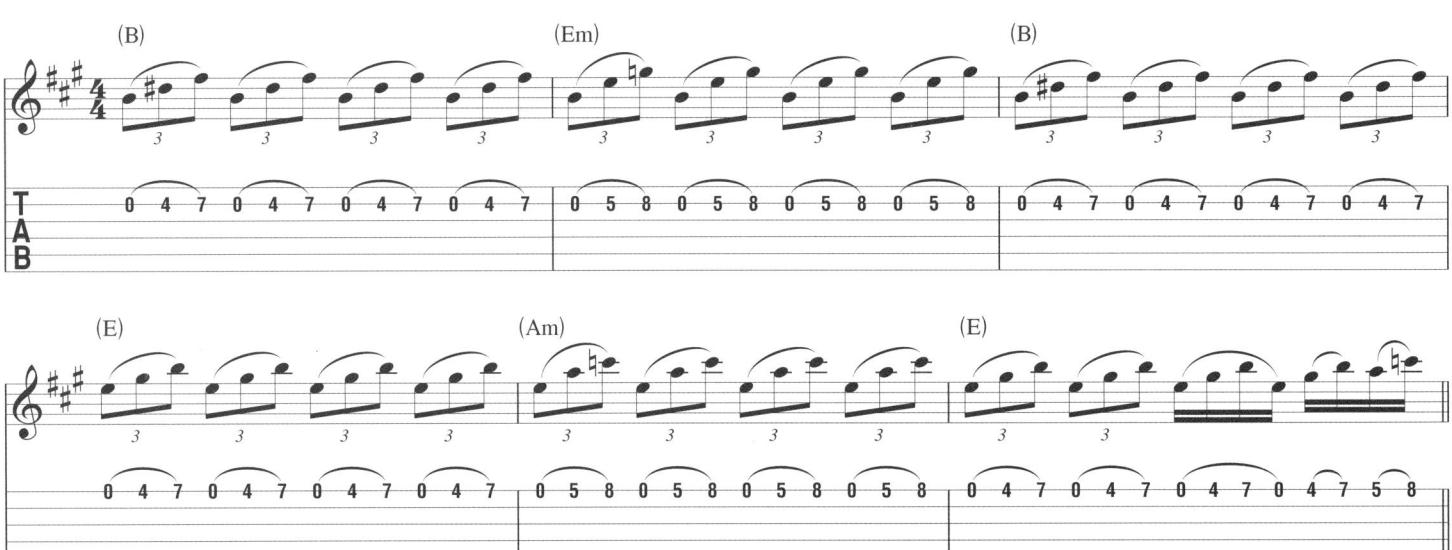

Music 37 is a minor line similar to the one I play in the third and fourth bars of my solo in "The God That Failed" [*Metallica*]. Here, I play an E harmonic minor (E–F♯–G–A–B–C–D♯) pattern on the B string while using the open high E-string note as a *drone*. I got the idea from "Paint It Black" by the Rolling Stones. In both songs, the droning string adds a distinctly Eastern, sitar-like vibe. Just so you know, I use strict alternate picking on this run: downstrokes on all the B-string notes and upstrokes on all the open Es.

Music 37

Track 37

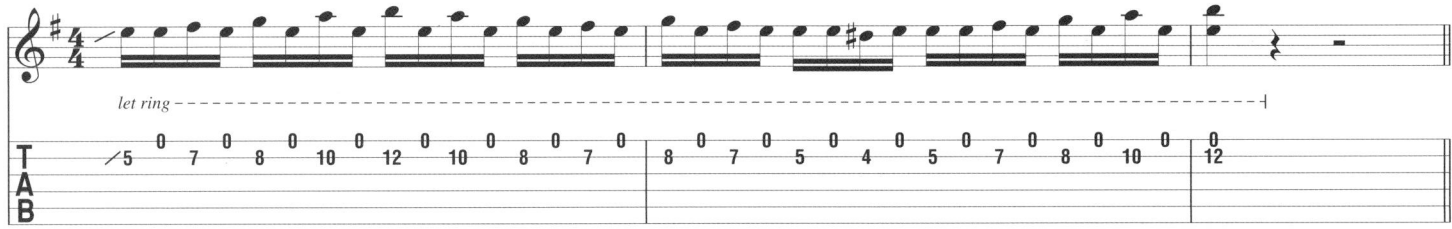

Ode to Jeff Beck

When I first started playing guitar, I read an interview with Jeff Beck in which he said something that really stuck in my mind and still does to this very day. He said that he likes playing things that are easy but sound difficult. And the intro to my "Of Wolf and Man" solo shown below in Music 38 is exactly that—it sounds difficult, but is actually pretty simple to play. I guess the thing that makes it sound complex is the timing and phrasing of the notes.

Music 38

Track 38

"Of Wolf and Man"
Words and Music by James Hetfield, Lars Ulrich and Kirk Hammett
Copyright © 1991 Creeping Death Music (GMR)
International Copyright Secured   All Rights Reserved

I wanted a really dynamic and interesting intro to that solo—something that had an exciting, percussive groove. At the time, though, I just couldn't come up with something no matter how hard I tried. So, I put my guitar down, played the track without soloing, and just kinda sang what I wanted to hear. The very first time through I came up with something I liked, so I picked up my guitar again and figured out how to play what I'd just sung. I played it over the rhythm track and it worked really well. I was really happy because I'd been struggling with the beginning of that solo for what seemed like forever.

Once again, open-string notes play a pivotal role (sorry, awful pun not intended!) in this particular example. The opening two bars are more rhythmic than melodic, and then the chromatic climb up the A string using the open A note as a pedal point sounds a lot more complicated than it really is due to the wide intervals created by continually pulling off to the open A.

To be frank, Music 38 is 50% Jimmy Page and 50% Angus Young! The first half is Jimmy and the second half is Angus. Jimmy Page always seems to play those off-kilter, polyrhythmic, pull-off patterns like in bar 2, and Angus would always do pull-offs to an open string while he moved up the neck chromatically, especially on early AC/DC stuff like "Dirty Deeds (Done Dirt Cheap)."

Talking of the great Jimmy Page and using open strings, legend has it that another guitar giant, Edward Van Halen, first got the idea for his innovative two-handed tapping from some of Page's clever use of an open-string-note as a pedal point in a solo. Which segways us neatly into Kirk's next topic.

55

Tapping into Tone—A Look at the Taboo Technique of Two-Handed Tapping

We've just explored a few very effective ways of introducing wide intervals into our playing—wide fretboard-hand stretches, string-skipping, and using open-string notes. So, the next logical topic for us to discuss is *two-handed tapping*. To be honest, I almost decided to ignore the technique altogether because it's been done to death. But then I realized that if I didn't touch on it, I'd be implying that two-handed stuff isn't cool. Just so you know, I think that tapping *is* cool—as long as it isn't overused or employed mindlessly. Also, contrary to what certain narrow-minded people think, tapping doesn't automatically make you an *"Edward Van Halen clone!"* That's a totally ridiculous notion. The only time it holds true is if you merely regurgitate Eddie's two-handed licks, note-for-note.

On the surface, the appeal of the two-handed technique is that it enables you to perform lightning-fast, wide interval runs that are virtually impossible to play any other way—such as the E minor passage shown in Music 39.

Music 39

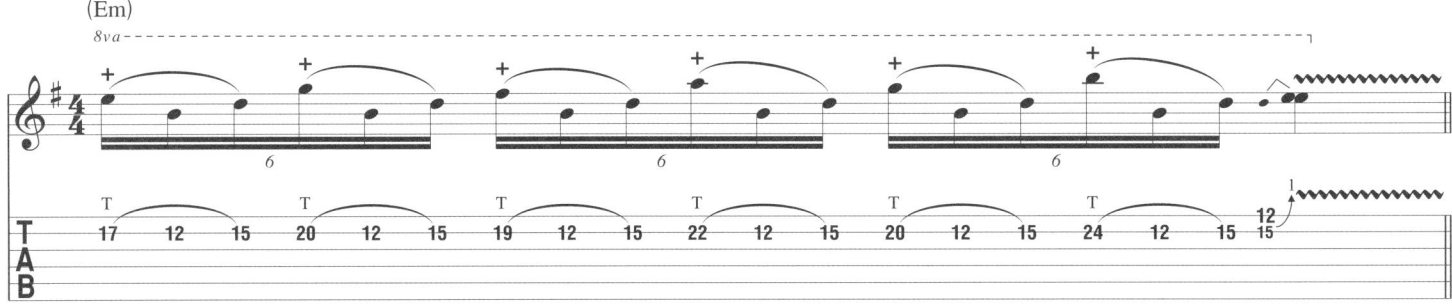

To me, though, the great thing about tapping is the fluid tone it produces. For example, compare the simple A minor pentatonic lick in Music 40 with the tapped version shown in Music 41. I'm sure you'll agree that Music 41 sounds much smoother.

Music 40

Music 41

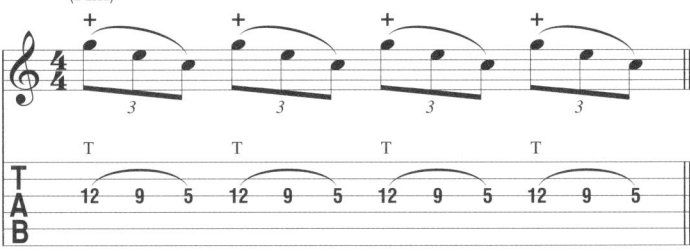

Continuing with this comparative theme, Music 42 is the two-handed version of the F♯ and G arpeggios in Music 43 . . . the tapped version of which is similar to a section of my "To Live Is to Die" solo on . . . *And Justice for All.*

Music 42

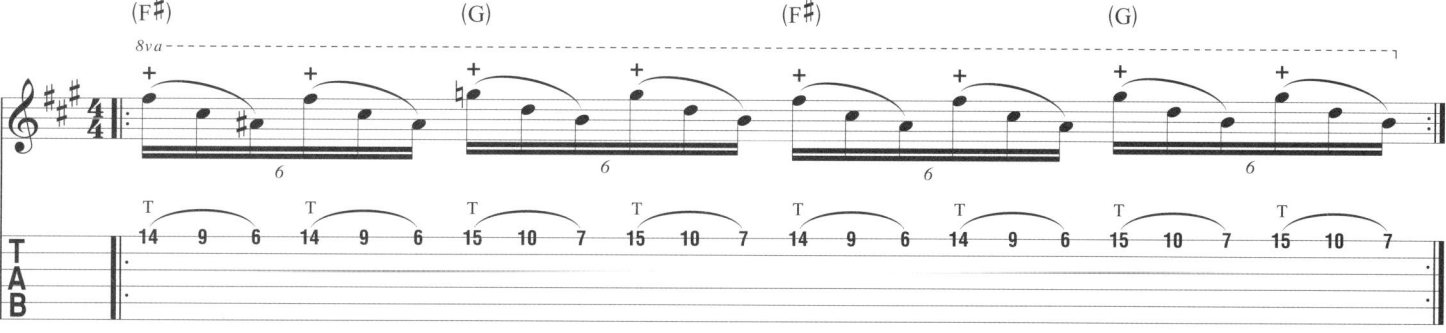

Music 43

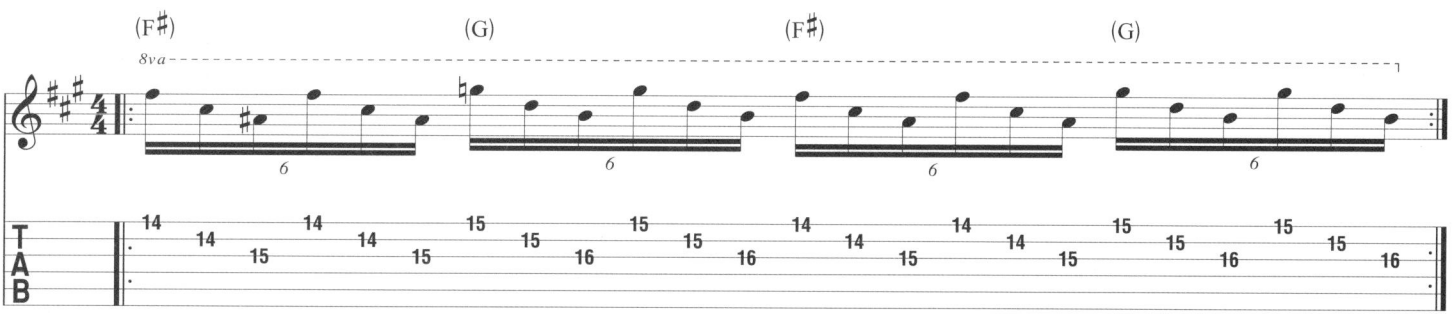

Try coming up with two-handed versions of your own licks and runs—doing this might open up some new doors in your soloing approach while also giving you some subtle tonal options to think about.

Liquid Tonal Gold

Aside from the obvious sonic difference in attack between tapped and picked notes, the main reason the two-hand technique produces such a "liquid" tone is that, no matter how fast you play, the notes you play never overlap. This happens because the majority of tapping runs use only one string, meaning that only one note can sound at any one time—think about it! As we've seen in the examples we've just gone over, when you try to play the exact same run without tapping, you'll invariably have to use more than one string, and this means that notes running into each other is a distinct possibility, especially if you're playing really fast. Sure, sometimes having more than one note ringing when you're soloing can be the shit, but not always! Compare how the F♯ and G arpeggios in Music 42 and Music 43 sound when you play them as fast as you can and you'll definitely hear what I'm talking about.

Texture Tool

To my way of thinking, tapping is much more of a textural thing than the main, feature part of a solo. So, on the rare occasions I do tap, I tend to use the technique more as an effect than anything else. The reason I used two-handed tapping at the beginning of my solo in "One" is that it sounded much more dynamic and also more exciting than playing the same exact thing by regular means. What I'm playing in the first four bars is basically four three-note arpeggios—Em, C, Bm, and G. And, as was the case with the previous example, with two-handed tapping you can get these arpeggios sounding much cleaner and smoother than you could by playing them without tapping—especially at speed. Compare Music 44, a tapped version, with Music 45, a "regular" (i.e., untapped!) version of the first two bars, and once again you'll hear what I mean.

To add extra vibe to the splendid "ad-libbed" version Kirk's given us of the first four bars of his "One" solo, I've also added James's rhythm part to Music 44.

Music 44

Track 44

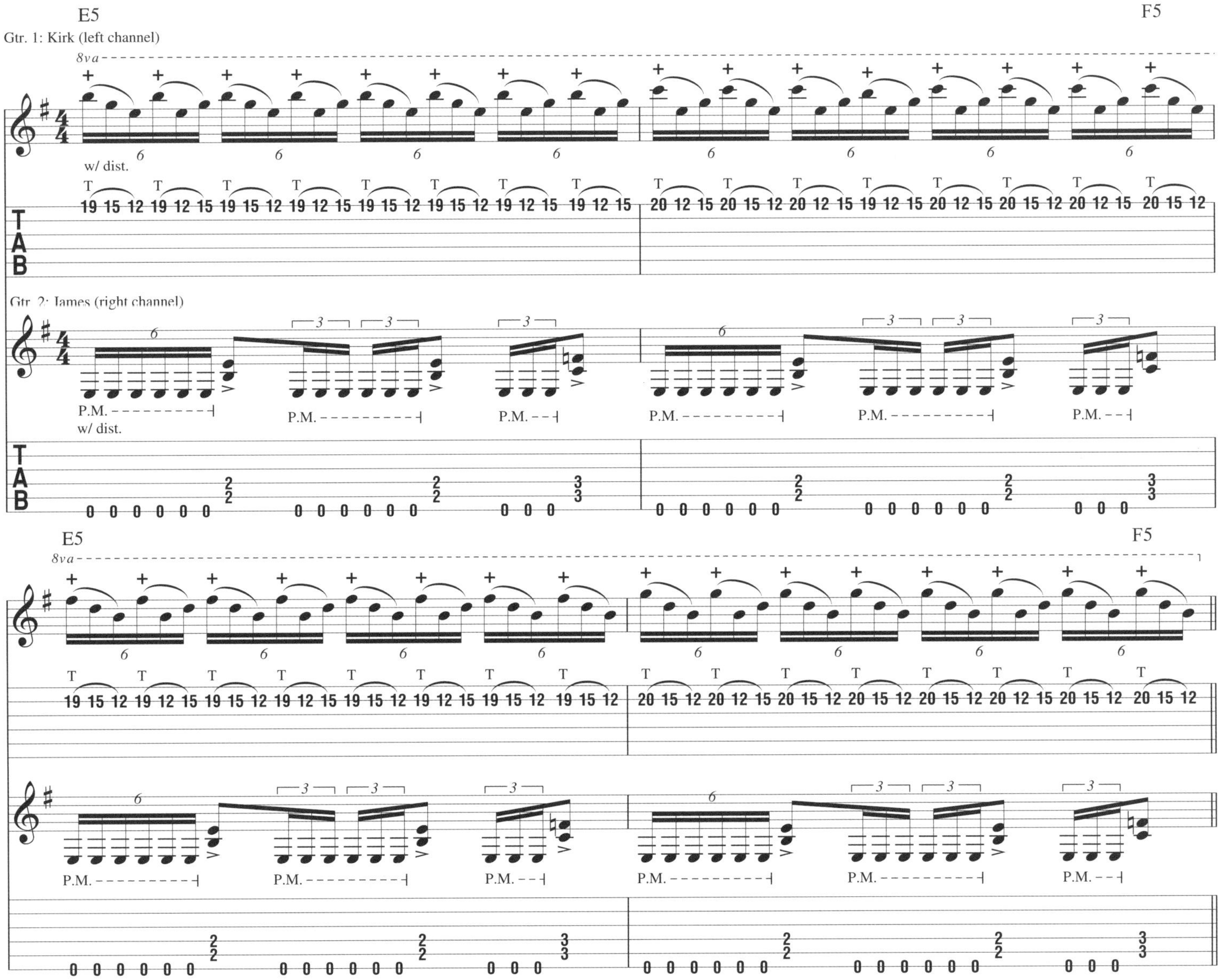

"One"
Words and Music by James Hetfield and Lars Ulrich
Copyright © 1988 Creeping Death Music (GMR)
International Copyright Secured   All Rights Reserved

As Kirk points out, in addition to sounding smoother and cleaner, it's also much easier to achieve sub-human speeds via tapping. Try getting Music 45 (the "untapped" version of the first two bars of the solo) up to the speed of "One" on the album, and you'll immediately see and hear what I'm talking about here.

Music 45

Track 45

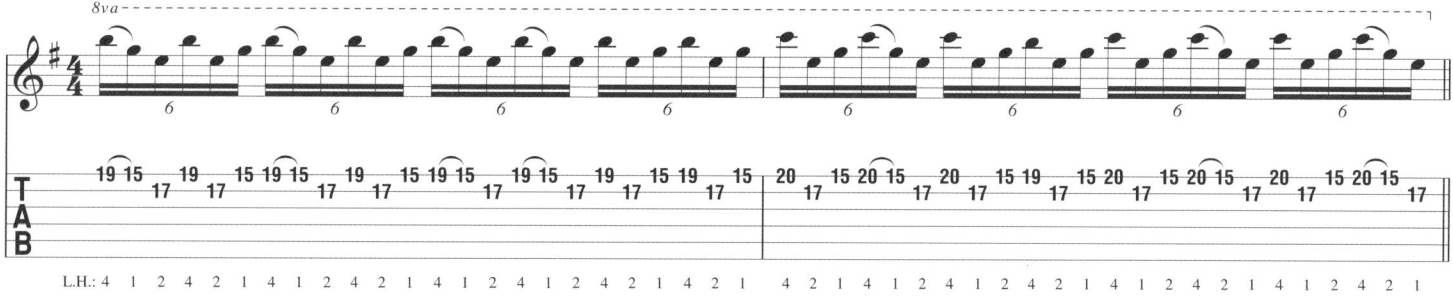

"One"
Words and Music by James Hetfield and Lars Ulrich
Copyright © 1988 Creeping Death Music (GMR)
International Copyright Secured   All Rights Reserved

Let's take a look at a few more two-handed tapping ideas that are worth investigating.

Open Up

A great and pretty obvious way to increase the wide interval possibilities of tapping is to incorporate open-string notes as well. The E minor tapping run in Music 46 is a good example of what I'm talking about here. The one and only Eddie Van Halen used this idea to great effect at the start of his "Spanish Fly" solo piece on *Van Halen II*.

Music 46

Track 46

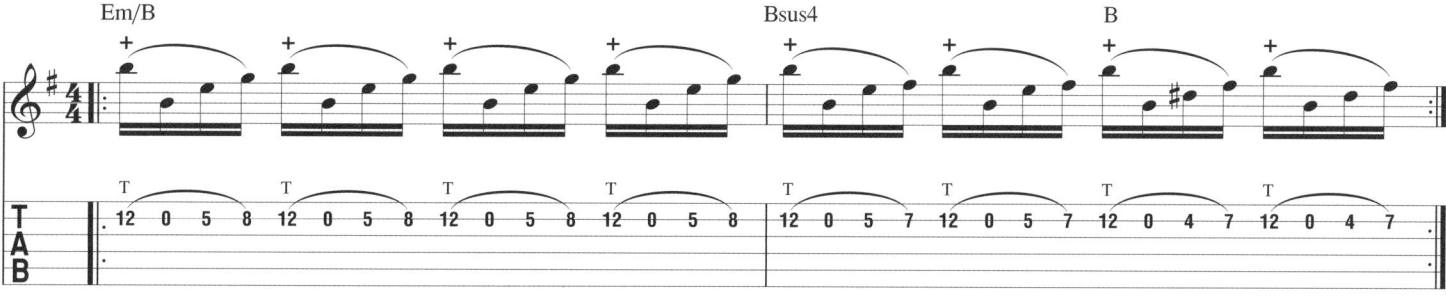

Pick Juggling and How to Avoid It

I tap with the middle finger of my right hand. Some players tap with their index finger, but this means that they have to juggle around the pick before and after tapping because the most common way to grip a pick is between your right thumb and index finger. Some players "palm" their picks, and I've even seen some guys put the thing in their mouths whenever they tap! I never have to worry about this because, by tapping with my middle finger, my pick can stay exactly where it is.

59

Take Your Pick

Speaking of picks, one way to get a completely different tone when tapping is by using the edge of your pick to tap with. I used to take lessons from Joe Satriani, and he taps with his pick all the time. The late, great Randy Rhoads used to do the exact same thing, too. Personally speaking, I feel that it sounds warmer when you tap using the flesh of your fingertip rather than the edge of your pick. Tapping with your pick produces a brighter, sharper attack that definitely works in certain situations—try both and let your ears decide.

In addition to preferring the tone it produces, another reason I like tapping with my fingertip is that I know I'm definitely hitting the note I'm supposed to be hitting! When you tap with your pick, sometimes you might not be hitting the string straight on. To me it's about accuracy and feel, in addition to being a sonic thing. Tapping with my finger feels more natural to me, too.

Funnily enough, a few people have written in saying that they read in an article that I use the edge of my pick to play the two-handed tapping section of my "One" solo. Well, just to confirm, I don't—I use my middle finger there. Maybe it's just the way I hold my pick that fools people . . . or maybe it's because I keep forgetting to cut the nails on my right hand so it sounds like I'm tapping with the edge of my pick!

Bend 'n' Tap

Sometimes I'll bend a string while I'm tapping it so it goes up in pitch, which can be a neat effect. I do this bend-and-tap technique I'm talking about here very briefly in "Damage, Inc." from *Master of Puppets*. After the main solo there are two fills, and I do this on one of those. When we recorded the song in the studio, I performed the fill in question by tapping all the way up the neck—I just moved my tapping finger up the neck chromatically (one fret at a time). But whenever we play that song live, I just tap the same fret while I'm bending the crap out of the string because it's more fun that way and it sounds a lot cooler, too!

This is another instance when I definitely prefer tapping with my finger rather than with the edge of my pick. When you're tapping with your finger it's very easy to follow the bend with your tapping finger all the way to the target note. Doing the same thing while tapping with your pick definitely doesn't feel as solid and is much more of a hit-and-miss affair.

Tap 'n' Slide

A cool-sounding two-handed approach is to do slides with your tapping finger. You can slide off a tapped note to an indefinite point, as shown in the A minor motif in Music 47, or you can slide between specific notes, as shown in Music 48. Doing the latter may prove difficult at first because it's unlike anything you've probably done before, but persevere with the technique because it's definitely worth mastering.

Music 47

Track 47

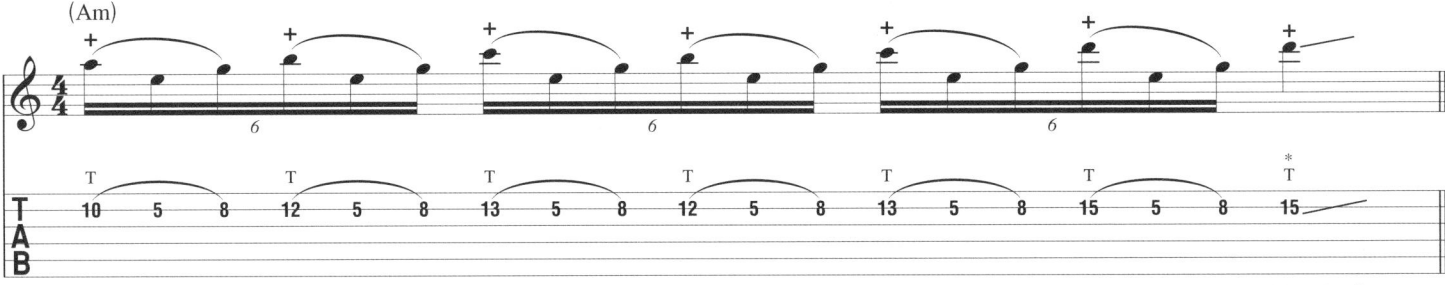

*Slide up neck with tapping finger (or edge of pick) to an indefinite point.

Music 48

Track 48

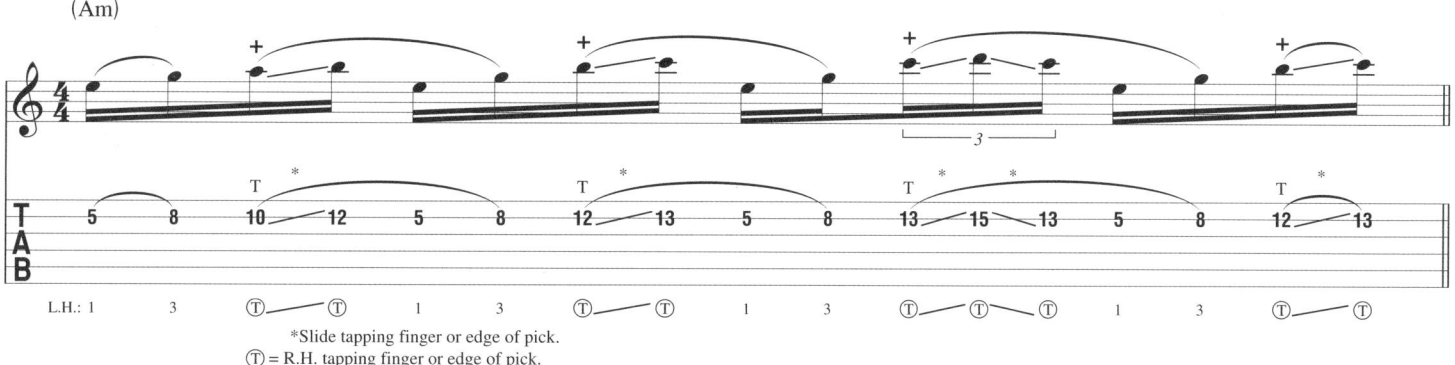

*Slide tapping finger or edge of pick.
Ⓣ = R.H. tapping finger or edge of pick.

Once you've become more familiar with the idea, you'll be able to do relatively lengthy and complex slides like those shown in Music 49—an E minor run that also incorporates the open G-string note. Try doing slides like this with the side of your pick as well because of the inherent tonal difference between the two techniques.

Music 49

Track 49

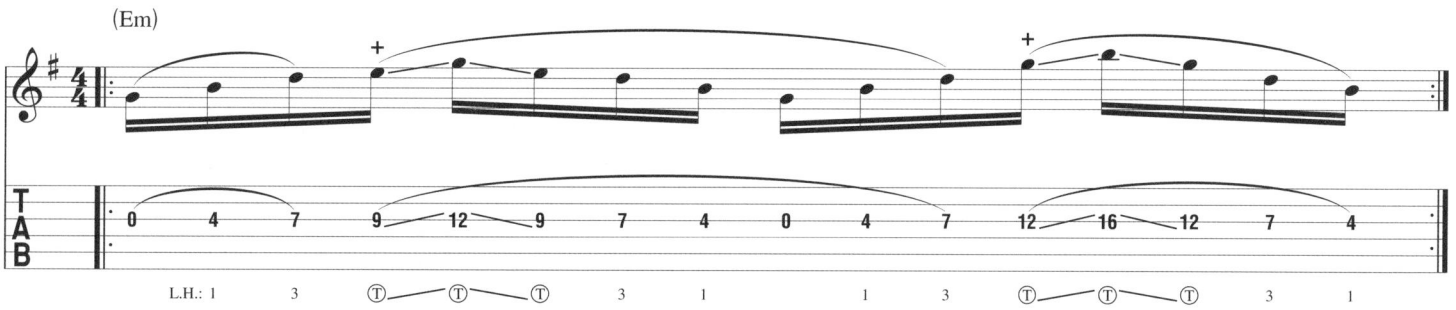

Have fun with this and don't be afraid to experiment . . . ever.

Get in the Ring! Making the Most of Natural Harmonics in Your Lead Work

Let's take a quick look at how we can make the most of *natural harmonics*. I've always loved the sound of natural harmonics [indicated by "Harm." in the music] ever since the first time I heard them being used, which was by Steve Howe of Yes in the song "Roundabout" [*Fragile*]. When played properly, they really stand out, as they have an almost bell-like pureness to them. A lot of metal and hard rock guitarists tend to only use them for screaming whammy bar dives. This can be very cool and dramatic, *but* as I'm hopefully going to illustrate over the following few pages, there are a lot more things you can do with natural harmonics—providing, as always, you use a little bit of thought.

61

As you probably already know, natural harmonics exist all over the guitar neck at specific *node points* on all six strings. Sounding a natural harmonic is easy: All you do is lightly rest one of your fret-hand fingers on a string directly over a node point (e.g., the 12th fret on the low E string) and then pick the string. Providing you do this properly, you can then lift your finger off the string and hear the desired harmonic continue to ring. To be perfectly clear, when I say "lightly resting your finger on the string" I mean that you're touching the string but not actually pushing it down to the fretboard. Photo 11 illustrates what I mean here.

Photo 11

The easiest places on the neck to get natural harmonics happening are directly above the 12th, 7th, 5th, and 4th frets on each string. If you've never really messed with these before, experiment with them and figure out what notes you're getting (no, I'm not gonna tell you—use your ears!). Then, once you're comfortable with making them happen, try and use them creatively in a riff or solo *without* grabbing your whammy bar and flooring it!

Music 50 shows you an E minor lick made up entirely of natural harmonics at the 7th fret. This simple but effective fill is definitely influenced by Eddie Van Halen and is similar to the one used in the intro of our cover of Diamond Head's classic "Am I Evil."

Music 50

Track 50

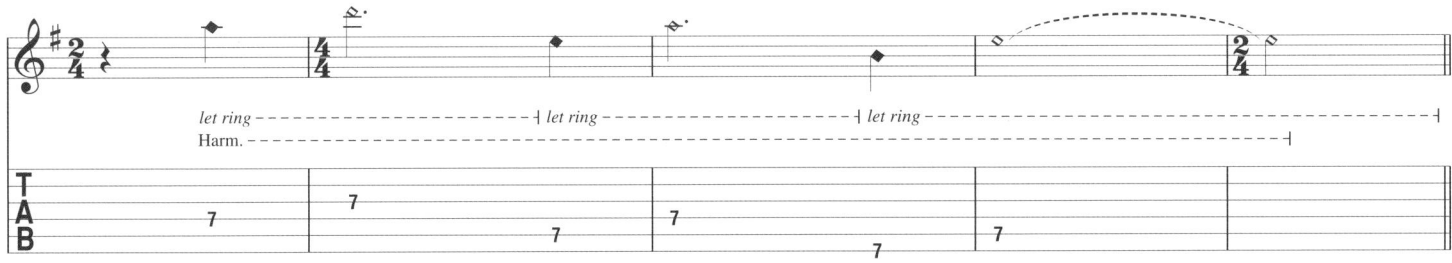

Here are a few more examples of how I like to incorporate natural harmonics in my lead work. Music 51 is similar to something I do in my "Shortest Straw" [*. . . And Justice for All*] solo and is a good example of using harmonics melodically in a lead break—instead of merely hitting one and then abusing the whammy bar while you work out what you're gonna play next! I got this idea from an old Rush song (I can't remember what it's called, sorry!) where Alex Lifeson plays a really lyrical solo that ends with harmonics phrased as a run.

Music 51

Track 51

Another guy who's great at using harmonics musically is Jeff Beck. Check out what he does on "Blue Wind" [*Wired*] for example. And then, of course, there's that guy I've already mentioned, Eddie Van Halen, who's a true master of the art.

As I've already pointed out, a lot of guitarists tend to only employ natural harmonics when they want to create a screaming dive-bomb effect with their whammy bar. This kind of thing can definitely sound cool, but only if you do it very occasionally and with some thought—not if you do it 20 times in every solo! And believe me, I've seen some players do exactly that . . .

Whenever I want to come up with a dramatic dive bomb with the bar, I really like using the natural harmonics at the 3rd fret. They're not as easy to hit as the other harmonics we've been talking about but, when you nail 'em just right, they really do scream.

Hint: The more distorted your sound is, the easier it is to get tricky harmonics like the ones that reside at the 3rd fret to ring out.

Music 52 is a simple A minor blues run that finishes with me hitting the harmonics at the 3rd fret on the B and G strings together and then diving them down with the bar. If you want to get more into making weird noises and cool screams with natural harmonics, then check out the amazing Dimebag Darrell (R.I.P.) of Pantera and Damageplan fame . . . the ones he does at the end of "Cemetery Gates" [*Cowboys from Hell*] where he mimics the vocal screams are mind-blowing.

Music 52

Track 52

Bar . . . None!

If you don't have a whammy bar on your guitar and you want to do some wild things with harmonics, one simple thing you can do is hit a harmonic and then push the string in question behind the nut (i.e., between the nut and the tuning peg). Doing this will enable you to "bend" the harmonic you've hit upwards, and this can sound really effective if done tastefully. Music 53 is an A minor run that finishes with me repeatedly "bending" and releasing the natural harmonic at the 5th fret of the G string using this "behind the nut" string-bending technique.

Music 53

Track 53

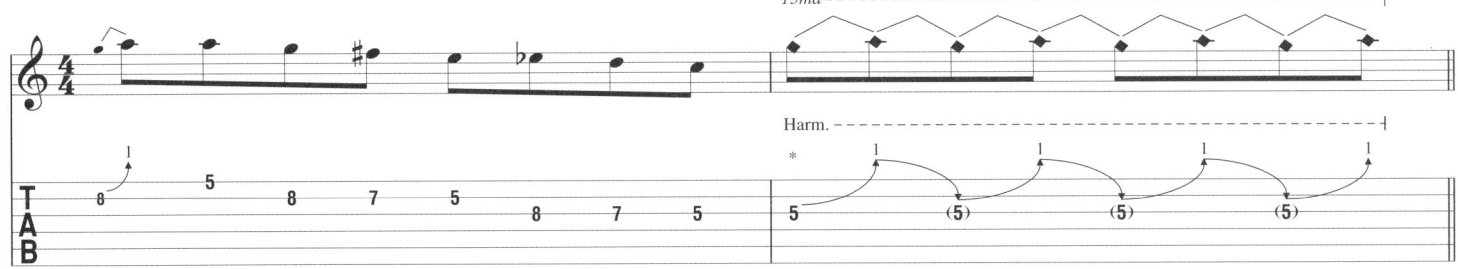

*Bend string behind nut (see text).

I don't do this maneuver too often because almost all of my guitars have locking nuts. I was watching the Hendrix *Rainbow Bridge* video and noticed that he started "bending" harmonics in the exact way we've just been talking about. That totally freaked me out because, to my knowledge, it's never been documented that he did that. And, if it's good enough for Jimi . . .

If you aren't already experimenting with natural harmonics, I hope what we've just covered gets you started, because there are a lot of cool things you can do with them.

Open up and Say "Wah!" Kirk Waxes Lyrical about his "All-Time Favorite Pedal," the Wah-Wah

If there was one aspect of soloing with which Kirk is truly synonymous, it would have to be his use of his beloved wah-wah pedal. In fact, he's so attached to the device he once told me this: "I'm a total wah-wah freak—in fact, I think I'll probably die with one underneath my feet!" The following excerpt from his eloquent Foreword to *The Wah-Wah Book* that I worked with him in December 1993 speaks volumes as to our subject's strong feelings and unbreakable bond with his beloved Cry Baby.

When certain guitarists play a wah-wah, I sometimes wonder if they're doing it for themselves or for the audience. I definitely play mine for myself. Even if our fans hated it, I'd still use one, because when it comes to my tone I'm totally selfish! Every single time I step on my wah-wah it seems to kick-start my playing because its sound gives me instant inspiration. When the pedal is all the way down (closed) it gives me super aggression, and when it's all the way up (open) it adds a fluid coolness. Also, sweeping the thing through its complete tonal range is a great way of accenting certain notes and phrases.

Although the wah pedal is a hot item right now, it hasn't always been that way. In the mid-'80s people were always giving me crap like: "Why are you using that dinosaur thing, man? The Crybaby went out with Jimi Hendrix." I gotta tell ya, that's totally the wrong thing to say to me! Hendrix was a musical genius, and his wah-wah work was masterful. Although I really dig what Jimi did with the pedal, the guy who totally turned my head around was Brian Robertson of Thin Lizzy. He had a totally unique technique and he made me realize there are stylized ways of using the wah. Instead of using the pedal to accent individual notes, like most people do, Brian would do long, slow sweeps over a succession of notes to create and augment tension. His solo in "Opium Trail" [*Bad Reputation*] is a classic, and pretty much everything he did on Thin Lizzy's *Jailbreak* album is amazing, too.

Whenever I play my wah, I always try to do everything I've learned to do with it in one solo! In addition to accenting notes and phrases, I also try to utilize its broad scope of tones. I used my wah-wah pedal a lot on the *Metallica* album, and sometimes our producer, Bob Rock, would purposely hide the thing so I wouldn't be able to use it that day! After a while I'd start getting itchy feet and would end up having to search the whole damned studio for my wah-wah while Bob laughed at me!

There are a lot of great things you can do with a Crybaby, and anyone who dismisses it as being a one-dimensional effect obviously hasn't looked or listened deeply enough. To me, the wah-wah is a tonal crayon you can use to color a great many aspects of your playing, and it's right there at your feet! I love this pedal to death. In fact, the only way you could keep me from playing one is by chopping off my legs!

Wow! Talk about passion. When it comes to the wah-wah, Kirk is the ultimate evangelist and he dedicated an entire column to his beloved pedal. Here it is. Enjoy and learn.

Cry, Baby, Cry—Make the Most of a Crybaby Wah-Wah Pedal

I'd like to talk about using a wah-wah pedal and how it can make your playing sound more "human." A lot of people say that guitarists hide behind the wah-wah and use it as a crutch. I don't buy that. If anything, the wah-wah brings out ideas, stimulates your creativity, and makes you play more emotionally and conversationally. This pedal helps me emphasize certain notes and transform them into gut wrenching screams and cries. It's really become a part of my style. There's also something physically satisfying about bending a note and laying into the pedal with my foot. It's as if I'm putting my whole body into the note.

To all intents and purposes, the wah-wah is a foot-operated tone control which enables you to vary the timbre of whatever you're playing . . . kinda like the way you use your mouth to form different vowel sounds. This adds a whole new dimension to your phrasing possibilities. It's really important to learn to use your wah-wah properly, and the key to doing that is a simple one: Use it *musically* to highlight the contours of what you're playing.

When the pedal is all the way down [i.e., closed, indicated by a "+" below the tablature] it gives me super aggression, and when it's all the way up [i.e., open, indicated by an "O"] it adds a fluid coolness. Also, sweeping the thing through its complete tonal range from open to closed, or vice-versa, is a great way to accent certain notes or phrases. I often rock the pedal forward when I want to emphasize a high note within a phrase, like I do in my "Enter Sandman" [*Metallica*] solo.

One of the coolest things about the wah-wah pedal is that, unlike a lot of effects boxes, you can control the speed and depth of it with your foot and make it fit with the rhythm of what you're playing. When you first try out a wah-wah, the natural thing to do is instinctively rock it back and forth in time with the music, just like you're tapping your foot. By doing this you can use the pedal to create a cool rhythmic effect while holding a single note or chord. You can hear Eric Clapton doing this to great effect in the bridge of "White Room" by Cream.

Although the "tapping your foot" wah approach can sound pretty cool, if that's all you do with the pedal, it'll get old real quick. Music 54A ("Wah Option 1") shows a simple E minor pentatonic lick being played in this fashion. To totally alter the way the same exact lick sounds, all you have to do is the exact opposite—rock the pedal in time so it's "open" on every downbeat instead of "closed" (Music 54A, "Wah Option 2"). You could also try doubling the speed of your foot tapping to twice per beat (Music 54B) or slowing it down to one tap every two beats (Music 54C). You can also get that Brian Robertson slow sweep happening by slowly closing or opening the pedal as shown in Music 54D.

Music 54A

Track 54
:00

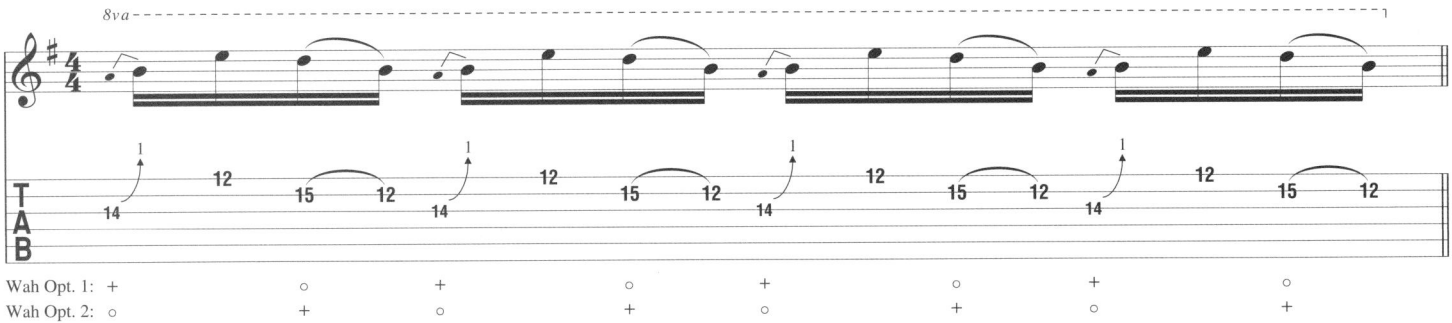

Music 54B

Track 54
:25

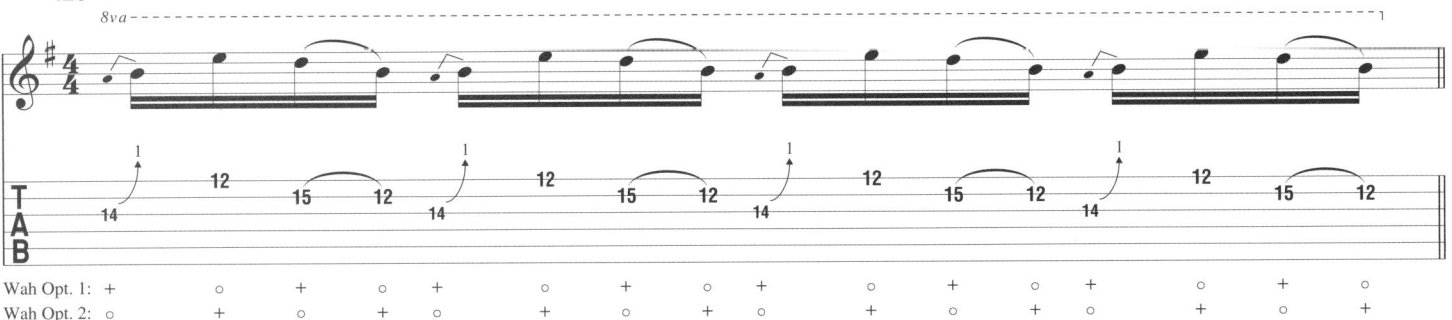

Music 54C

Track 54
:49

Music 54D

Track 54
1:12

As you'll hear, each of these wah-wah phrasing options gives the same exact lick a completely different character and feel. Realize that we've only just scratched the surface of the options open to us. For example, you could be playing a 16th note lick while opening and closing the pedal in a quarter note triplet feel—the possibilities are endless!

Jimi Hendrix was a true master of the wah-wah. When he used it on tracks such as "Voodoo Chile (Slight Return)," "Rainy Day, Dream Away," "Up from the Skies," and "All Along the Watchtower" it just sounded so natural it didn't draw attention to itself. Two other guitarists who really know how to use the wah pedal effectively are Jimmy Page and Stevie Ray Vaughan. Check out Led Zep's "Dazed and Confused," "How Many More Times," and "Living Loving Maid," or SRV's "Say What" or "Telephone Song," and you'll hear exactly what I'm talking about.

Another great thing about the wah pedal is that you can use it as a tone filter by opening it up until you find a tonal "sweet spot" and then leaving it there. I learned this trick from another one of my early influences, Michael Schenker.

The Art of Understatement—The Solo in "Hero of the Day"

To close this enlightening section on the art of lead playing, let's take a look a Kirk's wonderfully understated solo in one of the biggest songs on *Load*, "Hero of the Day." Kirk covered this in his January 2002 column in response to the following question from a reader.

Hi Kirk,

Although I love it when you rip out a really fast lead break, my favorite solo of yours is the very laid-back one you do in "Hero of the Day" [Load]. *How do you rate that solo? Is it one of your favorites or is it an also-ran? I look forward to reading your thoughts on this particular lead, as it is so different from your usual style and approach.*

Roger Bruno,
Nashville, TN

Good question, Roger. As you may remember, way back in the Feb 2000 issue, I answered a reader's letter that asked, "Out of all the solos you've recorded, which one is your personal favorite?" In my response, I revealed that my best-ever solo was probably one I did at four o'clock in the morning when no one else was around . . . and I still think that! I also mentioned the fact that "what's my favorite solo?" is a very difficult question to answer because I feel good about 95 percent of the countless leads I've recorded over last two decades. Now, I know this is going to shock people, but other than that early, unheard, late night/early morning lead I just mentioned, my solo in "Hero of the Day" is definitely one of my personal favorites. "Hero of the Day" is a really mellow song, and there are several reasons why I really like that solo so much—it is really melodic, it sits real well in the song, and, last but certainly not least, it's definitely not something I would just be able to play at the drop of a hat!

The "Hero of the Day" solo was a real challenge for me because I find it much easier to play something flashy that stands out and is a complete statement in itself. After all, that's exactly what I've been doing for the last 18 years or so! So, for me to come up with a solo like the one in "Hero of the Day" which is very simple, understated, melodic, and modest, was very difficult because I don't usually do that sort of thing. Like I've just said, it's invariably always an over-the-top, high energy, squealy kind of thing with me!

Music 55 not only shows you how I play this solo live, it also shows you James's rhythm part so you can hear exactly how the solo sits relative to it and how the two parts interact and compliment each other. "Less is more" is a cliché that's been used to death, but it definitely holds true in the case of this solo. One of the main reasons why my "Hero of the Day" lead is so simple and relatively sparse in terms of the number of notes played is because, as you can see and hear, the arpeggiated, chordal backing that James plays is pretty "busy" for the most part. So, in order to compliment and counter that without making things sound too cluttered, I felt a simple, sparse approach to this solo was definitely called for. To hear first-hand how the two parts work together, try recording the backing guitar part and then playing the solo over it. Or, better still, have a friend play the rhythm part while you solo over it because, at the end of the day, nothing beats jamming with other people.

I've seen several transcriptions of this solo and, although they invariably get the notes right, they always seem to assume that I play it in a different area of the fretboard than the one I actually do. All the transcriptions I've seen have me using the B and high E strings when, in fact, I play it higher up the neck on the G and B strings as shown in Music 55, Guitar 1.

Music 55

Track 55

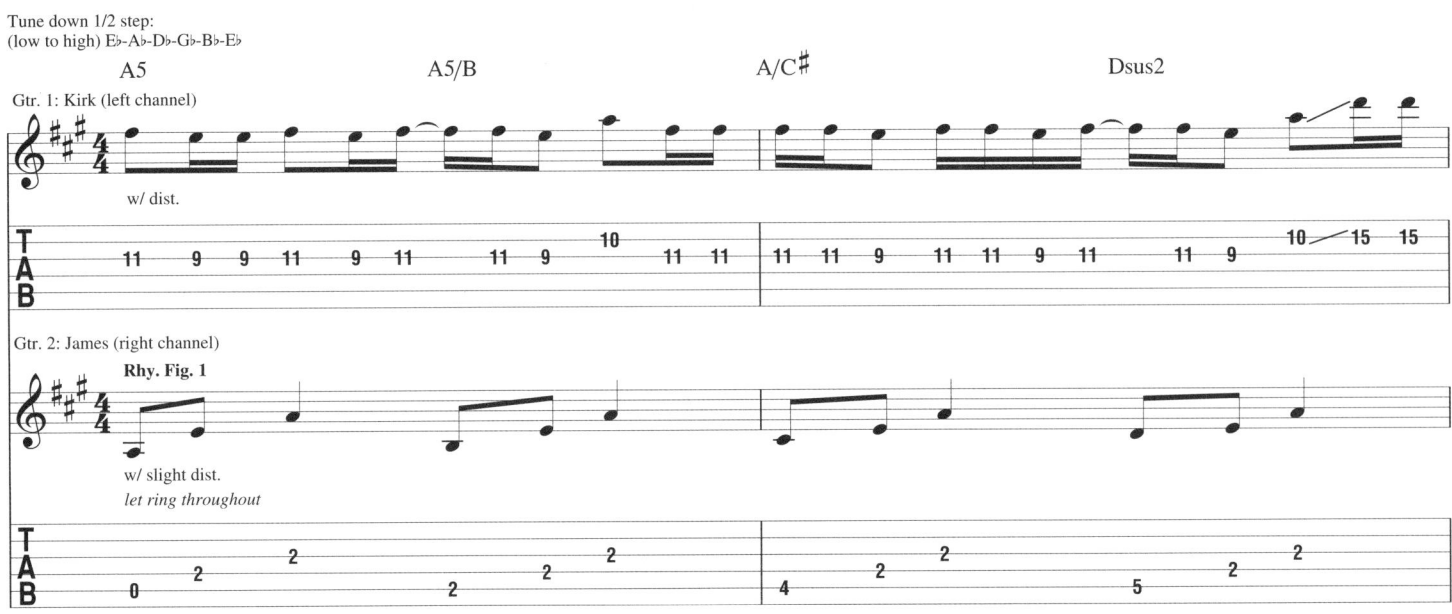

"Hero of the Day"
Words and Music by James Hetfield, Lars Ulrich and Kirk Hammett
Copyright © 1996 Creeping Death Music (GMR)
International Copyright Secured   All Rights Reserved

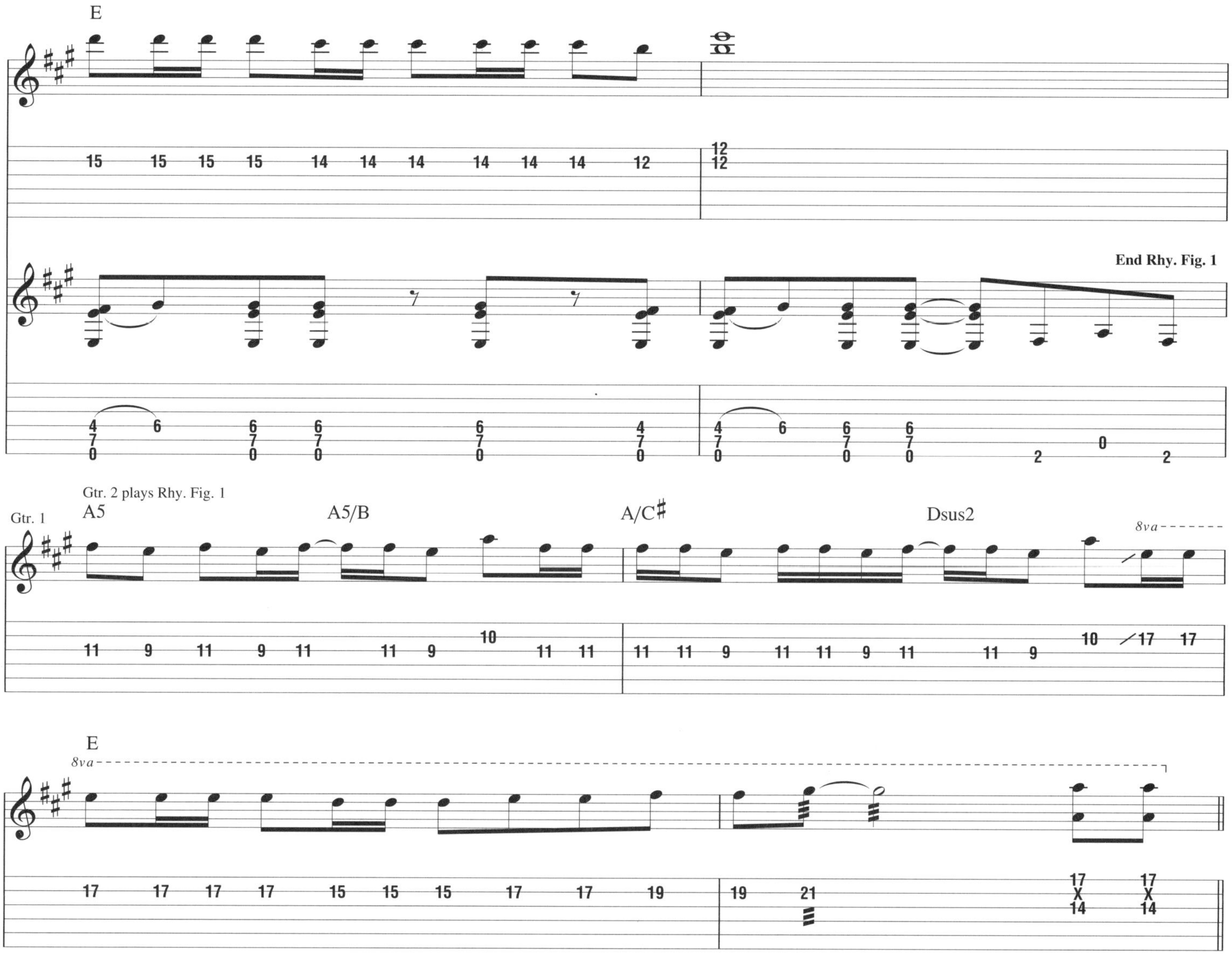
E
End Rhy. Fig. 1
Gtr. 2 plays Rhy. Fig. 1
Gtr. 1
A5
A5/B
A/C♯
Dsus2
8va
E
8va

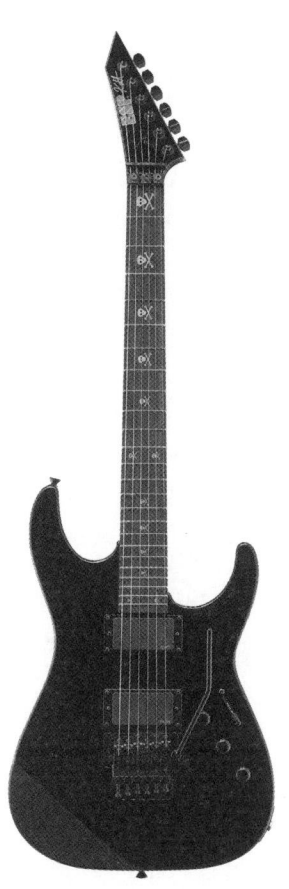

CHAPTER 7
MASTER OF RHYTHM
The All-Important Art of Rhythm Guitar

"Although I love playing lead, a good 95 percent of my time on stage is spent playing rhythm. Consequently, it doesn't matter how great your lead playing is—if your rhythm work sucks, you're not going to go very far." So states Kirk, and, for that reason, he dedicated a great deal of his column discussing and dissecting this all-important aspect of his craft. So, without further ado, let's dive in.

The Right-Hand Rules

When you're playing rhythm in a band like Metallica, what your right (picking) hand does is really important. Obviously, what your left hand does is also pretty damned crucial, but, as a lot of our riffs involve muted open-string notes and relatively-simple-to-finger power chords, it's really the right-hand picking and muting techniques that make or break a song! Before we talk about muting and picking, though, let's quickly touch on dialing in a good, crunchy rhythm tone. First, switch to your guitar's bridge pickup—preferably a humbucker—turn the volume and tone controls all the way up, and let's get to it.

Kaptain Krunch!

The first thing I've gotta say is that Metallica's crunch tones are a bit cleaner than some people expect. Distortion is great, but there's definitely a point where having too much of it in your rhythm tone turns your sound to mush—the low end loses its tightness and your overall tone gets flabby, with no definition or cut.

When you're first starting out, there's always the temptation to hide behind distortion because it lets you get away with murder! But when it comes to rhythm work, you've gotta back off that gain control—especially if you're playing with another guitarist. Actually, over the years James and I have found that as well as giving us more definition and cut, backing off the gain on our guitars makes us play our riffs better—because we can't get away with being sloppy!

The Mids Rule

Another thing a lot of people automatically assume about Metallica's rhythm tone is that we scoop out all of the mid-range frequencies. Well, we used to do that, but while making the *Metallica* album, we discovered how much louder and fuller our guitars sound with some mids in there!

As a result, our basic mindset regarding tone control settings is this: Turn your amp's bass control up as far as it can go without the amp starting to fart, then bring in the mids. When your tone starts to sound too nasal, you'll know you've gone too far. Once this is done, dial in the treble and presence until you've got the high-end cut you need.

Mute-allica!

Right off the bat, I'd have to say that 99 percent of our riffs involve right-hand muting. This important technique is pretty easy to master, so I'm not gonna dwell on it. Here are a couple of dos and don'ts.

1. To palm-mute a chord or note correctly, rest the lower part of your right-hand palm (the shaded area in the top drawing) on the strings, right where they go over the bridge. Don't go too far away from the bridge or the notes will lose their definition and become dull thuds.

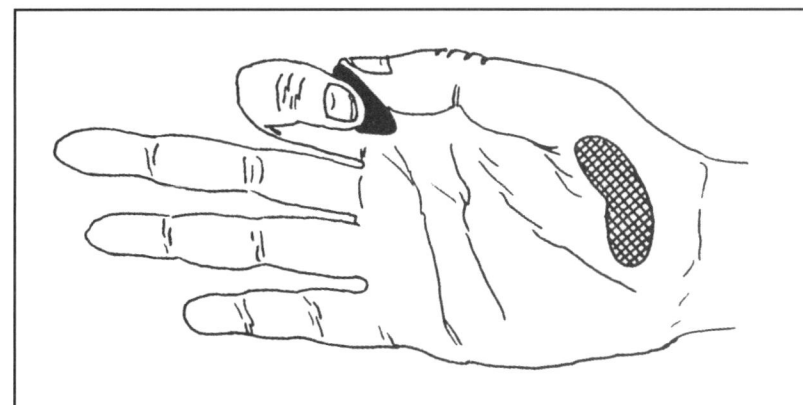

2. If you play a guitar with a fixed bridge (like a Les Paul or the ESP Explorer James uses), you can be pretty heavy-handed when muting. If, like me, your guitar has a whammy system that's set up to be "floating" so you can pull the bar up as well as push it down (see the bottom drawing), you've gotta be a bit more careful. If you lean too hard on a floating bridge when you're palm-muting the strings, you'll end up pushing the bridge down, and it'll sound like shit because your strings will all go sharp.

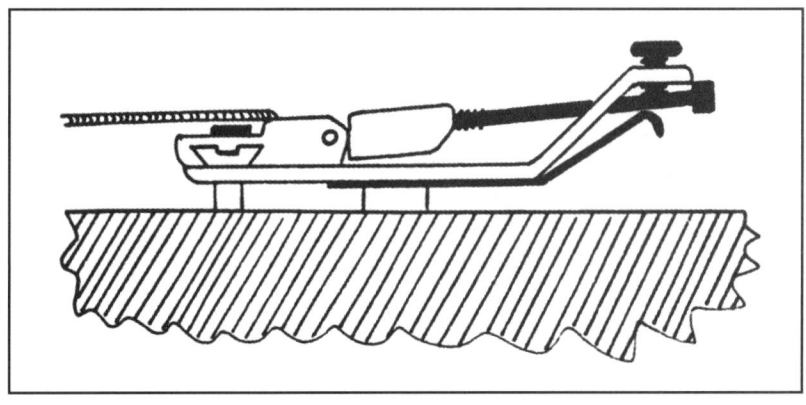

For this reason, some players who use whammy bars have their bridge set up so that the back of it leans against the body. Doing this means you can only push the bar down, so you can be as heavy-handed as you like when palm muting. Eddie Van Halen uses this type of whammy setup.

Going Down

To attain maximum balls, you've gotta pick using downstrokes only—it just sounds tighter, chunkier, and more rhythmic. Playing really fast riffs using all downstrokes is something James and I have been working on for years.

No matter how good you are at downpicking really fast, there is obviously a point where you can't do it anymore and have to resort to using upstrokes as well—even James has to relent sometimes! We play the intro riff to "Master of Puppets" [*Master of Puppets*] using all downstrokes, and although this riff isn't our absolute limit, it's definitely getting up there! As for a riff like the one at the start of "Whiplash" [*Kill 'Em All*] alternate picking is a must!

Talking of the intro riff to "Master of Puppets," not only is it one of the most classic metal riffs of all time, it is also one of the most wrongly transcribed, too. Music 56A (top of the next page) shows you how this section invariably appears in print—the notes, except for the final one (Kirk finishes on an F, but an open low E is often assumed), are right, but where they're being played on the fingerboard is totally wrong. Music 56B shows you the right way and also how Kirk fingers it!

Music 56A—"Master of Puppets" Intro Riff Played the Wrong Way

Music 56B—"Master of Puppets" Intro Riff Played the Right Way

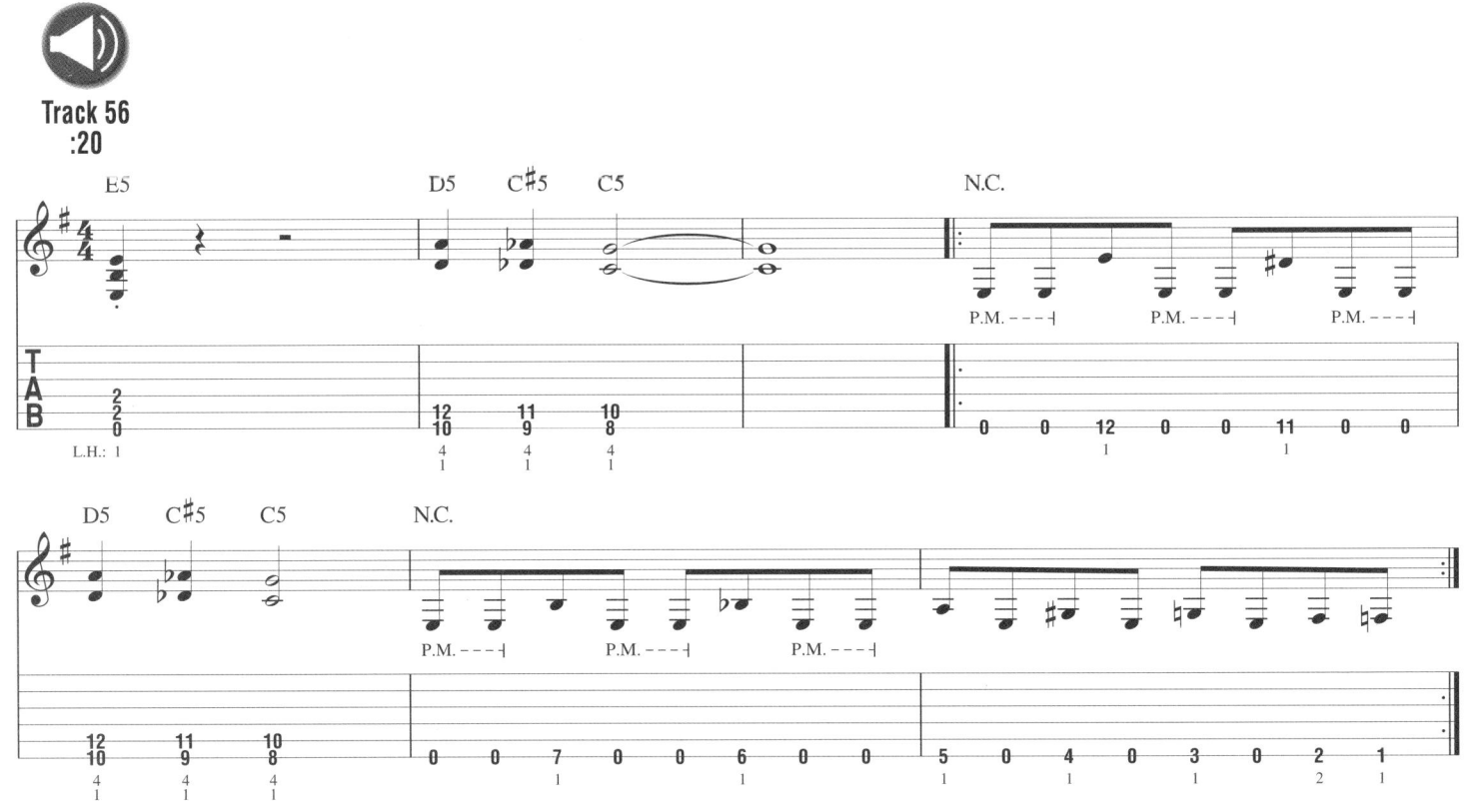

"Master of Puppets"
Words and Music by James Hetfield, Lars Ulrich, Kirk Hammett and Cliff Burton
Copyright © 1986 Creeping Death Music (GMR)
International Copyright Secured   All Rights Reserved

Now that you know the correct way to play this metal monster, let's get back to Kirk and the story of how this classic intro was born.

I can tell you how this riff came about, and I doubt James even remembers this. On the *Ride the Lightning* tour, he would play that riff in the dressing room but on the D string, and I'd play it simultaneously on the G string as a parallel harmony line to his. We'd always do that and then laugh about it because it sounded really dorky and funny. Then one day I showed up to rehearsal and James said, "Let me show you this really heavy song intro" and then played that exact same riff but on the low E string. I went, "Ah, so you finally found a use for that dorky little thing," and he goes, "Yeah, it sounds heavy, huh?" I said, "Yeah, it sounds good, finally! It's anything but dorky now."

Music 57 is the chromatic motif that immediately follows Music 56B and is also performed using downstrokes only. As already mentioned more than once in *The Sound & the Fury*, I've always been a big proponent of using all four fingers of your fretboard hand, and this riff is a good example of one that'd be difficult to play if you didn't use your pinky.

Music 57

Track 57

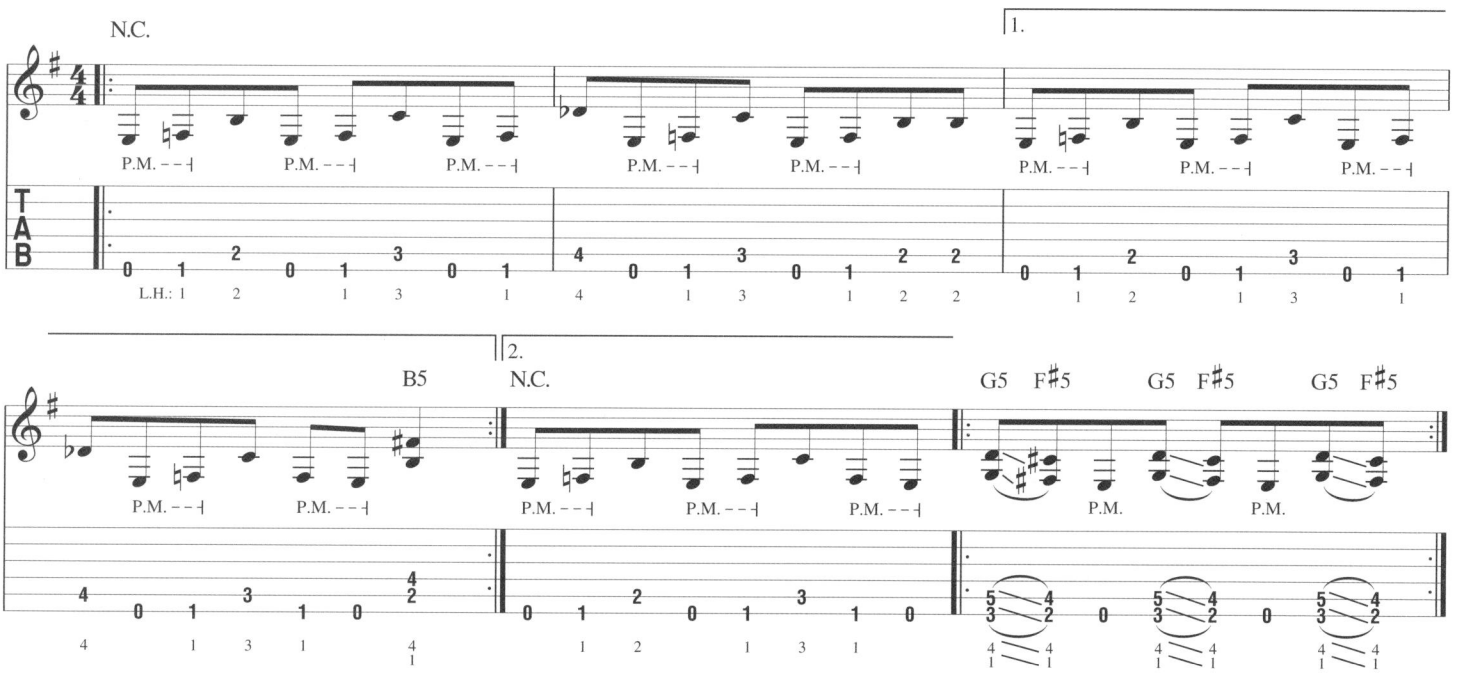

"Master of Puppets"
Words and Music by James Hetfield, Lars Ulrich, Kirk Hammett and Cliff Burton
Copyright © 1986 Creeping Death Music (GMR)
International Copyright Secured   All Rights Reserved

Grind Factors

When I'm playing rhythm, I hold my pick in such a way that only a tiny part of it is sticking out. I also tend to hit the strings with the edge of my pick as opposed to its tip. Doing this makes things a little more grindy sounding. Because of the way I hold the pick, the ends of the fingers I'm gripping it with also hit the strings, as the below diagram illustrates. This definitely adds to the grind factor! James does this, too.

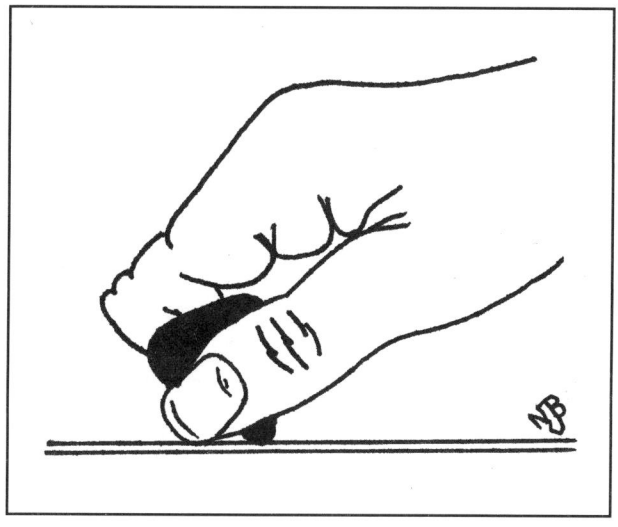

Wrist Watch—Building Downpicking Strength, Stamina, and Technique

One thing I've noticed over the years is that there are two distinct approaches to picking. Watching a lot of other guitarists, I've noticed that there are some players who pick from their wrist and others who pick with their whole forearm. I've found that you have a lot more control over your picking when you pivot from your wrist as opposed to pivoting from your elbow. This is because when you pivot from your wrist there's a lot less movement. So, by picking this way, you can fine-tune your right-hand technique into a very precise and economical wrist maneuver.

Getting this picking approach down can really make a big difference. As I've already stated a number of times in these pages, most of Metallica's rhythm work is done using downstrokes only—even some of our real fast shit! Believe me, pivoting from the wrist rather than from the elbow makes much more sense for the reasons just mentioned. Also, most of our stuff involves right-hand palm muting, and that's another reason why it's good to pivot from your wrist rather than your elbow. Think about it: It's a lot harder to palm-mute the strings with your right hand when your entire forearm is moving. When you pivot from your wrist, you can anchor the heel of your palm on the bridge because the movement of that area of your right hand is minimal.

One of the easiest ways to work on improving your picking technique is to practice simple rhythmic exercises on the open low E string. Because your fretboard hand isn't doing anything, you can totally zone in on ensuring that you are pivoting from your wrist and that your picking motion is as precise and economical as possible. As always, start off slowly and then build up speed. Providing you are willing to spend some time working on them, these two exercises will also help you build up the right-hand speed and stamina you need for intense, palm-muted, downpicked riffing.

I realize that chugging away on the open low E string for hours on end isn't exactly the most inspiring thing in the world, so once you're happy that your picking motion is happening, start practicing some actual single-note riffs using this technique. The opening riff to "Through the Never" [*Metallica*] is a pretty good one to work on because it's pretty fast and involves the A string as well as the low E. This riff is shown in Music 58. Remember to use downstrokes only and don't worry if you can't play it as fast as the audio example right off the bat. Start off at a tempo you're comfortable with and then build up speed as you become more confident.

Music 58

Track 58

"Through the Never"
Words and Music by James Hetfield, Lars Ulrich and Kirk Hammett
Copyright © 1991 Creeping Death Music (GMR)
International Copyright Secured   All Rights Reserved

It's also a good idea to do the same exact thing using root/5th power chords so you get used to hitting two or even three strings with each downstroke. Once again, to make sure that your picking action is correct, start by just chugging on a single chord, as doing this will enable you to zone in on what your right hand's doing without having to worry about your left hand. Then, once you're happy with what your right hand is doing, start playing power-chord riffs so your practice session is a little more interesting.

The second intro riff in "For Whom the Bell Tolls" [*Ride the Lightning*] is a good one to start with. Music 59 illustrates the riff in question. It's not that fast, but once you've played it over and over for a couple of minutes you'll definitely start to feel a burning sensation in your right forearm. Be careful not to push your muscles and tendons too hard, too soon, though, or you might develop tendonitis, which is something you definitely DO NOT want—hence the earlier chapter dedicated to warming up!

Music 59

Track 59

"For Whom the Bell Tolls"
Words and Music by James Hetfield, Lars Ulrich and Cliff Burton
Copyright © 1984 Creeping Death Music (GMR)
International Copyright Secured   All Rights Reserved

Easy Does It—Minimizing Left-Hand Movement

If you're a Metallica fan, I don't need to tell you that James Hetfield is one of the best rhythm players there is. Not only does he have killer tone and write amazing riffs, he performs them with the precision of a Rolex. And, in addition to that, he often has to sing at the same time he's playing these parts. Over the years, James has developed several really efficient ways of fingering certain power chords that enable him to move between them without having to shift his left (fretboard) hand up or down the neck.

This technique is often referred to as *economy fingering*, and being able to do it is a good thing for two reasons.

1. It means you can change between chords without having to look down at your fretboard.

2. You minimize the risk of making those annoying and unwanted "scraping" noises that often happen when you have to move your left hand up or down the neck between chords. This noise is especially noticeable when you're using a heavily distorted tone.

Quite a few of our riffs involve moving between an open E5 chord and the F5 shape at the 1st fret. Provided you finger the E5 chord with your middle finger (Diagram 7 and Photo 12) and the F5 with your index and ring or index and pinky (Diagram 8 and Photo 13), you can move back and forth between these two chord shapes without having to shift your left hand up or down the neck.

Photo 12

Photo 13

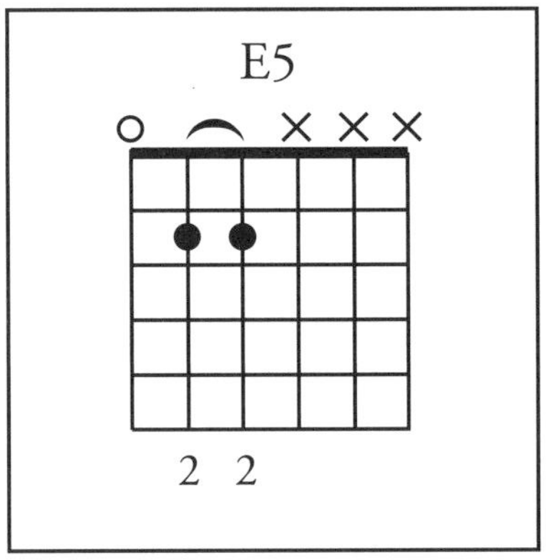

Diagram 7

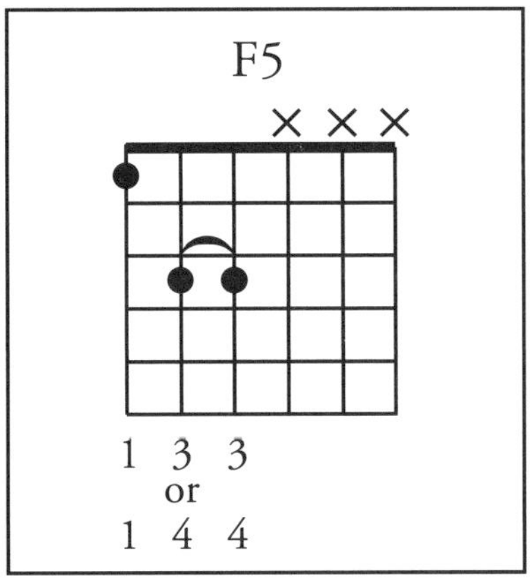

Diagram 8

A good example of this economy fingering in action between F5 and E5 is the verse riff to "Of Wolf and Man," which is shown in Music 60.

Music 60

Track 60

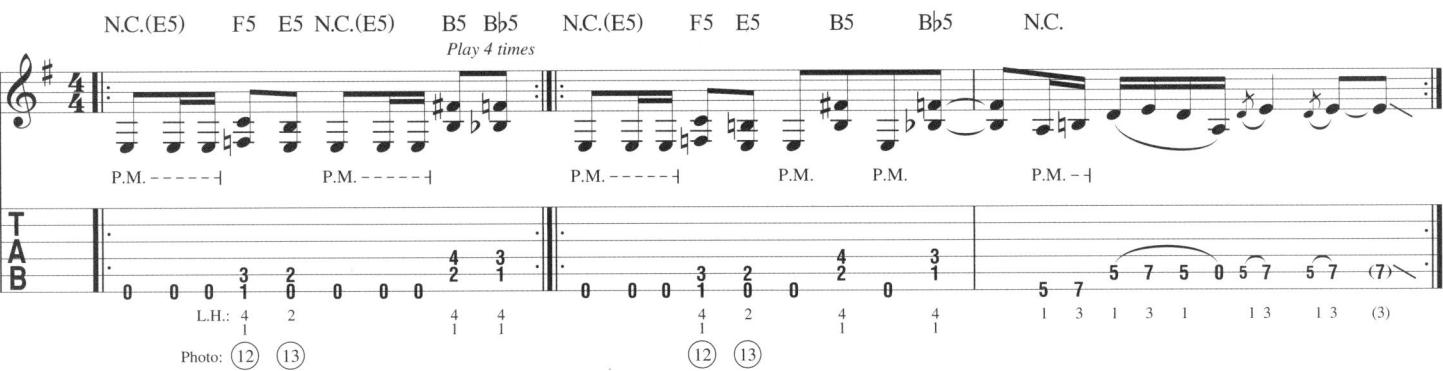

"Of Wolf and Man"
Words and Music by James Hetfield, Lars Ulrich and Kirk Hammett
Copyright © 1991 Creeping Death Music (GMR)
International Copyright Secured   All Rights Reserved

In fact, this simple economic fingering approach enables you to move between any combination of E5, F5, A5 (Diagram 9), and B♭5 (Diagram 10) with minimal left-hand movement.

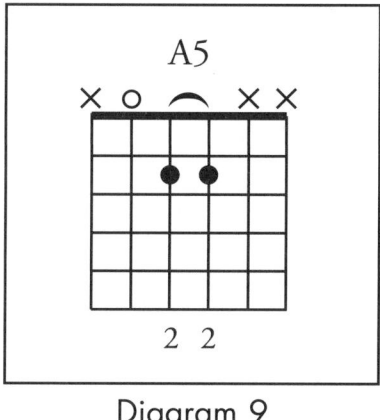

Diagram 9

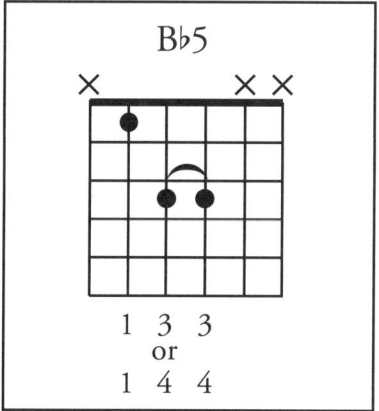

Diagram 10

Similarly, if you finger the open E5 and A5 chords with your index finger and the F♯5 and B5 chords with your index and ring (or pinky) fingers, then you can obviously move between any and all of the four shapes without having to move your fretboard hand out of 2nd position. Think about it!

Also, if you finger an open E5 chord with your index finger (Diagram 11, Photo 14) and a G5 power chord at the 3rd fret with your middle finger and pinky (Diagram 12, Photo 15), you can move back and forth between these two chords while keeping your fretboard hand in the same position. Fingering the G5 like this might feel a bit weird at first, but you'll get used to it after a while.

Kirk uses this exact economy fingering move when performing the staccato intro riff to "Dyers Eve" [. . . *And Justice for All*] which goes E5–F5–E5–G5. By using this awkward but very effective piece of economy fingering when going from E5 to G5, he successfully avoids making any unwanted string noise in the desired "holes of silence" between chords. "By fingering these two chords this way, you can minimize the potential of making any of those unwanted 'scraping' sounds which invariably happen when you have to move your hand up or down the neck when you're changing chords, especially when you're using a high gain sound," Kirk confirms.

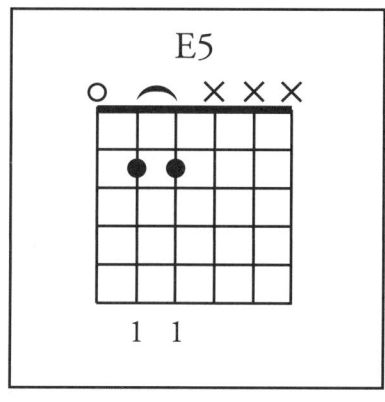

Diagram 11

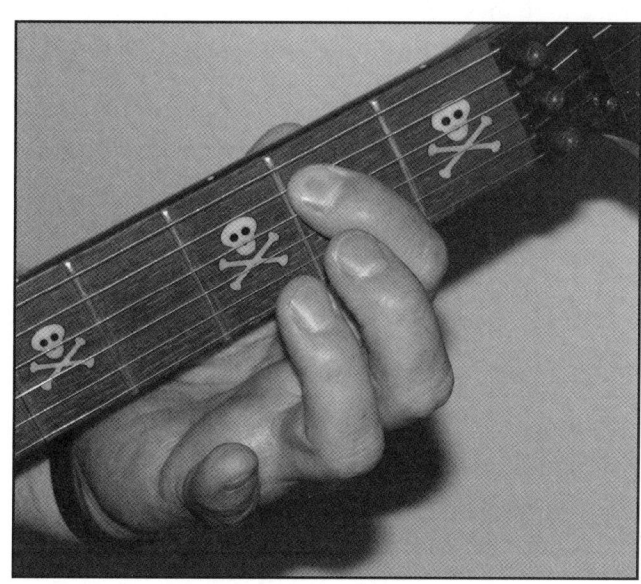

Photo 14

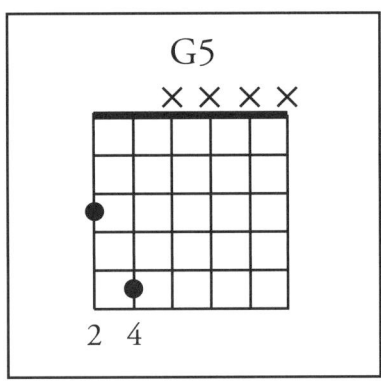

Diagram 12

Photo 15

We also have another economy fingering way of going between an E5 to a G5," Kirk continues. "What we'll sometimes do is play an E5 chord using the left-hand index finger at the 2nd fret (Diagram 11 and Photo 14 on page 77) and then we'll go to a two-string inversion of G5 at the 5th fret on the A and D strings (Diagram 13) instead of playing the low G note at the 3rd fret on the 6th string (Diagram 12 and Photo 15). And sometimes we'll also play the low open E note as well as this inverted G5 shape. This can sound pretty cool when you're playing in E minor because the combination of E and G gives you that minor 3rd feel. A good example of us doing this can be heard during "Better than You" from *ReLoad*.

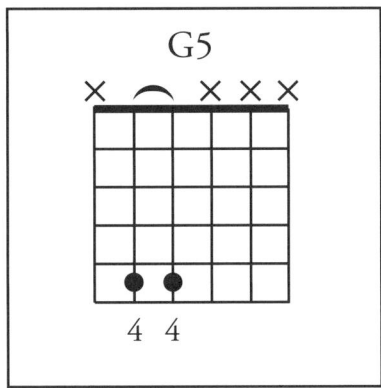

Diagram 13

Shaping Up and Riffing Out—Using Major and Minor Power Chords to Add Color to Your Riffs

As I've already mentioned, and I'm sure you know, the predominant chord shapes used in heavy music like Metallica's are those tried and trusted root/5th power chords. We rarely, if ever, play regular major or minor shapes (Diagrams 14–17) because the amount of distortion we use makes them sound like shit! They come out sounding muddy, and that's the last thing we want to happen.

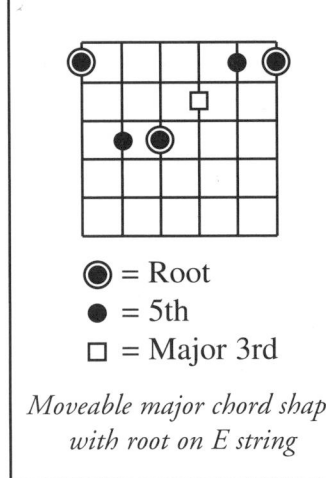

◉ = Root
● = 5th
□ = Major 3rd

Moveable major chord shape with root on E string

Diagram 14

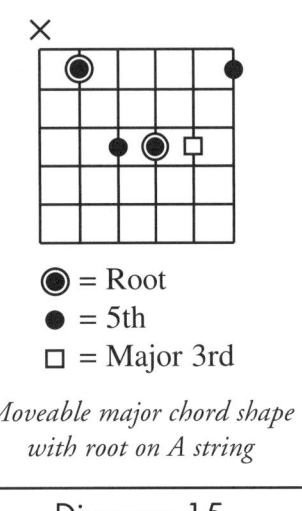

◉ = Root
● = 5th
□ = Major 3rd

Moveable major chord shape with root on A string

Diagram 15

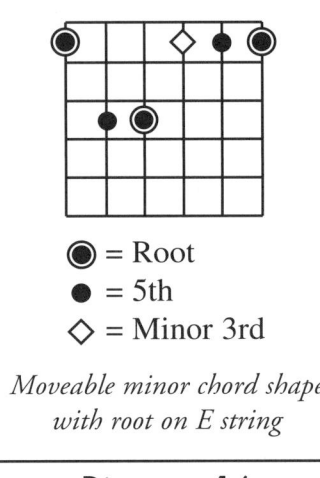

◉ = Root
● = 5th
◇ = Minor 3rd

Moveable minor chord shape with root on E string

Diagram 16

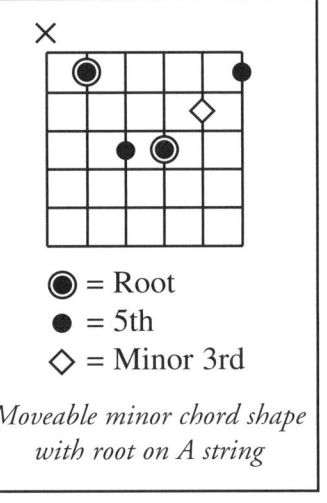

◉ = Root
● = 5th
◇ = Minor 3rd

Moveable minor chord shape with root on A string

Diagram 17

In our game, clarity and cut are just as important as crunch. That's why we use root/5th power chords almost exclusively . . . unless, of course, we're doing a clean passage and then almost anything goes (we'll look at some clean stuff shortly). Root/5th power chords are neither major nor minor—they're ambiguous. If you're not quite sure what I mean here, then take a quick look at the two chord frames below.

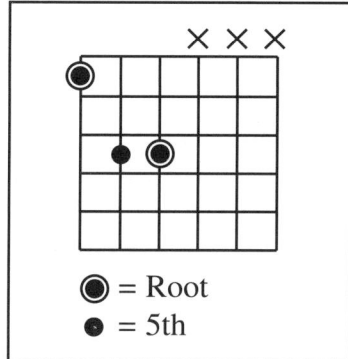

Diagram 18: Moveable root/5th power chord with root on low E string

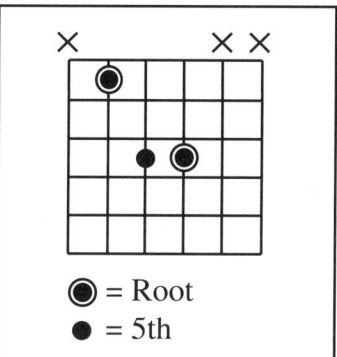

Diagram 19: Moveable root/5th power chord with root on the A string

As you can see in Diagrams 14–17, the root and 5th notes are present in both major and minor shapes. Whether a chord is major or minor is determined by the presence of a major or minor 3rd. The trouble is, when you're using a load of gain and you add a major or minor 3rd to a root and a 5th, you end up losing those two important factors I just mentioned—clarity and cut. However, if you ditch the 5th and play just the root and 3rd together, you can get away with it, even when using mondo distortion! Diagrams 20–23 are moveable major and minor, two-note (root and 3rd) chord shapes that work with a high-gain sound.

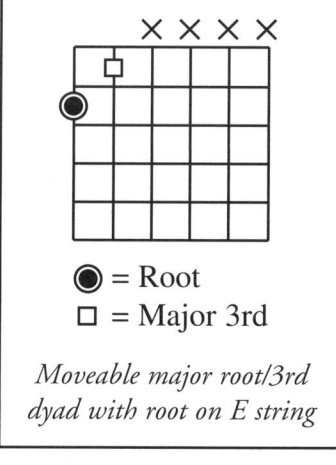

Moveable major root/3rd dyad with root on E string

Diagram 20

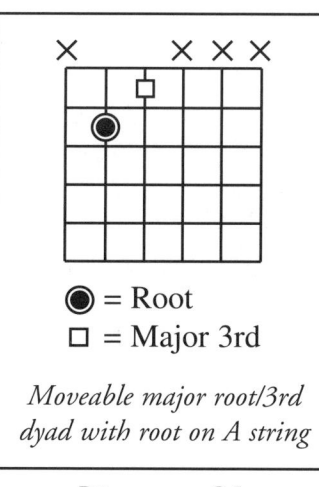

Moveable major root/3rd dyad with root on A string

Diagram 21

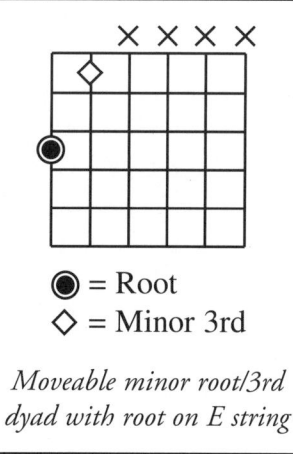

Moveable minor root/3rd dyad with root on E string

Diagram 22

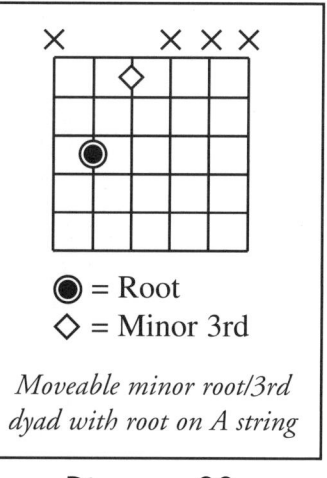

Moveable minor root/3rd dyad with root on A string

Diagram 23

 Every now and again, we use these suckers in our riffs to add some contrast and color. For example, the main riff to "Battery" [*Master of Puppets*] shown in Music 61 uses the minor two-note (also called a *dyad*) chord shape shown in Diagram 23 and Photo 16.

Music 61

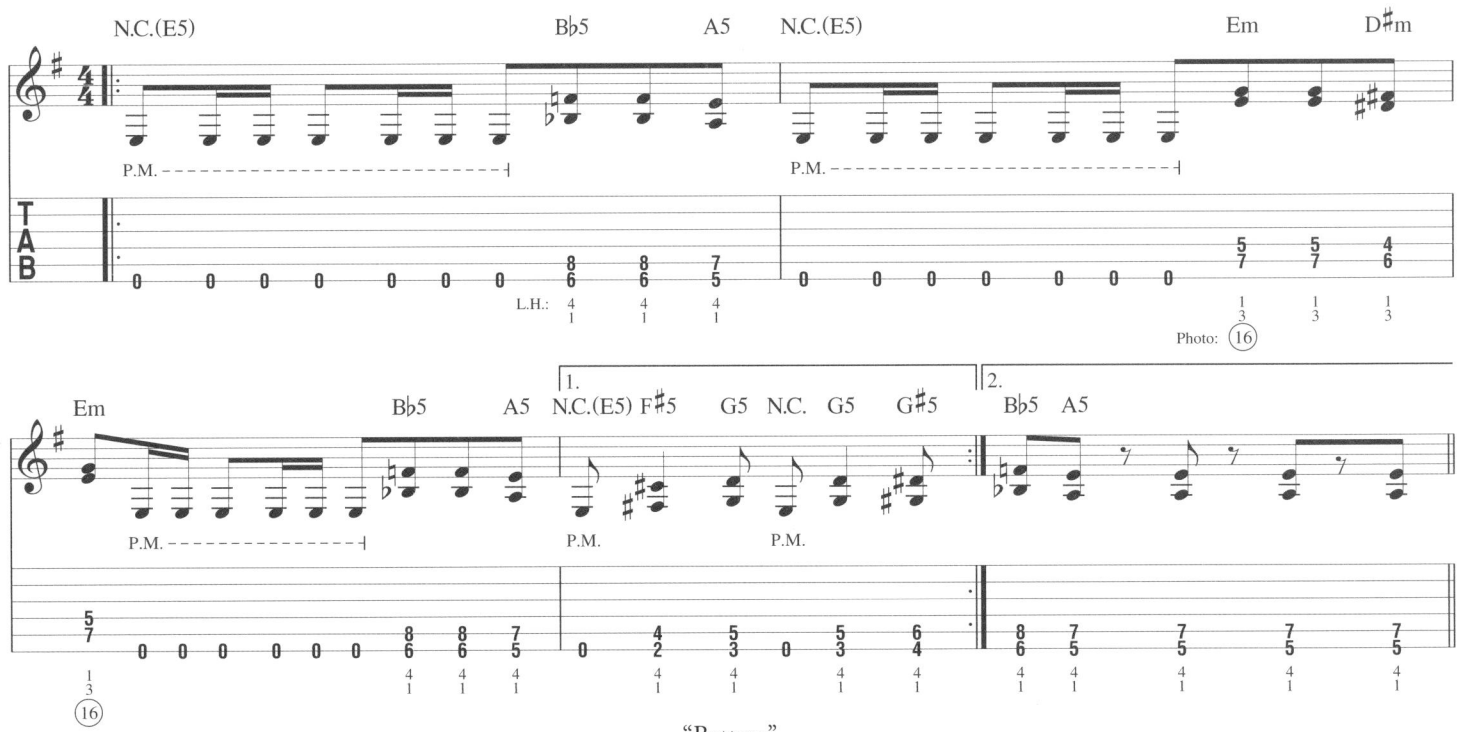

"Battery"
Words and Music by James Hetfield and Lars Ulrich
Copyright © 1986 Creeping Death Music (GMR)
International Copyright Secured   All Rights Reserved

Photo 16

Music 62 uses all three power-chord types under discussion here—major, minor, and root/5th. It's similar to a riff from the vaults we used in "Phantom Lord" on our very first album, *Kill 'Em All*.

80

Music 62

Track 62

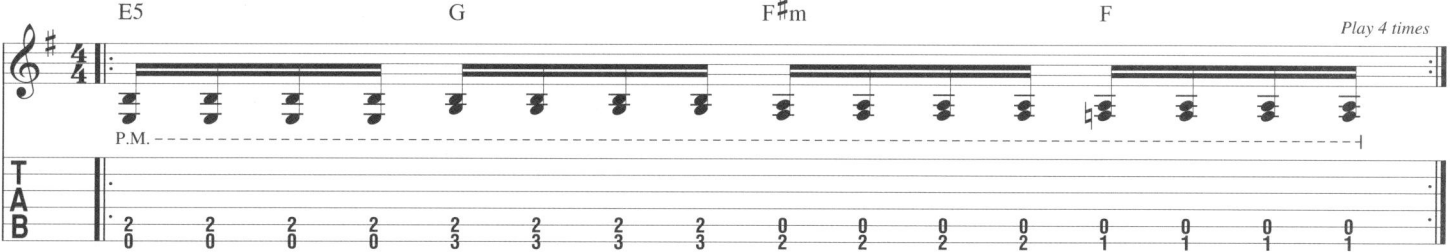

To hear and appreciate the difference the major and minor shapes make, play Music 62 back-to-back with the same exact E–G–F#–F root note progression but using regular root/5th G5, F#5, and F5 chords instead of G, F#m, and F.

Another thing you can do to use major and minor chords with a lot of distortion is to drop the root and just play the 3rd and 5th notes of the chord together. Diagram 24 shows a moveable minor dyad without the root, and Diagram 25 shows the same thing for a major chord. Diagram 26 and 27 show both shapes with the root marked for your reference.

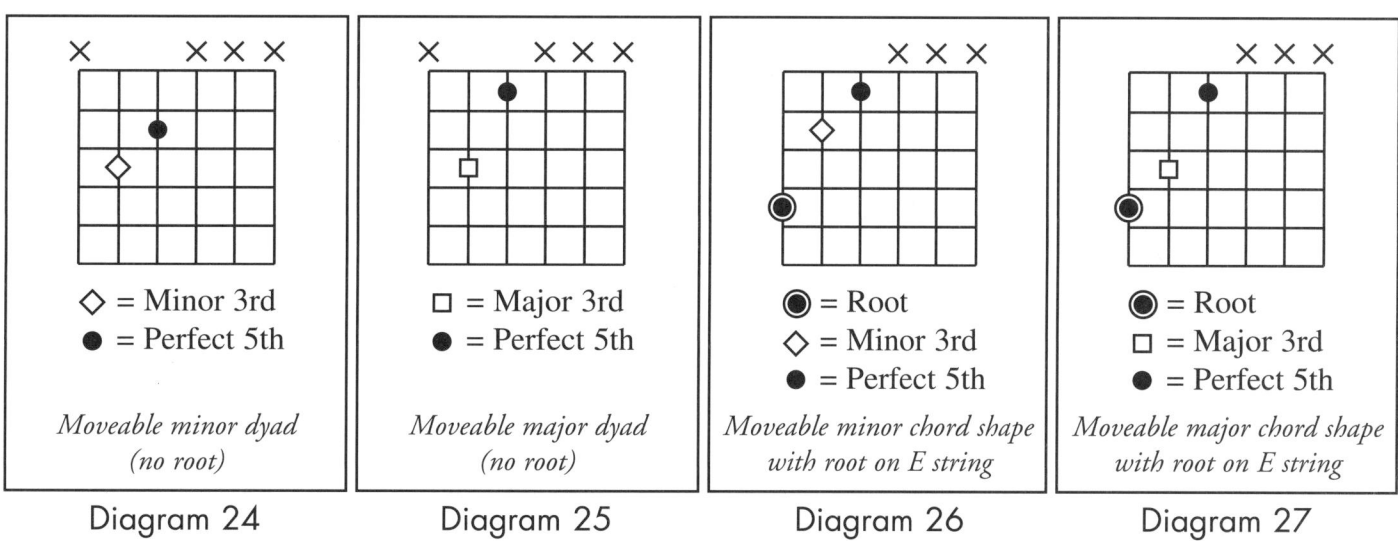

Diagram 24 Diagram 25 Diagram 26 Diagram 27

Music 63, the main riff to "Orion" [*Master of Puppets*], shows the rootless minor chord shape shown in Diagram 26 (Bm) in use.

Music 63

Track 63

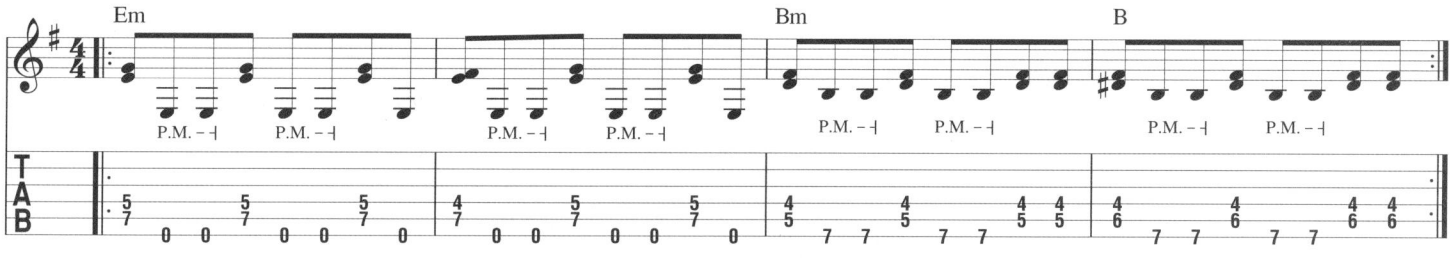

"Orion"
Music by James Hetfield, Lars Ulrich and Cliff Burton
Copyright © 1986 Creeping Death Music (GMR)
International Copyright Secured   All Rights Reserved

Experiment with these two-note, major, and minor power-chord shapes in your own riffs," Kirk concludes. "One word of warning, though—use them sparingly. If you don't, then their impact will be greatly diminished. Like the saying goes, you *can* have too much of a good thing!"

Octaves

Another alternative to root/5th power chords is the use of octaves as illustrated by the verse riff to "Master of Puppets" (Music 64), which is shown below. As you can see, the G–A slides in the final bar are strummed octaves—not power chords as they are often incorrectly transcribed.

Music 64

Track 64

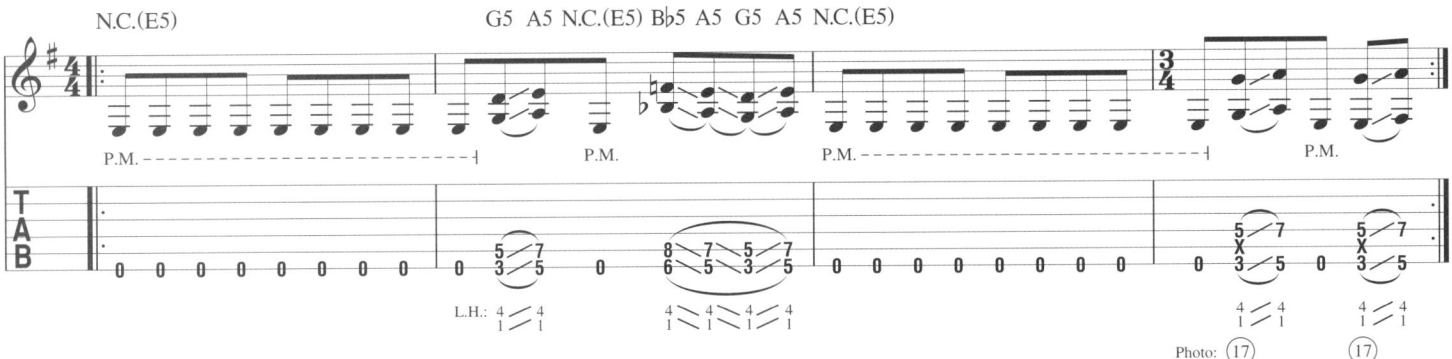

"Master of Puppets"
Words and Music by James Hetfield, Lars Ulrich, Kirk Hammett and Cliff Burton
Copyright © 1986 Creeping Death Music (GMR)
International Copyright Secured   All Rights Reserved

Playing octaves instead of root/5th chords, makes those notes jump out a little more," Kirk explains. "I play the low E-string note with my index finger and the octave note on the D string with my pinky. I stop the A string from sounding when I hit all three strings with my pick when I play the octave by angling my index finger back far enough so it mutes the A string by lightly resting on it (Photo 17).

Photo 17: Kirk fingering the G octave in the "Master of Puppets" verse riff

Light and Shade—Making Effective Use of Dynamics

Time for a new topic: Using clean passages as a way of adding dynamics and an extra dimension to a song. Sometimes there's nothing more dramatic sounding than a quiet, clean part that abruptly kicks into a raging, balls-to-the-wall, distorted riff. I've received quite a few letters asking me to show you how to play some of Metallica's clean passages—two of the most requested are the intros to "... And Justice for All" [*... And Justice for All*] and "Welcome Home (Sanitarium)" [*Master of Puppets*]. And, it just so happens that both represent a period of deceptive calm before the lightning crashes and a heavy storm kicks in!

The opening to "... And Justice for All" (Music 65) makes full use of the major and minor root/3rd shapes we've just looked at, and it's fairly "busy" in terms of notes. The fact that it's in 3/4 time (three beats per bar instead of four) also tends to make it sound more difficult to play than it really is. As long as you use the fretboard fingerings shown below Music 65, you should be able to master this passage in no time at all. As you can see, the only left-hand shifts happen at the beginning of each of the four bars when you change chords from E to D to C to Bm. The rest of the notes in each bar can be played without having to move your hand up or down the neck.

Music 65—"... And Justice for All" Intro

Track 65

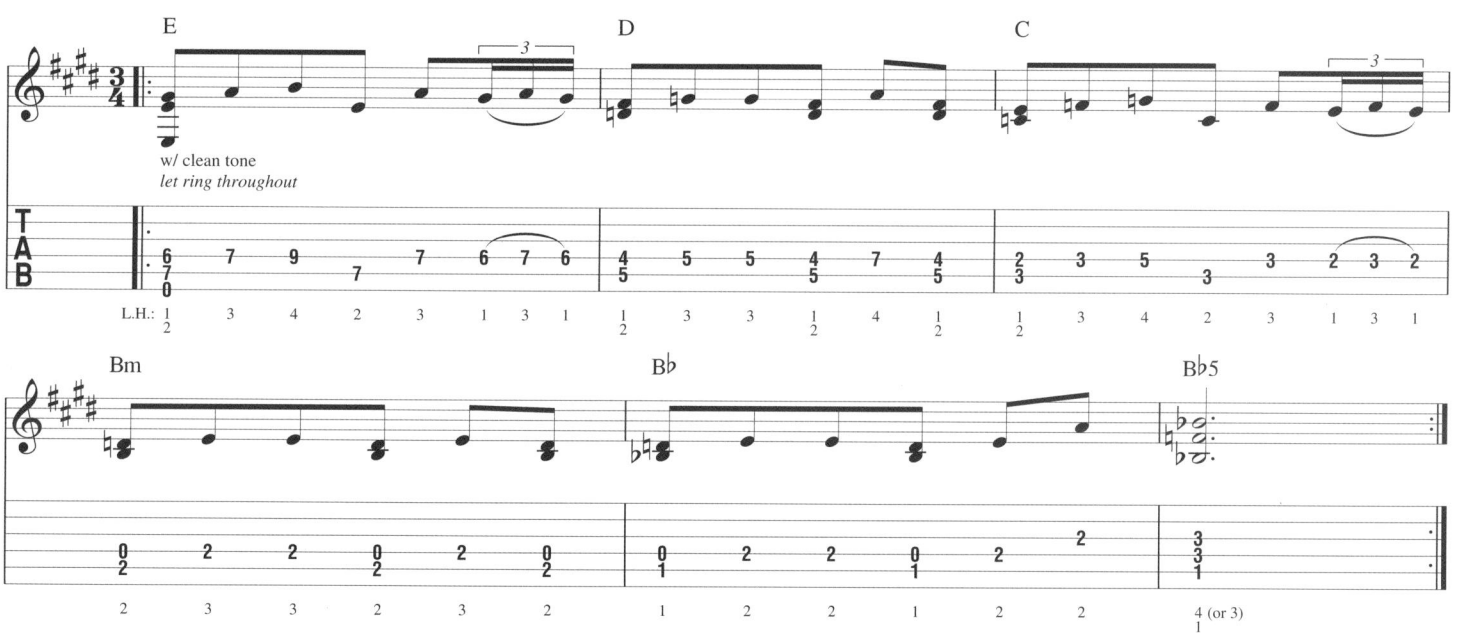

"... And Justice for All"
Words and Music by James Hetfield, Lars Ulrich and Kirk Hammett
Copyright © 1988 Creeping Death Music (GMR)
International Copyright Secured   All Rights Reserved

Get in the Ring (Revisited) and Shape-Shifting

The clean intro and verse riffs to "Welcome Home (Sanitarium)" illustrated in Music 66 and Music 67 feature two cool ideas you might want to experiment with when song writing.

1. Using natural harmonics in a riff. It's a pretty simple part that James plays in Music 66, but the harmonics really add life to it. I especially like the fact that the last three harmonics he plays make up an E minor arpeggio (E–G–B). A couple of old-school metal songs that helped get me into the idea of using natural harmonics in this way are "Killers" [*Killers*] by Iron Maiden and "Euthanasia" [*Wild Cat*] by a great NWOBHM [New Wave Of British Heavy Metal] band that not many people in

 America know about called the Tygers of Pan Tang. In both of these songs, natural harmonics are an integral part of the main riff. Man, every time I used to hear "Euthanasia," I'd crack up and think, "Wow, that guitarist [Rob Weir] is way cool!"

Music 66

Track 66

"Welcome Home (Sanitarium)"
Words and Music by James Hetfield, Lars Ulrich and Kirk Hammett
Copyright © 1986 Creeping Death Music (GMR)
International Copyright Secured   All Rights Reserved

2. Moving a chord shape up or down the neck while hitting an open string . . . or two, as in the verse riff (Music 67).

Music 67

Track 67

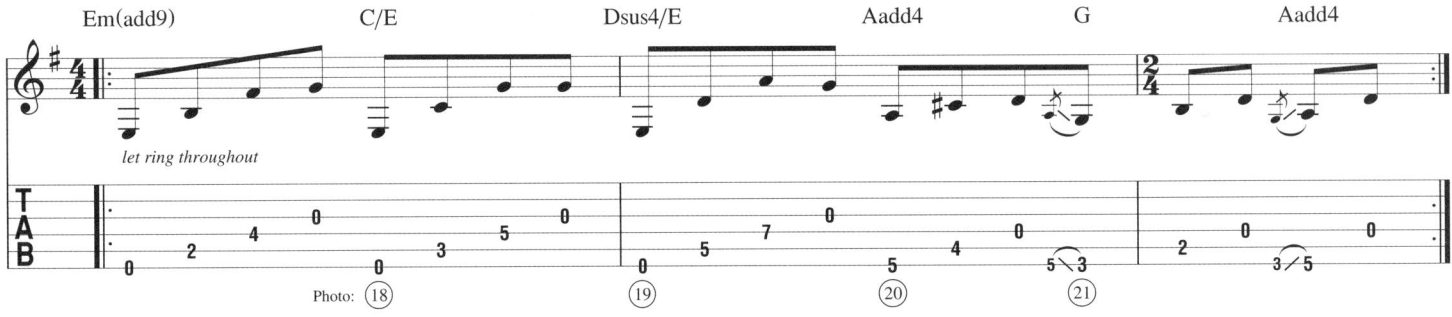

"Welcome Home (Sanitarium)"
Words and Music by James Hetfield, Lars Ulrich and Kirk Hammett
Copyright © 1986 Creeping Death Music (GMR)
International Copyright Secured   All Rights Reserved

Photo 18: Kirk fingering C/E

Photo 19: Kirk fingering Dsus4/E

If you look closely at the three chord windows below, you'll notice that the first three arpeggiated chords in Music 67—Em(add9), C/E, and Dsus4/E—all have two things in common.

1. They all include ringing open G- and low E-string notes.

2. They each use the same two-fingered chord shape—just in different positions on the neck (see the chord frames below). These ringing open notes are really important in the verse because they help give it harmony and a little more tension.

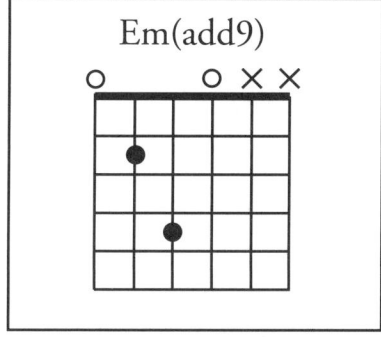

Diagram 28

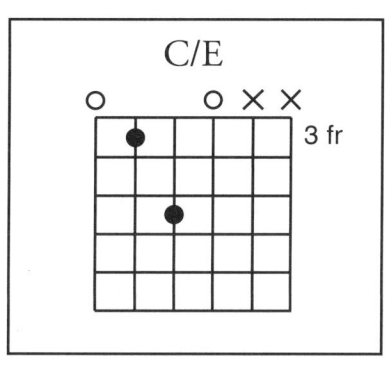

Diagram 29

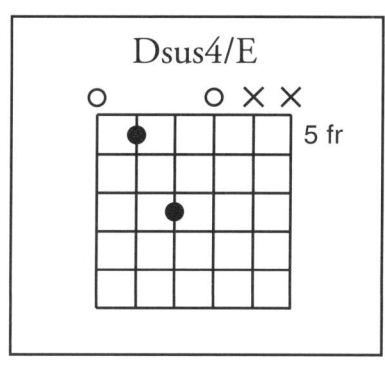

Diagram 30

85

Also, if you look at the next two chords that follow—Aadd4 and G—you'll see that the exact same idea is being employed except with a different left-hand shape and a ringing open D string.

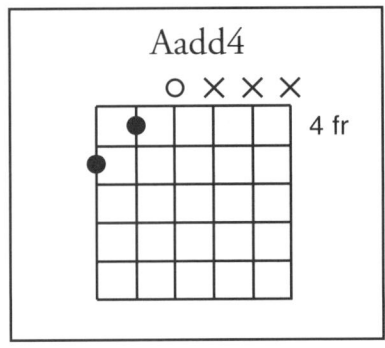

Diagram 31

Photo 20: Kirk fingering Aadd4

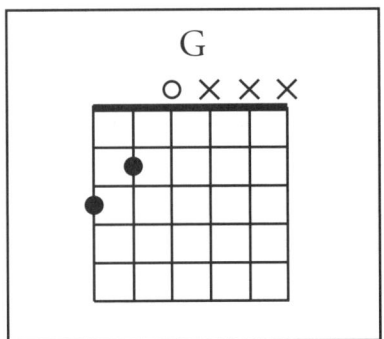

Diagram 32

Photo 21: Kirk fingering G

Just Plucking Around—Fingerpicking the Intro to "Nothing Else Matters"

Staying on the subject of "cleaning up our act," let's take a look at another clean passage a lot of you have written and e-mailed in asking about—the intro to "Nothing Else Matters" from *Metallica*.

The first thing you should know about the opening section of "Nothing Else Matters" is that both James and I ditch our picks and use our right-hand fingers to pluck the strings. I used to play a lot of classical guitar, and that's how I got into this particular style of playing. As you probably already know if you read my column regularly, I'm always going through phases of listening to and playing different styles of guitar music—one month it'll be blues, the next month it's jazz, then it's classical, and so on. I think jumping around from style to style like this is a pretty healthy habit. It definitely helps broaden my musical horizons and tastes, and it also means that I never risk getting bored by playing the same type of stuff day-in and day-out.

When you use your fingers to pick it, definitely gives you a better connection with the strings. Fingerpicking also results in a softer, warmer-sounding tone than you get when using a pick. Because of this, I'll often use my thumb, rather than my pick, to strum certain clean chords. Try strumming the Em chord shape shown in Diagram 33 with your pick and then with your thumb, and you'll hear exactly what I'm talking about here. In fact, if you watch the footage of us working on "Nothing Else Matters" in the *Year and a Half in the Life of Metallica* home video, you'll see that I keep putting my pick down on the music stand in front of me so I can either fingerpick or strum certain chords with my thumb.

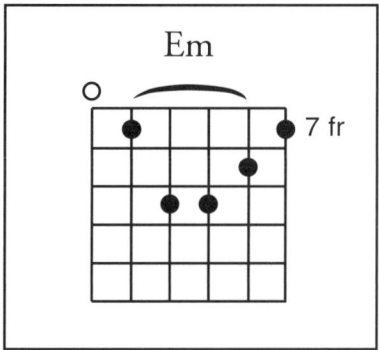

Diagram 33

Another subtle but cool thing about fingerpicking is that it enables you to achieve simultaneous attack on several strings when you play certain chords, because you can pluck *all* the notes at the exact same time, as opposed to strumming them in quick succession. Doing this definitely affects how a chord sounds. To hear the difference I'm talking about here, try this quick comparison: First strum the Am shape shown in Diagram 34 and then play it by plucking the A, G, B, and high E strings simultaneously.

When I play the intro to "Nothing Else Matters" (Music 68 on the next page), I use my thumb (indicated by *p*) to play all the open low E- and A-string notes (the downstemmed notes). I'll pluck the rest of the notes on the higher strings with either my index finger (*i*), middle finger (*m*), or ring finger (*a*). As you can see in Music 68, all the upstemmed notes in the intro happen to fall on the top three strings. So, if you wanted to get real anal about it, you could pick all the G-string notes with your index finger, all the B-string notes with your middle finger, and all the high E-string notes with your ring finger . . . or you could do what most rock players do and go with whatever feels the most natural to you.

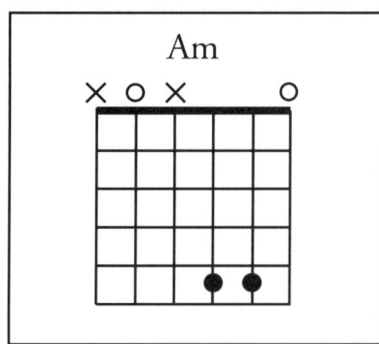

Diagram 34

Music 68

Track 68

p = thumb, i = index finger, m = middle finger, a = ring finger

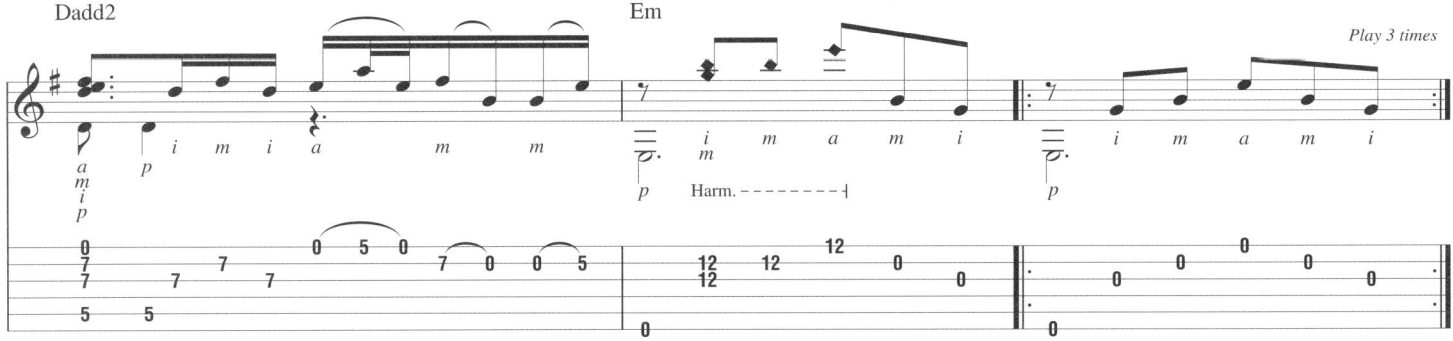

"Nothing Else Matters"
Words and Music by James Hetfield and Lars Ulrich
Copyright © 1991 Creeping Death Music (GMR)
International Copyright Secured   All Rights Reserved

If this is the first time you've ever tried finger-picking, the repeated six-note motif in bar 1 that opens "Nothing Else Matters" is a great starting-out exercise because it only uses open-string notes. This means you can focus all your concentration on what your right hand is doing because you don't have to worry about fretting any notes with your left. Once you've got this down so that it feels natural and sounds nice and smooth, you're ready to tackle the rest of the piece. Don't be afraid to learn it real slowly, one bar at a time if necessary. If this style of playing is new to you, then it might take a while to nail this one. But hang in there and have fun with it.

Double Trouble—Making the Most of Two Rhythm Guitars

The final section of this eye-opening chapter was sparked by the following letter from a reader.

Kirk,

I've been a big fan of yours for years. I really dig the fact that on both Load *and* ReLoad *you're playing rhythm, because the way you and James [Hetfield] compliment each other sounds great. I'd really appreciate it if you could talk about how you come up with parts that are different to what James is playing, and how they work within the context of a song.*

Hugh Nelson
Nashville, TN

It's really weird for me to hear people say, "Hey Kirk, it's great to see that you're playing rhythm as well as lead now," because I've always played rhythm—I just never got to record my parts until the last few albums! We were constantly rehearsing and playing the songs as a band on all the albums before *Load* and *ReLoad* while we were writing and recording them. So, even though James ended up recording all the rhythm tracks while I recorded pretty much all the leads, I was always playing rhythm anyway. It wasn't like I was just playing lead the whole time and nothing else! So, the only real difference for me when we record now is that I have to get all my rhythm stuff on tape as well as my leads.

Just so you know, one of the main reasons James used to record all the rhythm parts in the old days was because we were both playing the exact same parts 99% of the time. So, when it came to getting an exact doubling of the guitars on tape, which is the vibe we wanted at the time, it made much more sense for James to do 'em all. Plus, it gave me a bit more time to work on my leads.

The other thing that's changed about our rhythm work on *Load* and *ReLoad* is that James and I often play different parts. Even though the riffs are still the most important part of our songs, we rarely play the exact same thing. Instead of merely aping what James is doing, I go out of my way to find a different guitar part that works in conjunction with his. I try my hardest to come up with something that will add extra texture, mood, or dimension, while complimenting his part at the same time. For example, when James is doing something like a heavy chug, I'll try to find a different, much lighter part, which will help emphasize the heaviness of what he's doing.

Trying to find a part that works well is pretty challenging. I enjoy doing it but it can also be pretty frustrating! I mean, sometimes you find a part right away, sometimes you can't find a part for weeks, and sometimes you think you've found the greatest thing ever but then you go into the studio and discover that everyone else hates it! It's just one of those things you have to strive to do because ultimately it makes the song sound better.

A lot of the time it doesn't take much to add extra dimension and interest to a rhythm part. For example, take the chorus of "The House Jack Built" (Music 69 on the next page). James and I are following the exact same chord sequence—the only difference is that I'm playing power chords while James is playing arpeggios.

Music 69

Track 69

Tune down 1/2 step:
(low to high) Eb-Ab-Db-Gb-Bb-Eb

"The House Jack Built"
Words and Music by James Hetfield, Lars Ulrich and Kirk Hammett
Copyright © 1996 Creeping Death Music (GMR)
International Copyright Secured   All Rights Reserved

Timing Tip: As you can see from the time signature above, this riff is not in the usual 4/4; it's in 6/4. Don't sweat it though—this is a very easy part to play and, for that reason, serves as a great introduction to odd time signatures if you're new to them. All you have to do is count in groups of six as opposed to four. To help you in this task, I've included the count. So, listen to the recording a few times, start counting as indicated, and go for it. Master it slowly at first and then work up to Metallica's tempo of 101 b.p.m. Towards the end of Chapter 9, Kirk covers another riff in 6/4 and gives you further advice on playing in this slightly oddball time signature. In the meantime, get that foot tapping or that metronome ticking, and good luck!

When it came time for me to do my rhythm work on both *Load* and *ReLoad,* James' core parts had already been recorded. So I'd listen to a section and think to myself, "Is there anything I can do that will act as a counterpoint to what he's playing?" Then I'd start experimenting around with different ideas and sounds. It was obvious on certain riffs that we should both play the same parts—like the main riff to "King Nothing" [*Load*] or the intro to "Bad Seed" [*ReLoad*], for example. But then there were certain passages where it wasn't so obvious, and I'd often spend days working out a different part.

Rather than waste time and money in the studio, I did a lot of pre-production for my guitar parts at my own studio in the basement of my house. Sometimes I'd sit there for hours at a time just experimenting with different sounds because I've become really interested in using the guitar as a textural instrument. Having my own studio was invaluable for this purpose. Hell, there are even some parts on our albums that I recorded in my basement! For example, the backwards guitar with heavy modulation during the first instrumental break in "The House Jack Built" is something I did in my home studio with my engineer and ProTools. When it came to doing that part on the album, rather than try and duplicate it again, we just dumped it onto a CD and then flew it straight in.

As I illustrated in the chorus of "The House Jack Built," it is often something really simple that makes for the most effective counterpoint part. For instance, in the chorus of "King Nothing," while James is playing the power chord progression E5–C5–B5–A5–E5–C5–B5–F5, all I'm doing is pounding out 16th notes on an open low E until we both chug on the F5 chord together—and it sounds great. Another simple thing that can often add dimension and texture very effectively is playing the exact same part an octave lower or higher. The intro riff to "Damage Case," one of the Motörhead songs we covered on *Garage Inc.*, is a great example of us playing the same basic riff but an octave apart.

A good example of two different but complimentary rhythm parts happens just before the first verse of "Poor Twisted Me" from *Load*. As you can see in Music 70, not only are our parts completely different, but sometimes James is playing when I'm not, and vice-versa. When two rhythm guitars "trade off" like this it can be really interesting—provided it is done sparingly and with thought and taste.

Music 70

Track 70

"Poor Twisted Me"
Words and Music by James Hetfield and Lars Ulrich
Copyright © 1996 Creeping Death Music (GMR)
International Copyright Secured   All Rights Reserved

Not only are James and I often playing contrasting rhythm parts on *Load* and *ReLoad*, there are also a lot more guitar textures and layers going on. Because of this, we get to pick and choose which layers we want to play live, which is kinda fun. You can play the solid riff the song was written around, or you can play the counterpoint part, or you can play the texture parts, or you can try and simulate some little studio trick you did. Because of all these choices, I sometimes find myself playing a combination of two or more layered parts. For example, in "Bleeding Me" [*Load*], I play a blend between the main riff and the arpeggiated chord part, which is kind of neat. And, in addition to that, I also do a guitar line that James recorded because he doesn't want to play it while he's singing—he just wants to bang out chords. So I combine all three parts into one.

And that, my friend, brings this fine slab of "rhythm 'n' bruise" to a close. If you're hankering to learn how to play a few more Metallica riffs the correct way, though, don't fret—Kirk covers another batch in Chapter 9: *. . . And Answers for All*.

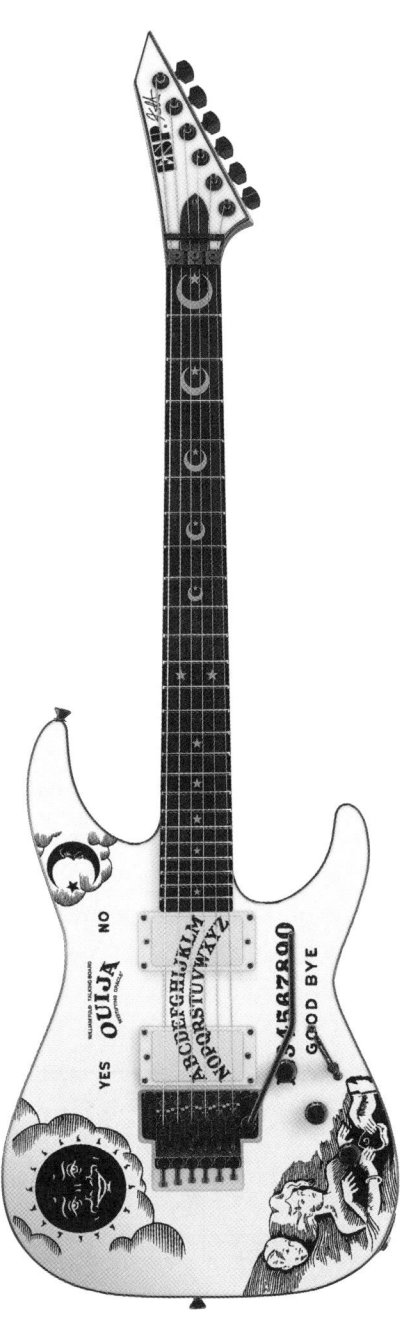

CHAPTER 8
COMFORT ZONE BUSTERS
Getting out of Those Darned Ruts

Early on in this book, Kirk touched on the fact that employing certain playing techniques such as string-skipping and wide stretches can help lift your playing out of a rut. As he promised back then, this chapter is dedicated to rut busting! Take it away, Mr. H.

When you're serious about your guitar playing, there's nothing worse than getting stuck in a rut. As already mentioned earlier in this book, each of us has what I call a "comfort zone," which is basically a library of well-trodden "hot" licks and runs that we turn to out of habit because we know they work. In a nutshell, being caught in a rut means that you're trapped in your comfort zone and can't get out! Whenever this happens, though, don't despair because:

1. It happens to us all from time to time, and . . .

2. There *are* things you can do to get out of this six-string nightmare, and that's what we're going to address.

Listen Without Prejudice

To my way of thinking, one of the most obvious ways to get out of a rut is to listen to a style of music you don't normally listen to and then try to learn something from it. You can do this by either trying to learn some of the licks and runs you hear or by merely trying to solo over it. The latter is great because you'll get chords and progressions thrown at you that you aren't used to playing over. Because of this, you'll invariably get so caught up in trying to discover what will work that you'll get disoriented and will invariably forget all about your own comfort zone. That's what I usually do when I'm in a bit of a rut. I especially like doing it with jazz music—I love trying to solo over that stuff because it always gives me a totally new perspective.

Because doing this type of thing can be really helpful, don't cut yourself off from some potentially great stuff by being narrow-minded. Instead, give everything a chance. For example, if your favorite bands are Slipknot, Korn, and Pantera, you might think, "Shit, I'm never going to listen to funk or R&B because they're both lightweight and wimpy." Even if you feel this way about a particular genre of music, I urge you to listen to a decent cross-section of it before you write off the whole damn genre! You never know—you might learn something and you might even find something you like.

For instance, not all country music sounds like Shania Twain or "Achy, Breaky, Heart"! I mean, check out some of Albert Lee's stuff, for example. He's an amazing guitarist in anyone's book. And what about the Allman Brothers? Their unique blend of blues, rock, *and* country is unbelievable and, in my mind, every guitarist can learn something from the late, great Duane Allman.

Steal from Other Instruments . . . Tastefully!

Another thing I do that not only gets me out of a rut but also expands my playing vocabulary is to listen to other instruments and then try and play their licks on guitar. There's nothing wrong with copying stuff from other people, as long as you personalize it and make it your own. I mean, David Bowie once called himself "a very tasteful thief," and that's what you should aim to be, too.

I've found that listening to and copying ideas from great jazz horn players opened up completely new musical horizons for me. There are so many great trumpet and saxophone lines that you can adapt to play on guitar. I've gotten loads of inspiration from Miles Davis (trumpet) and John Coltrane (saxophone), and, of course, the amazing Thelonius Monk. I don't mind admitting that I'm totally obsessed with Monk's piano playing. His phrasing is just so brilliant and out there. He definitely puts notes in places no one has put them before!

If you're interested in exploring the stuff these guys do, here are three albums I feel you *have* to have: Coltrane's *Blue Train*, Miles Davis's *Kind of Blue*, and *Straight No Chaser* by Thelonius Monk, which is just killer. Although all three of these guys play some mind-blowingly complex stuff, some of their greatest moments are relatively simple. For example, I once learned the E minor lick shown in Music 71 from John Coltrane's playing.

Music 71

Track 71

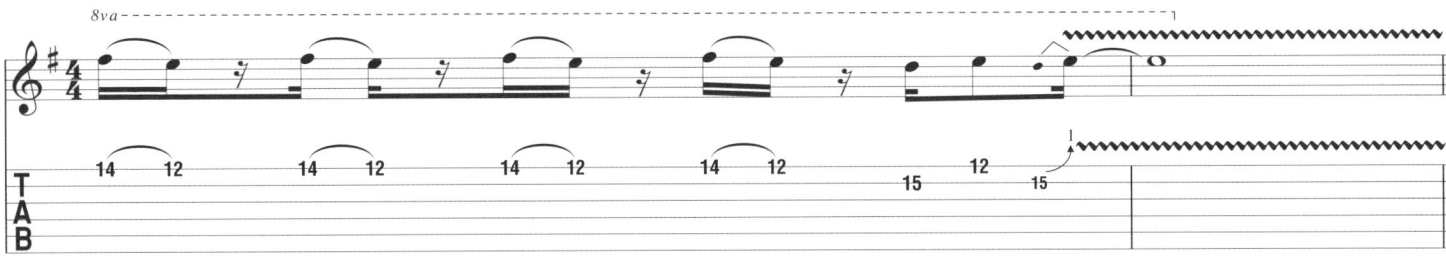

As you can see, it's unbelievably simple, but it's so percussive and melodic at the same time that it floors me every time I hear it. The line just jumps out and grabs your attention. Now, obviously, not every jazz lick or run will work in a metal context, but the simple action of making your hands do something different from what they're used to will help break you free of your comfort zone.

Vocalize It

In addition to checking out other instruments, I love listening to great singers like Frank Sinatra, Billy Holliday, and Ella Fitzgerald, and one of my favorite things to do is try and figure out their vocal melodies on the guitar. Take Ella Fitzgerald for example: She really went out on a limb and was hitting notes over chords that most people wouldn't dare try. When you listen to her doing that stuff, you don't even notice it at first because you take it for granted that she's just "scatting." But then, when you pick up a guitar and try and figure it out, you realize that there are some really bold things that she was doing and pulling off. She's a monster and she totally blows me away.

To summarize this first section: Try to keep yourself open to everything musically or your creativity and versatility could suffer. Obviously, you're not going to like every single thing you hear, but, as I've already said, please be prepared to at least give something a fair shot before dismissing it. Although I'm a metal player at heart, over the years I've learned to listen without prejudice and recognize quality in all forms of music—everything from early Hank Williams (as far as I'm concerned, his approach to music has more in common with Robert Johnson than it does with Shania Twain or Garth Brooks), to '50s blues guys like Guitar Slim, to jazz vocalists such as Ella Fitzgerald, to classical music, to Rage Against the Machine . . . and almost everything in between. My taste is so broad at this point that I can jump straight from Fear Factory to Frank Sinatra and the Nelson Riddle Orchestra!

Listening to all types of music, singers, and instruments other than the guitar has definitely opened up my horizons and helped me grow as a player. And I know that whenever I get together with the band that all these other influences are going to start coming out of the speakers in a Metallica context. As far as I'm concerned, my non-metal leanings just give me more colors to help paint our music with. So, listen with an open mind and open ears, and without prejudice!

Let's Get Phrasey! Use the Simple Blues Scale to Bust out of a Rut

Some people seem to think that the only way to come up with new soloing ideas is to learn more scales. I definitely don't agree with that. I mean, if that's the case, what happens when you run out of new scales and modes to learn? In my opinion, you don't need to know every exotic scale under the sun to be able to come up with creative and exciting leads. Take for example a standard minor blues box shown in Diagram 35 below.

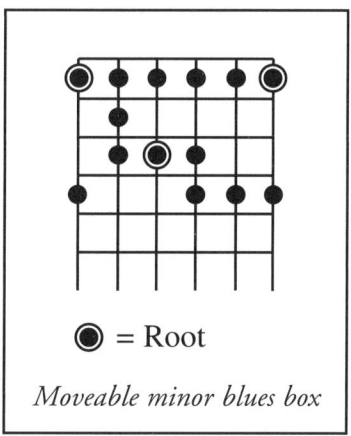

Diagram 35

There are only six different notes in there, but there's so much you can do with them. I always find myself stumbling across different ways to spice up my well-worn blues licks . . . ways that are often so simplistic it's unbelievable. In fact, sometimes the thing that makes all the difference is so very basic that if you sat down and deliberately tried to do something different, you'd probably never think of it.

For an example of what I'm talking about here, compare Music 72 and 73. As you can see, they're virtually the same exact A minor blues scale (A–C–D–E♭–E–G) lick, except that in Music 73 you bend up to the last note (G) from a half step below (F♯). This simple, subtle nuance gives that final note a completely different type of vibrato sound plus a crying, vocal-like quality that adds emotion to the lick.

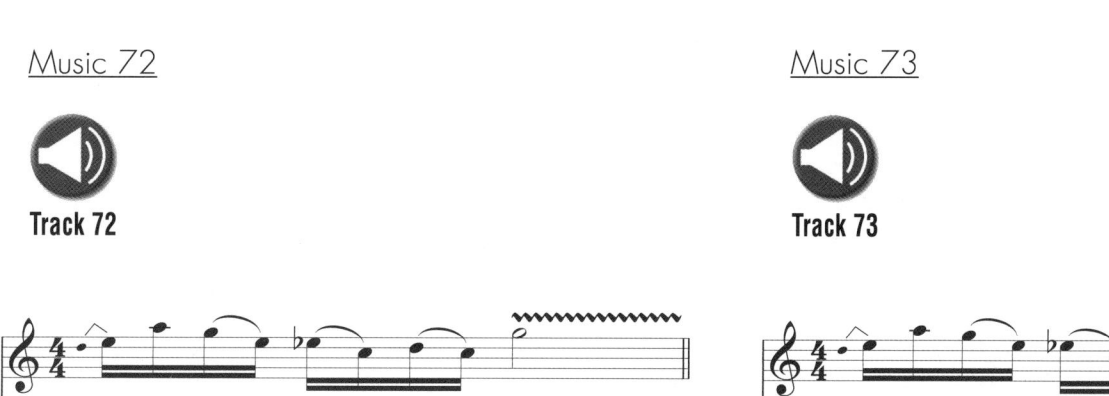

Now compare Music 74 and 75. Music 75 is basically the same E minor-blues (E–G–A–B♭–B–D) lick as the one in Music 74, but with a couple of trills, double-stops, and a slide thrown in for extra excitement.

Music 74

Track 74

Music 75

Track 75

Get the picture? As these two examples illustrate, it doesn't take much to breathe new life into a seemingly tired idea.

A really great and effective way of rejuvenating an old lick is to see how many different ways you can *phrase* it. In case you're not 100 percent sure what I'm talking about here, I'll quickly explain: To phrase a run or lick differently, you don't change the order of the notes you're playing—instead, you just mess with their timing. Basically, phrasing is all about two things: 1) how you attack each note, and 2) how long before you move onto the next one. Confused? If you are, don't worry—the following example should make this concept crystal-clear.

Check out the simple A minor blues lick shown in Music 76. By keeping the running order of the notes the same and merely changing the timing of each note, you can come up with a bunch of variations in no time. Music examples 77–81 are just a few of 'em. Get it? It's real easy to do, and those five variations are just the start. There are literally an infinite number of ways this short sequence of notes can be phrased without altering their order or adding extra slurs or passing notes.

Music 76

Track 76

Music 77

Track 77

So, the next time you find yourself guilty of recycling the same exact licks over and over again, try taking a few of them and seeing how many different ways you can phrase them. I realize that this is an unbelievably basic concept, but then again, most of the great ones are—and for that very reason, are often overlooked. Don't dismiss this one—it could well save your ass the next time you find yourself caught in a "lick recycling" rut!

Exorcise Your Repetitive Demons

Sometimes you can be in a rut and not even know it! When I first started playing, I used to make my sister sit down and tell me when I was repeating myself. Then, when she'd recognize something I kept doing, I'd write the lick in question down and say to myself, "Okay, I'm not going to play that one for a while." This is a great way of exorcising your repetitive demons: You're consciously flushing them out of your system because you're writing them down on a piece of paper and then throwing them away—and it works!!

For instance, one of the things my sister noticed that I wasn't even aware of was that I used to finish almost every lick or run with a phrase I stole from Pat Travers. Music 82 shows the phrase in question played in A minor and then Music 83 is an E minor blues run that ends with it.

Music 82

Music 83

Once she'd pointed this out to me, I was able to put this little phrase away for a while and get out of the rut I didn't even know I was in. Oh, and if you don't have a sibling or a friend you can persuade to police your playing like this, you can always do it yourself by taping your playing and then listening back with a critical ear.

Take a Break . . . I Think!

Even though I love to play and do so almost every single day without fail, one thing that occasionally works for me when I'm in a rut is not to play for a while. Sometimes, after a big tour, I won't touch a guitar for a couple of weeks. Then, when I pick it up again, I start playing completely different stuff, which is always great.

I left this idea for last because, to be honest, I'm not even sure I should be recommending it to you! I say this for two reasons.

1) You can only do this if you've been playing for a long time.

2) Although it works for me, it might not work for you because everyone is different.

As it just so happens, Kirk further expanded on this "take a break" idea in the January 2006 issue of *Guitar World*, which was dedicated to rightfully giving "the ultimate metal album," *Master of Puppets*, a 20-year salute. In this issue, the cover artist (Mr. Hammett, of course!) answered a bunch of questions, including this next one.

What Do You Do When You Hit a Creative Wall?

"Go surfing. Go watch a movie," was Kirk's reply. "Just do something that pulls you out of yourself and into a completely different realm. It's important, because if you just keep at it, you're going to dig yourself a deeper hole. Go dig a ditch . . . whatever."

Kirk's closing comments: "I hope some of the ideas we've looked at will help you out the next time you find yourself in a rut. So, take that lick you keep repeating and rephrase it or put that Coltrane CD on and become a tasteful thief!"

CHAPTER 9
...AND ANSWERS FOR ALL
Readers Asked, Kirk Answered

As touched on at the very onset of this tome, Kirk dedicated a slew of column space to answering many of the questions he received from his *The Sound & the Fury* fans. As he put it in the May 2001 issue, "Your questions keep flooding in via snail-mail and e-mail so, once again, in this month's column I'm going to answer some more of your queries."

I've already assimilated several of these questions and answers into relevant chapters, but as Kirk's responses were always so telling, here's a collection of some of the best.

Tone Talk—Pickups, Guitars, and Other Tonal Topics

Hi there, fellow tone nuts. All the following questions I'm going to answer relate to tone in one way or another. I've gotta tell you—whether I'm on stage, in the studio, or just jamming in my bedroom—having a cool guitar tone is vitally important to me. If my tone is hurting, then I become a sack of wet noodles! It's like that old Samson and Delilah legend—if you cut off all his hair, then he has no strength. Well, take away my tone and I'm worthless! Also, like most serious guitarists, I'm always looking for ways to improve my sound. So, to this day, I'm still constantly tweaking my gear and experimenting with different stuff.

Tone is such a vast and fascinating subject because there are so many variables. As well as having a mind-boggling assortment of different types of guitars, pickups, amps, and effects to choose from, there are so many subtle things you can do with your pick and your fingers to alter your tone. For example, the way you hold your pick or where you pick the strings has a drastic affect on your tone. For instance, if you pick near the bridge you get a very bright, twangy tone, whereas if you pick near the neck, you get a smoother, rounder, jazzier sound.

How hard or soft you pick is another very important tonal factor. When I'm playing blues, I tend to dig in really hard and, as a result, I end up hitting the string with the tip of my right (picking) hand as well as with my pick. The result is not quite a pinch harmonic but something very close to it.

Hi Kirk,

Thanks for doing such a cool column. I recently formed a metal band with some friends and I'm thinking about buying myself a better guitar. I know someone who's selling a pretty good axe but it only has one pickup—a humbucker in the bridge position. I really want one with a neck pickup as well, but he tells me that metal guitarists never use that pickup anyway. I haven't been playing for very long—is he telling me the truth or is he just trying to sell me his guitar?

Danny Nichols
Cleveland, OH

I obviously can't speak for every metal player, but I definitely feel that if your guitar only has a lead (bridge) pickup then you'll be selling yourself short because a rhythm (neck) pickup is so versatile for many different things. It can give you a great, smooth feel when you're playing lead with a super amount of distortion and it sounds just as good on a clean tone, too. I personally love using the neck pickup on a two-humbucker guitar such as my ESP Les Paul copy because it has such a cool, fat, singing tone to it. I also dig the sound of a single-coil pickup in the neck position because it's so lyrical. On a Strat, the middle-position, single-coil pickup is magical, too, for that totally Hendrix-style, "Little Wing"–type tone.

Dear Kirk,

Do you have any advice on buying guitars and amps you could pass on, please? For example: Should I be influenced by what my favorite players use or not? My brother says I should, but I'm not sure. Help!

Joey Tennate
Bronx, NY

If there's a player you really admire and you also really like his sound, then in my opinion, the gear he uses is a really good guide. I mean, if you really like Stevie Ray Vaughan's tone and you buy a Les Paul and a high-gain Marshall stack then you're not going to get that sound—in fact, you're not even gonna get close! You might get close if you buy a Strat, though you'll probably get even closer if you buy a vintage Strat— and you'll probably get even closer if you buy a vintage Strat *and* a vintage Fender combo amp.

Dear Kirk,

You're one of my favorite guitarists, and I've seen you play live a bunch of times. Although I've noticed that you change pickups every once in a while, I've never seen you mess around with your guitar's volume control—even when you're using a clean sound. Some guitarists seem to mess with that control all the time, but I get the impression that you just turn it all the way up and then leave it there. Is that the case, and if so, why?

Titch Colbert,
Salt Lake City, UT

I've always felt that if you back off your guitar's volume control, then the pickup doesn't pick up the full vibration of the strings. I don't know if that's true, but it's definitely my mindset! That's why I always try to get clean sounds with my pickup full-on—that way, I know that my pickups are working 100% to capture my guitar's tone.

Hey Kirk,

Is there a really cheap way I can get more tonal variation out of my existing rig?

Ken Dowling,
Canoga Park, CA

Try getting hold of a half-decent wah-wah pedal. The great thing about a wah is that if you have a good guitar sound, then you can use the wah as a tone filter [by switching on the pedal, opening it to a "sweet spot," and then leaving it there] and get several variations of that one sound instantly.

Dear Kirk,

Your column has really helped me improve my technique and speed and, thanks to you, my "comfort zone" has expanded virtually all over the fretboard. Every month I buy my new Guitar World, *I turn to* The Sound & the Fury *first. I'd like to know exactly what you use to get your sound because I love it. I own a Kirk Hammett Series M-2 that I love and I've come really close to perfecting your tone, but something's just not right. Please help.*

Brad Burris,
Marlton, NJ

Thanks for the letter, Brad. I'm glad to hear that my column has helped your playing out. As I've already said in *The Sound & the Fury*, if there's a player you really admire and you'd really like to get his sound, then the gear he uses is a real good guide to getting a tone similar to his. I use the word "similar" because even if you play your favorite guitarist's personal axe through his own personal rig, you're still going to sound like you—and that's the beauty of the guitar.

Soloing, Shredding, String Raking, SRV, 'n' Stuff

Dear Kirk,

I find it hard to solo over certain things and I read in interviews that some lead players like to come up with their own specific rhythm parts for lead parts and even have a backlog of chord progressions that they like to solo over. Is this a good idea?

"Cookie King Todd" Altekruse,
Findlay, OH

In my opinion, it's definitely not a good idea because all you're doing is playing it safe—you're resting on your laurels and heading back to the security of your "comfort zone." Whenever you come across a chord progression or riff that's difficult to solo over, don't give up and decide to change it right away—instead, get excited and rise to the challenge. All it means is that none of the licks and runs in your comfort zone are working, so you'll have to come up with some brand new ideas. This can be frustrating at first, but stick with it because, at the end of the day, the challenge will broaden your horizons as a player . . . and that's definitely a cool thing!

Talking about broadening your lead playing horizons, one thing I used to do a lot was just switch on the radio and then play over everything and anything that came along—even jingles. This is a lot of fun, and will really push you because a lot of the time you'll have no preconceived notions of what you're going to be soloing over next.

Dear Kirk,

Your thoughts on "rut busting" have been real helpful to my playing. I'm a big fan of your lead work. How do you approach it? Do you have a specific M.O. or is it different every time? I'd like to know what goes on in your head, and I'm sure a lot of other readers would, too. Keep up the good work and please tour England soon. Cheers!!

Lance Perkins,
Evesham, England

Although I don't have any set game plan for my solos, I'm totally from the school that says, "Start out with a great idea, resolve it, introduce a second great idea, resolve it, and then end with a bang!" I try to make every note count—to have no dead spaces, except for the occasional passing note. Basically, I believe that a solo is a song within a song, and that's definitely how I feel when I'm working on a solo . . . I feel like I'm composing a song.

One approach to building a memorable solo is to have one or two themes that you repeat and build upon. A good example of a song with a repeating theme within it is "The God That Failed" [*Metallica*]. In bars 3 and 4, I do something similar to the open-string lick we looked at in Music 37 [page 54] and then, three bars later, I do an octave run similar to Music 84 that mimics the first half of that motif.

Music 84

Track 84

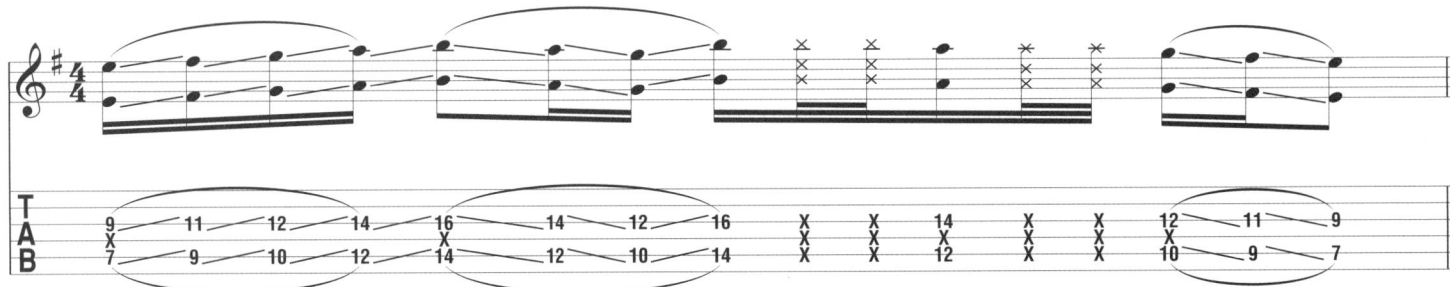

Regardless of my goals for a particular solo, I try not to consciously think of scales and modes too much. Ultimately, when it comes to making music there are no rights and wrongs: If a note sounds great, then use it, regardless of what the rules of theory say!

Dear Kirk,

Are your solos worked out, ad-libbed, or a mixture of both?

James Roberts,
Dallas, TX

As I've just pointed out, I view a lead break as a song within a song and so, from that standpoint, all my solos are composed. But, having said that, I must add that a lot of them get written right on the spot! Often, the first time I try one, I play something that's so right that very few things need changing. Some backing tracks are so "improviser friendly" that I feel I can come up with something good right off the cuff, so I purposely leave those areas open for spontaneity in the studio.

Then there are other progressions that are so #@$%ed up and complex that I have to sit down and specif- =ically work out something that fits. I basically take each situation at face value and then determine what I need to do to make the solo work.

Dear Kirk,

I learn a lot of my lead stuff by copying other players' solos off albums. A friend of mine, who's a much better player than me, says that learning solos note-for-note isn't cool. Is he right or wrong?

Jeffrey Vaughan
Port Chester, NY

There's nothing wrong with learning other guitarists' solos note-for-note. I mean, most guitarists have done it at one time or another, as I have. Just don't get to the stage where all you do is regurgitate other peoples' ideas every time you play a lead. I strongly recommend that you learn all you can from other guitarists but, when it comes time for you to solo, just play from inside yourself. I believe that playing what *you feel* is really important. It doesn't matter how fast you can sweep pick or how many exotic scales you know—capturing your emotions and then conveying them to others through your playing is what music is all about.

Hi Kirk,

I remember reading an interview with James Hetfield, just after Metallica *was released, where he said, "When we hear Kirk sweep-picking an arpeggio we wanna hit him!" Are you guys really that down on shred techniques like sweep-picking arpeggios?*

Roger Pinto
Farmingdale, NY

I can remember James saying that! Anyway, with regards to sweep-picked arpeggios, whether you like it or not, ever since Yngwie [Malmsteen] emerged, that has become one of the biggest lead-playing clichés of modern metal. As a result, I think that technique alienated certain people—they'd hear a string of lightning-fast arpeggios and immediately go, "See ya!" This isn't because sweep-picking arpeggios is necessarily a bad thing, but just because the idea got so overused, it's still automatically associated with being musically pretentious. That's why the technique became a definite "no-no" in Metallica.

When I was younger, I was definitely into cramming as much fast and impressive stuff into my solos as I possibly could. As I matured into a musician, though, I began to realize that sometimes you've got to give the big finger to technical stuff and do what's best for the band's music. And, as I've often said, a lot of the time, what's best is often something relatively simple and bluesy.

Although I still enjoy playing in a high-tech way once in a while, nowadays I'm definitely into space and sustain, too—I'm always trying to get more space in my playing. A lot of shredders don't seem to realize how space can be used constructively—they're just hell-bent on impressing you with how many notes they can fit in! To me, those guys sound like they're hyperventilating musically. The reason shred has earned such a bad rap is because so many players don't use the technique tastefully or constructively. Sure, Yngwie can play incredibly fast, but there's *always* a lot of feeling and emotion in what he does—and that's what it's all about. Remember, music isn't supposed to be pretentious.

I'm certainly not knocking everyone who plays lightning-fast, sweep-picked arpeggios, as my above comments on Yngwie demonstrate. It can be mind-blowing, providing the technique is used sparingly and musically. I mean, Uli Roth employs sweep arpeggios amazingly and Yngwie—the guy largely responsible for starting the craze—uses them brilliantly, too!

Actually, thanks to John Coltrane, I developed a new-found respect for arpeggios, because he played a hell of a lot of them and they were *always* part of a very melodic idea. He never used them just as a means to jerk off! One thing people don't realize about arpeggios is that you don't have to follow the exact same chord sequence that the rhythm guitar is playing in order to come up with a cool arpeggio line that works. A good example of what I'm talking about here happens in the title track of our *Ride the Lightning* album.

During the solo, there's a section where the rhythm guitar plays a power-chord sequence that chromatically descends from C5 to A5, similar to how Guitar 1 does in Music 85. If I'd wanted to use arpeggios and play it safe, I guess I could have just played a straightforward mixture of major and minor arpeggios that follows the C–B–B♭–A sequence—like C–Bm–B♭–Am, for example. Instead, though, I came up with an Am–G–Gm–F♯m arpeggio sequence similar to the one played by Guitar 2 in Music 85.

Music 85

Track 85

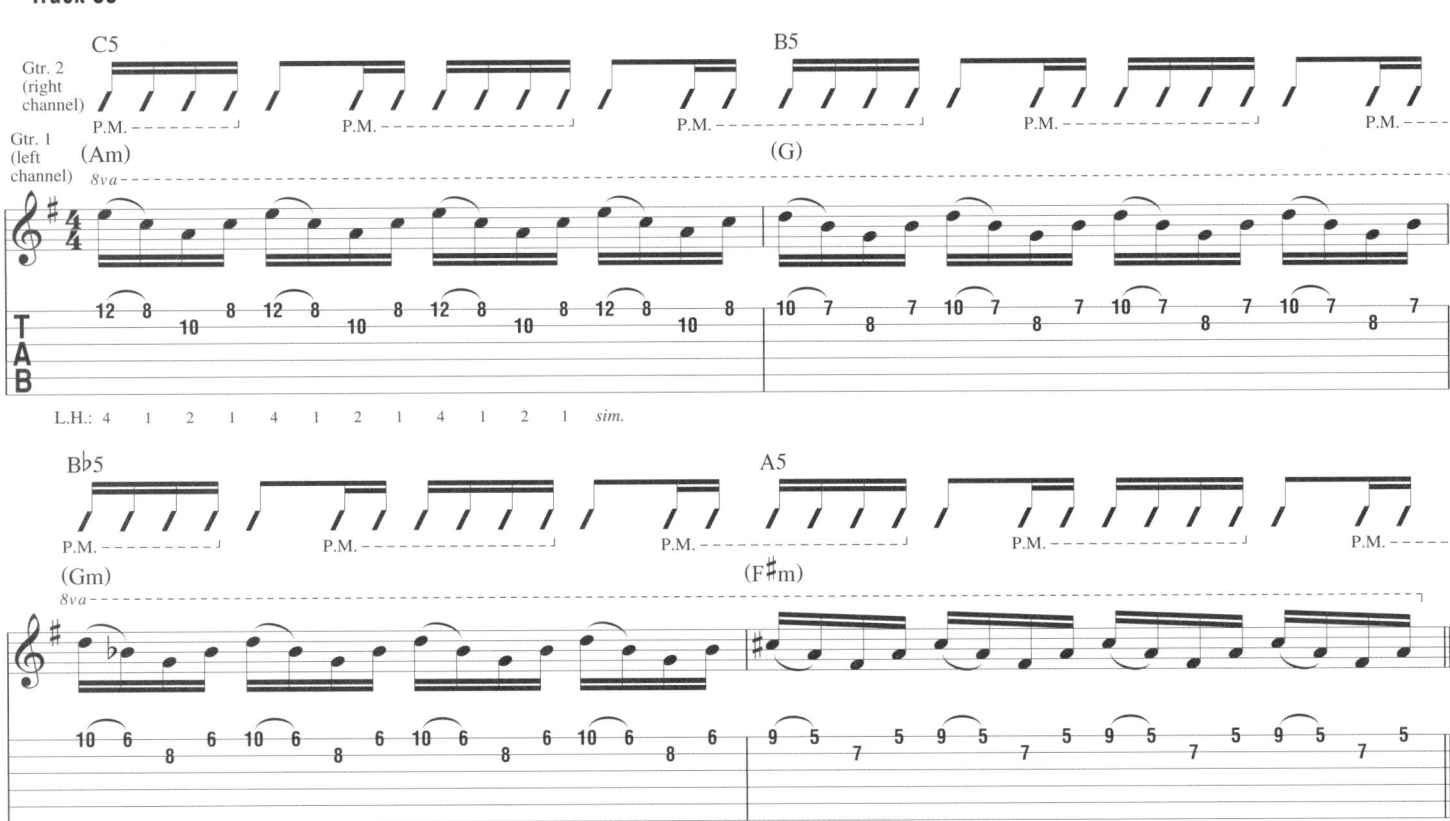

At first glance, my choice of arpeggios might seem completely unrelated to the backing chords but, believe me, it's not! Let me explain: If you look at the second and fourth 16th notes of each arpeggio, you'll see that the C–B–B♭–A sequence is being followed. Just so you know, each of these four notes is called a *common tone* because it is found in both the backing chord and the arpeggio being played over it.

Try experimenting with this common-tone idea when playing arpeggios over some root/5th power-chord sequences of your own and don't be afraid to make mistakes! We all make them from time to time and, if you're wise, you can learn from them. Also, don't be afraid to incorporate some breathing space into your solos. Otherwise you'll hyperventilate, and that's a definite no-no!

Dear Kirk,

Your columns have really helped my playing, especially the one about phrasing. If you have any other little hints that can help me "spice up" the runs and licks I already know, I'd really appreciate it. Thanks in anticipation and keep up the good work.

Jason Armstrong
Denver, CO

Thanks for the compliments, Jason—it's always great to hear that some of the ideas I've been throwing out there have been sticking! Regarding your question, a relatively easy way to "spice up" your lead work is by using a technique called string-raking. As you're about to discover, this relatively simple technique is kind of like percussive sweep-picking. Music 86 is a pretty simple C minor blues lick that begins with a string rake.

Music 86

Track 86

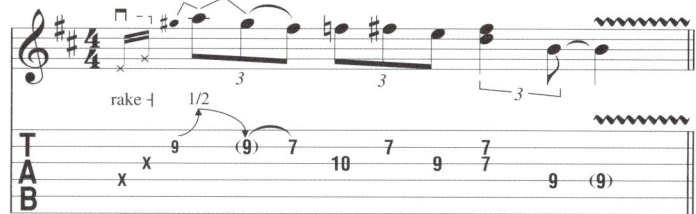

As you can see from the tab, all you have to do is this: Mute the D and G strings by lightly resting your left-hand [i.e., frethand] index finger on them and then quickly rake your pick across them using a single, smooth downstroke that ends with the half step bend at the 10th fret on the B string. Raking the muted D and G strings like this definitely adds extra emotion, attitude, and emphasis to the initial string bend in this lick. Try playing the same exact lick without the rake and you'll hear exactly what I mean here.

Music 87

Track 87

Music 87 is an E minor lick that also starts with a string rake, but this time across the D, G, and B strings. Because your left-hand index finger is being used to fret the first note of this run, you'll need to mute the D, G, and B strings with either your middle or ring finger . . . or both!

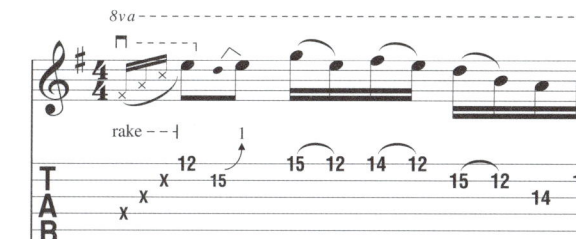

Music 88

Track 88

I do a lot of upstroke string-raking when I'm soloing too. I guess I got into this by listening to Ritchie Blackmore—he does it all the time. Music 88 is an E minor lick that uses upstroke string rakes. Once again, I use my index finger to mute the raked strings if it isn't being used to fret the note I'm raking to. If it is, I use my middle or ring finger for the muting.

If you want, you can actually sound the note or notes you rake to create a different feel altogether. As long as you're playing within the blues box, you're safe! Music 89 is an A minor example of what I'm talking about here.

Music 89

Track 89

Stevie Wonder—How to Play Like the Late, Great Bluesman, Stevie Ray Vaughan

Dear Kirk:

After reading a recent interview with you in which you raved about how great Stevie Ray Vaughan was, I figured I'd check him out. All I can say is, "Thanks a million," because now I'm hooked! I'll always be a diehard metal fan, but listening to SRV has opened up my ears. I'm having real trouble dialing in a tone that is even close to his, though—do you have any suggestions? Also, if you could give me any insight into a few of the quirks that helped make Stevie's playing so unique, that'd be cool as well.

Jared Hill
Phoenix, AZ

As you've no doubt already ascertained, Stevie Ray Vaughan is one of my all-time favorite guitarists. Ironically, I was never really into Stevie while he was alive. Then, shortly after he died, I got hold of a video of him playing a live show and was just totally blown away by his timing, his tone, his feel, his vibrato, his phrasing—everything. Some people are just born to play guitar, and Stevie was definitely one of them. VH1's *Behind the Music* program on Stevie showed some old footage of him playing guitar when he was a little kid—he was so good it made me want to cry.

When it comes to emulating SRV's tone, that's a tough one because his hands and soul definitely had a lot to do with it. Having said that, as I've already said earlier in this chapter, if there's a player whose sound you really admire, one way to emulate his tone is to look into the gear he used. So, if you really want to get a sound similar to Stevie Ray's you might get close if you buy a Strat and probably even closer if you get a vintage Strat and a vintage Fender amp because that's what he used. I also know that Stevie used an old Ibanez Tube Screamer and a Vox wah, too.

Other real big factors in Stevie's killer tone were pretty high action [i.e., the height of the strings from the neck], the gauge of his strings, and how hard he used to play. A lot of people try to do the SRV thing using a set of .009s, and you just can't do what he did with slinky strings like that. Stevie used real heavy strings—.013 (high E) to .058 or even .060 (low E). So, to get even close you need to start with at least a set of .011s.

In addition to using heavy strings, you also really need to attack the guitar if you want to get that big, percussive sound Stevie had. He was a super aggressive player and he didn't really pick from his wrist, he picked with his entire arm! If you watch video footage of him, you'll see exactly what I mean. Stevie also used a lot of downstrokes and a lot of string-raking, which really added to the unique rhythm and lead sound that he got.

Like all great players, Stevie's style contained a bunch of cool nuances—some of which are really hard to nail. Take the intro riff to "Scuttle Buttin'" [*Couldn't Stand the Weather*] for example. I've been messing around with it for years, but I still can't play it with Stevie's feel. There's a weird slide he does near the beginning that I just can't get exactly right, no matter how hard I try. I can play the riff note-for-note, but there's that little nuance that I just can't get, and I've been chasing it for a long time.

As I just mentioned, SRV often used string-raking, which is a topic we've just discussed. Another SRV move that definitely adds both bite and a nice bluesy tension to a solo is doing quarter tone bends on certain notes so they end up sitting right between two notes. Music 90 is an A minor run that features both these techniques.

Music 90

Track 90

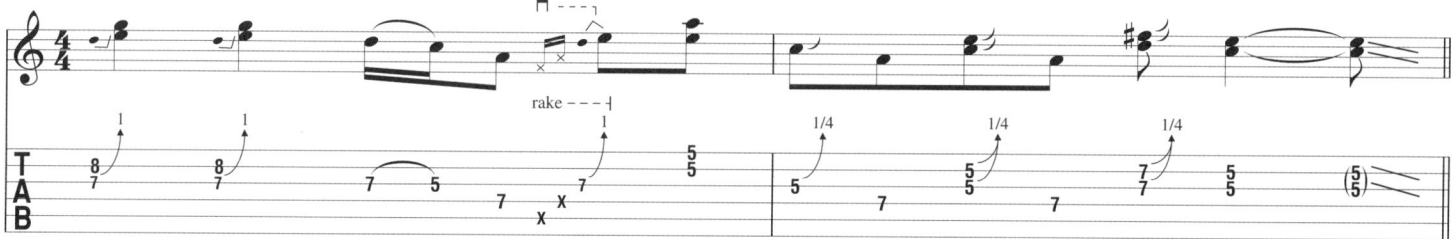

As you can see, several notes are bent up a quarter step—like the first note in the second bar, which is bent up so that it sits right between C and C#. Great blues players do this kind of thing all the time, and Stevie was especially good at it—hell, he'd even add a quarter note bend to notes he'd already bent up by one or even two steps.

Being able to shake a note in a way that compliments both the song and also mood of the solo is another highly expressive art that Stevie Ray Vaughan definitely perfected. I especially love his vibrato, because it is so damned wide and muscular. Unfortunately, this technique is almost as difficult to describe as it is to do. So, to learn more about this I recommend that you listen closely to his albums and also watch videos of him in action, zoning in on what he does with his left hand. Check out SRV's *Live at the El Mocambo* video—it's a jaw-dropping experience and, if you watch and listen closely, you'll learn a lot.

Dear Kirk,

I've been a loyal fan of Metallica and your lead playing ever since I bought Kill 'Em All *back in 1984. I've watched your lead style evolve with interest ever since then and am intrigued to know where you feel it's going next. Any clues would be appreciated! Also, please keep the column going as it's my favorite part of the magazine.*

John Kirkland
Nashville, TN

That's a good question, John. As you've no doubt noticed, my playing has changed a lot over the years. I started out playing very fast, flashy stuff that was very modal and also very metal. I did that throughout the '80s, but when the '90s came I got a little tired of that approach. As a result, my leads got a lot simpler—they became less modal and became more pentatonic, bluesy, laid-back, and melodic.

When I listen back to albums like *Kill 'Em All*, *Ride the Lightening*, *Master of Puppets*, and *. . . And Justice for All*, though, I realize that I still really like the way I played in the '80s. Also, when we were working on the covers album, *Garage Days Revisited*, going back and listening to all those bands I used to listen to was a musical time-travel trip for me. It helped me tap back into a style of playing that I used to really enjoy but I kind of lost track of. It really kicked my playing in the ass and woke me up again to that whole modal, three-octave scale approach (Music 91 and 92) that I abandoned for a while because I was listening to so much blues.

Music 91

Track 91

Music 92

Track 92

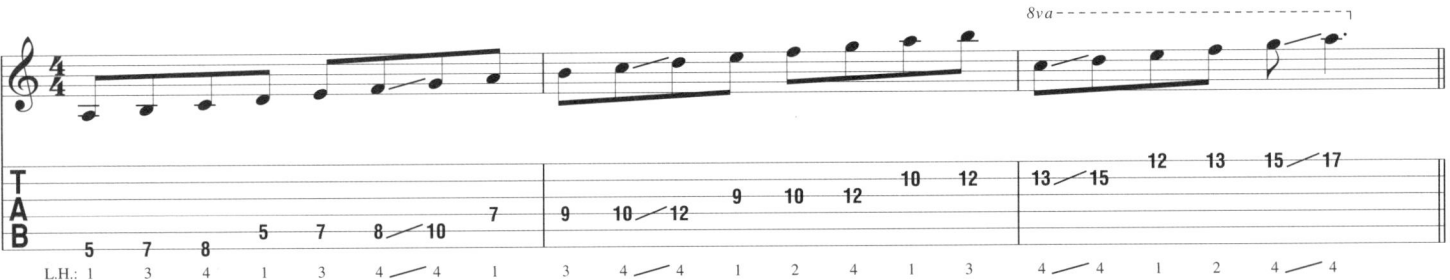

The thing is, I love the blues and I love pentatonics. I love major pentatonics and minor pentatonics because I grew up listening to that sound. All my favorite guitar players used those scales—Jimi Hendrix, Eric Clapton, Stevie Ray Vaughan, Joe Perry, Pat Travers, and Brian Robertson. Having said this, I also like the modal sound of players like Michael Schenker, Joe Satriani, Steve Vai, Eddie Van Halen, and Ulrich Roth.

So, ideally, what I'd like to find is a middle ground between those two approaches. By blending the two styles, I'm convinced that somehow, someway, something new and interesting will come out of it. So that's what I've been working on—melding the two approaches by mixing my pentatonic obsessions with modes, three-octave scales, and the blues. I'll also continue to take lessons; you can never learn enough!

Dear Kirk,

Of all the solos you've recorded, which one is your personal favorite?

James Bernard
Florida

That's a hard one to answer because I feel good about 95 percent of the solos I've recorded. I really like the solo in "Wherever I May Roam"—that's definitely one of my finer moments. I also really like how the lead I did in "Bleeding Me" turned out. That solo does a pretty good job of summing up my influences and also contains a pretty good dose of my own style. I pretty much sweep through my entire lick catalog on that one—from ones I would've played on *Kill 'Em All* to brand new ones.

"Hero of the Day" is another one of my very favorite solos because it's just so melodic and fits the song so well. It's not ripping, but I feel it nails the emotion the song puts across. I also like the solos in "Master of Puppets" and "The Thing That Should Not Be." I also really like my lead in "Devil's Dance" as that was the first time I ever abused a Digitech whammy and it turned out really well.

Ironically, though, as much as I like all the solos I've just mentioned, the very best playing I've ever done normally comes out in a hotel room at four o'clock in the morning!

Hey Kirk,

I love all your solos. Are there any you've recorded that you wish you could do over?

Jim Sawyer
St Paul, MN

There are a few solos I've recorded that I listen to and think, "What the hell was I trying to do on that one?!" Unfortunately, there's been the odd occasion in the recording studio where a pressing deadline has caused me to rush and sometime the art suffers because of that, which sucks. For example, there are a couple of leads on *Kill 'Em All* that were rushed and so was the one on "Frayed Ends of Sanity," which I had to do at four in the morning when I was exhausted because we were leaving for the Monsters of Rock tour. I really wish I could go back in time and redo that one. Having said that, though, the funny thing is that I've met people who've told me that's their favorite solo on *Justice*, so what do I know?!

Hi Kirk,

I recently started jamming with a band, and some of the fast lead runs I've been practicing just aren't in time with the rest of the guys. I'd like to blame the drummer, but I can't because he keeps great time! Do you have any advice for me?

James Ryan,
Hoboken, NJ

It sounds to me like you probably need to get hold of a metronome or a drum machine, James. To really maximize your practice time, it's sometimes a really good idea to play along with a steady pulse because you need to feel that sense of rhythm, so that when you hit a note, you know you're playing it in time. A lot of times when you're playing by yourself, you might think you're playing a lick or run in time, but you're not, and there's no real way of telling because you've got no real objective point of reference. So, even though you think you've mastered something, when it comes time to play it in a band context, you might be rushing it, or playing it too far back, or a combination of both.

Playing with Others

Dear Kirk,

A friend of mine is really into us jamming together. The trouble is, he's a much better guitarist than me, so I'm not sure that us playing together is such a good idea. What would you do?

Brian Mead,
Washington, DC

I'd definitely go for it if I were you because, in my opinion, playing music with other people is ultimately what it's all about. It doesn't matter if you're jamming with another guitarist, a drummer, a guy playing the harmonica, or even someone who's just hitting a beer bottle with a pair of chopsticks; the resulting human interaction will definitely bring things out of you that won't ever happen if you're just playing by yourself. I wouldn't let the fact that your friend is better than you bother you either, because I love it when that happens to me. In fact, I think that's probably the main reason why I'm still taking guitar lessons! My teachers have all been great players, and sometimes I just can't wait for my lesson, just so I can jam with them. Jamming with a monster player often brings a lot of stuff out of me that wouldn't normally happen.

Hey Kirk,

What's the story behind the white tape you wrap around your picking hand?

Brett Fergis
London, England

It's there to stop me from cutting myself. If your hands are anything like mine, you'll have some wrinkle lines on the side of your hand just below your little finger. Due to my aggressive playing style and all the muting I do, when we're on tour my right hand gets a pretty good beating and those wrinkles eventually get cut open and start bleeding. The tape is just there to help prevent that from happening because it's pretty painful, especially if a string gets in there once my hand's cut.

Riff Raff—In Search of the Ultimate Riff

Hi Kirk:

The Sound & the Fury rules! I learn something cool from it every single month. Some of my favorite Metallica songs ("Welcome Home (Sanitarium)," "Eye of the Beholder," "Of Wolf and Man," "King Nothing," and "Fixxxer," to name but a few) have been co-written by you. How do you come up with new riffs and song ideas? What inspires you? Do you deliberately sit down with the intention of writing new stuff, or do the ideas just come to you? Also, do you record them or write them down, or can you just remember the good ones? And lastly, if you had to pick one or two songs/riffs you'd written as your favorites, which ones would they be?

Joey McDonald
Mesa, AZ

I've never sat down with my guitar and tried to force out a song or riff idea by going, "Okay, it's three o'clock, time for me to try and write something." If I get inspired, though, I'll obviously pick up a guitar right away, but inspiration definitely doesn't follow any kind of timetable; it can strike anywhere and at any time, which is why I have guitars lying all over my house! In fact, I actually have a guitar in each room of my home because I always like to have one close by. Unfortunately, quite a few of them are missing a string because I'm too lazy to change a string when one breaks. Every time I break a string, I just put that guitar down and grab another one, which means I eventually end up with a house full of five-string guitars!

This said, pretty much every single time I pick up the guitar it inspires me anyway and, because of that, I invariably end up searching for *the* riff—you know, the next "Smoke on the Water," "Smells Like Teen Spirit," or modern-day equivalent. Mind you, you don't necessarily have to be physically playing the guitar to be creative. You can take a mental approach, too. I've often found that I can stimulate my creativity by listening to something I really like and then taking that feeling to the guitar and expressing it.

When I'm working on a riff idea, I tend to look for a group of notes that sounds interesting together without sounding forced. I like the notes to flow together naturally so the riff sounds organic and has a good groove to it. I also like riffs that sound somewhat familiar, but not completely so. When some guys come up with a riff and someone says to them, "Hey, that sounds like something I've heard before," they immediately go, "Fuck it" and drop the idea. When that happens to me, though, I immediately tend to think, "Cool! I could be onto something here—I must be on the right track." To my mind, it's good if a riff taps into a feeling you've had before—within reason, of course. Obviously, if people tell you that your killer "new" riff reminds them of, say, "Paranoid" by Black Sabbath, and the reason it does is because it's note-for-note identical to Tony Iommi's original riff, you *do* say "Fuck it" and drop the idea! For me, you just can't beat a killer riff, and the funny thing is that 99.9 percent of the truly great ones only have four or five notes in them. It all has to do with timing and feel. It's how you play those notes rather than how many notes are in there.

When it comes to remembering ideas, I always record them because, unfortunately, I just can't trust my memory. I mean, I must've learned thousands of solos and God knows how many licks, but I've forgotten them all. Damn, I wish I had a photographic memory when it comes to the guitar because I'd be one hell of a guitar player if I did. So, because my memory sucks, I rely on this little Sony Walkman that records in stereo and has a built-in speaker and EQ. I've been putting riffs on it since around 1992 and carry it with me pretty much all the time, especially when we're touring so that I have it on hand whenever a cool new idea surfaces.

As for my favorite riff of all the ones I've written—that's easy! It's "Enter Sandman" [*Metallica*], (Music 93), because it's pretty much the best one I've come up with so far. I also really like the riff in "King Nothing" [*Load*], (Music 94), which is kind of similar to "Enter Sandman" in as much as they both contain the flatted 5th interval [two notes that are three whole steps apart; E to B♭ in both instances here], which is such an important part of our sound. Looking back, that flatted 5th note is everywhere in so many of our songs, and has been since the very beginning. The intro riff to "Seek & Destroy" [*Kill 'Em All*] is a good example of its use in an early Metallica riff.

Music 93

Track 93

"Enter Sandman"
Words and Music by James Hetfield, Lars Ulrich and Kirk Hammett
Copyright © 1991 Creeping Death Music (GMR)
International Copyright Secured   All Rights Reserved

Music 94

Track 94

Tune down 1/2 step:
(low to high) E♭-A♭-D♭-G♭-B♭-E♭

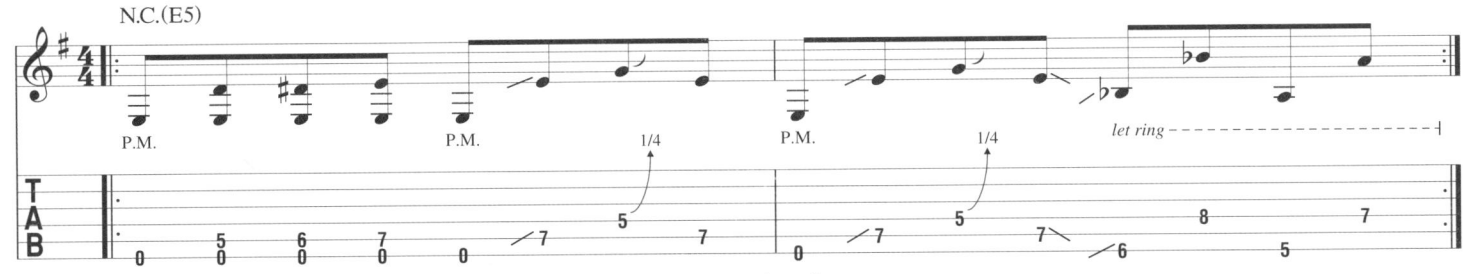

"King Nothing"
Words and Music by James Hetfield, Lars Ulrich and Kirk Hammett
Copyright © 1996 Creeping Death Music (GMR)
International Copyright Secured   All Rights Reserved

Because we've used the flatted 5th so often, I actually try to avoid it now so that everything doesn't end up sounding too similar. Consequently, the flatted 5th only creeps into our new songs on very rare occasions and only ends up being used if the riff in question sounds different and not forced in any way. I mean, the whole flatted 5th thing has been done to death now—ever since Black Sabbath used it in "Black Sabbath" [*Black Sabbath*] some 35 years ago!

Rhythm 'n' Bruise—A Batch of Metallica Riffage That Resulted from Readers Asking "How Do You Play That?"

Yo Kirk,

There's a killer Metallica riff I just can't seem to get right no matter what I do—the main E minor riff in "Creeping Death" (Ride the Lightning). *How do you play it so fast, dude? If you could explain that it'd really help me out.*

Scott Treutlein,
Massapequa Park, NY

As you correctly point out, Scott, the "Creeping Death" riff you're asking about is in E minor and a transcription of it is below.

Music 95

Track 95

"Creeping Death"
Words and Music by James Hetfield, Lars Ulrich, Cliff Burton and Kirk Hammett
Copyright © 1984 Creeping Death Music (GMR)
International Copyright Secured   All Rights Reserved

112

As you can see, if you use the suggested fretboard-hand fingering you don't have to move that hand up or down the neck. This is good as it allows you to focus in on the other aspects of playing this riff correctly. To master it, I suggest you start off by playing it real slow and then build up speed as you become more confident—as the saying goes, you can't run before you can walk.

To give this riff maximum balls, you should pick it using downstrokes only. If you're not used to picking using downstrokes exclusively and you can't play this riff at full speed right away, don't fret: Speed and stamina will come with time and practice. The other three things you need to be aware of to play this riff correctly are:

1. Make sure you mute each open low E-string note with the heel of your picking hand.

2. Make sure that the E5/B power chords are *staccato* (short and sharp) and aren't still ringing when you play the next note in the riff.

3. Execute the quick, four-note hammer-on/pull-off motif that concludes the riff cleanly, without sounding any unwanted open-string notes.

Human Suffering—Learning to Play "– Human"

Hi Kirk,

I'm having a real hard time with the first riff in "– Human," from Metallica's S&M *album. I think you tune your guitar down to C♯, but that's about it. Is there some weird time signature involved? I'm just not getting it, and I'm sure other readers must be having the same problems. Help!*

Allan Hetfield (no relation, unfortunately!)
St. Louis, MO

Actually, the tuning we use on "– Human" isn't standard tuning dropped down to C♯ (low to high: C♯–F♯–B–E–G♯–C♯). What we do is just drop the low E string down a whole step to D and, as we were tuned down a half step to begin with, that note is really C♯ or D♭. So the tuning we use is dropped-D a half step down (low to high: D♭–A♭–D♭–G♭–B♭–E♭). Now that we're clear on the tuning, let's look at the opening two guitar riffs.

As you'll know from the *S&M* album, "– Human" starts out with just the orchestra playing. We don't come in with the first intro riff (Music 96) until 0:35.

Music 96

Track 96

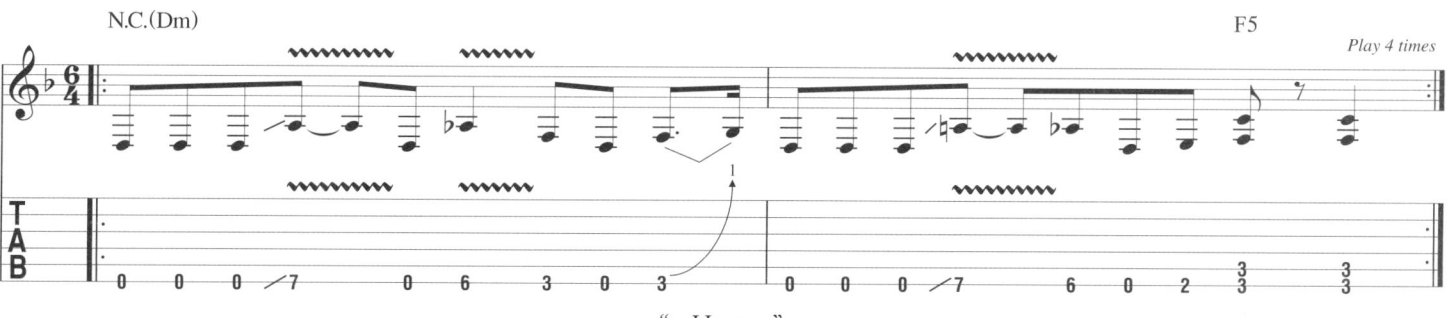

"– Human"
Words and Music by James Hetfield and Lars Ulrich
Copyright © 1999 Creeping Death Music (GMR)
International Copyright Secured   All Rights Reserved

As you can see, this riff is all played on the 6th string except for the two one-fingered chords at the very end. So, in terms of the notes used, it's a pretty simple riff. The reason you're having trouble nailing it down is probably due to the "weird" time signature you mentioned. As indicated at the beginning of Music 96, this riff is in 6/4 time (six quarter notes per bar), as opposed to the usual 4/4 (four quarter notes per bar), which is the meter that most rock songs are written in.

Because this riff is in 6/4 time, it definitely throws your ear for a loop because the riff doesn't turn around (stop and restart) where you'd expect it to. All 6/4 means, though, is that is you're going to play six beats per bar instead of the four that you're so used to. So, what you have to do is tap your foot and count "one–two–three–four–five–six, one–two–three–four–five–six," etc. Because you're so used to counting in 4/4 ("one–two–three–four, one–two–three–four," etc.), counting in 6/4 will probably feel a little weird at first, but stick with it; you'll get used to it after a while. Once you've gotten used to counting in groups of six instead of four, the "– Human" riff won't seem so weird any more. The other way to learn it, of course, is to listen to it over and over again until you can hum it. Once you can do that, just follow the notes indicated in the tablature, and you should be able to play this riff with no problem. As the old saying goes, "If you can hum it, you can play it!"

Masterful Riffs—Three Classic Riffs from *Master of Puppets*

To close this dissection of classic Metallica riffs, let's take a look at three monstrous motifs from *Master of Puppets*, exactly as played by Kirk.

2006 marked the 20th anniversary of this metal masterpiece. In order to celebrate this momentous occasion, *Guitar World* dispatched me to Metallica's H.Q. in San Raphael to conduct a private lesson with Kirk on the album. Here are a few of my favorite comments.

"Welcome Home (Sanitarium)" Chorus Riff

Music 97

Track 97

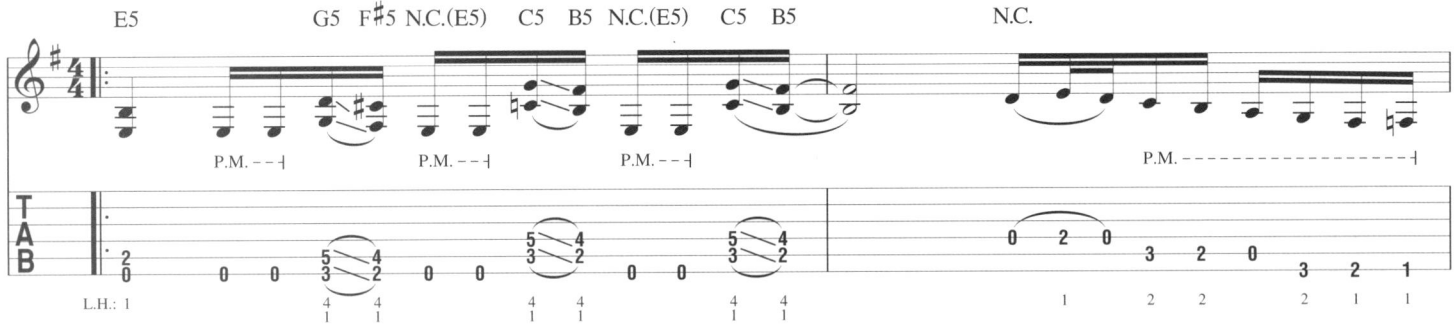

"Welcome Home (Sanitarium)"
Words and Music by James Hetfield, Lars Ulrich and Kirk Hammett
Copyright © 1986 Creeping Death Music (GMR)
International Copyright Secured   All Rights Reserved

Aside from being my favorite riff on the album, having Kirk show it to me confirmed something I'd long suspected—most transcriptions of it are wrong, as they omit the F note at the end of the second bar.

"Damage, Inc." Bridge

After revealing that this was my favorite riff on the album, I asked Kirk what his was. He answered my question by playing Music 98—the catchy E minor pedal-point bridge to "Damage, Inc." "It was influenced by a certain Deep Purple riff," he stated with a grin, "and that's all I'm going to say!"

Music 98

Track 98

"Damage, Inc."
Words and Music by James Hetfield, Lars Ulrich, Cliff Burton and Kirk Hammett
Copyright © 1986 Creeping Death Music (GMR)
International Copyright Secured   All Rights Reserved

Ode to Iommi—"The Thing That Should Not Be" Intro

To conclude the lesson, Kirk showed me Music 99, the clean-then-heavy intro to "The Thing That Should Not Be." "I believe this was the first time we ever tuned down low," he revealed as he played it, "It was definitely a Sabbath influence." As per Metallica's riffing M.O., downpicking is the order of the day. "Absolutely," Kirk affirmed. "Everything is always downstrokes with us, unless it's physically impossible to play that way."

Music 99

Track 99

"The Thing That Should Not Be"
Words and Music by James Hetfield, Lars Ulrich and Kirk Hammett
Copyright © 1986 Creeping Death Music (GMR)
International Copyright Secured   All Rights Reserved

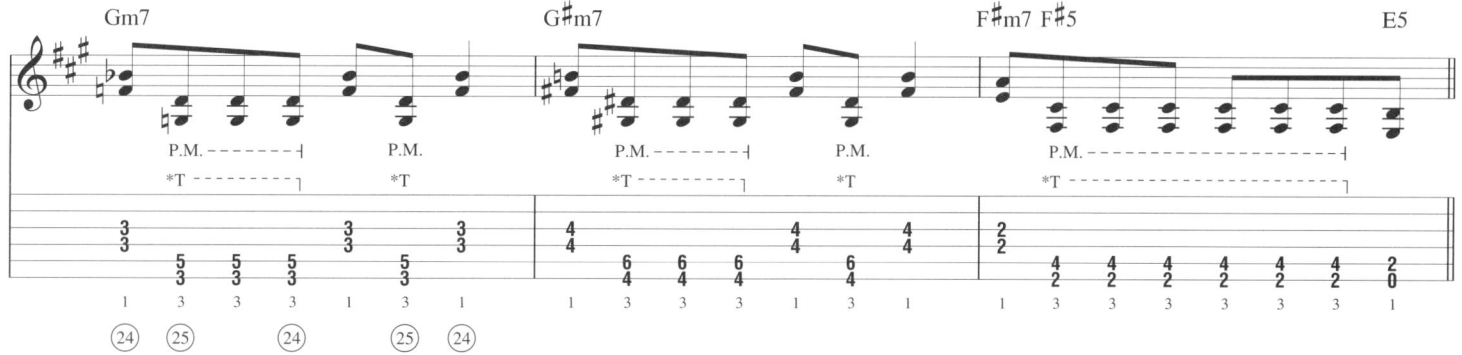

Note how Kirk uses his left-hand thumb to fret the low E-string notes in the last few bars. This is a trick well worth learning, as it ensures ease and accuracy when it comes performing this final passage. Photos 22–25 were taken while Kirk played the riff so you can see exactly how the master does it!

Photo 22

Photo 23

Photo 24

Photo 25

EPILOGUE
I Disappear
"Everything You Know Is Wrong" by Kirk Hammett

When Kirk penned the last column of his second series of *The Sound & the Fury* in Feb 2002, he promised he'd be back. Until his schedule lets up enough for him to do so, hopefully the contents of this book will tide you over—and also give you as much enjoyment in reading it as it gave me while I was putting it all together.

It's only fitting that the last word should be from our excellent and dedicated six-string teacher, and I strongly feel that the following from Kirk is a beyond-apt "sign off." Way back in the late '90s, the now-defunct US magazine *Guitar* let Kirk be the guest editor for their March 1998 edition. They literally let him call the shots from cover to cover. Needless to say, he did an amazing job. The piece Kirk penned to close the issue was enigmatically titled "Everything You Know Is Wrong." This thoughtful piece of writing was incredibly powerful at the time, and its message still resonates loudly today. For this reason, I'm going to leave you with Kirk's telling missive, as I honestly believe that, at the risk of sounding corny or obsequious, its conclusion truly does offer "words to live by" for any serious guitarist, regardless of style.

> When you're in a successful band, you can spend a lot of time wondering how your group got there and where it's all going to lead to in the future.
>
> It's never easy to figure these things out, because it seems like you're always working against some prevailing attitude, something that goes against everything you think you should do. When you're in a band in Metallica's position, you're often the target of this sort of thing. And we experience it a lot. During the whole grunge period, we were basically a metal band, and that was considered "unhip." You can see that same attitude in some of the reactions to *Load* and *ReLoad*, two albums whose un-Metallica style turned off some people who couldn't see beyond our past accomplishments.
>
> The bottom line is that you can't please everyone all the time. I know that's a really trite statement, but it resonates—probably more with guitar players than with anyone else—because it's a lot like that with guitar playing. If you know a lot about technique in this day and age, some people consider that wrong; if you don't know enough technique, that can be considered wrong, too, maybe even by the same group of people.
>
> Whichever way you go, someone is going to tell you that you're wrong. My point is that you should just go with your heart and just play what you want to play and not what's fashionable or trendy at the moment. I can remember in the '80s a lot of guitar players tried to chase credibility by saying they were heavily influenced by classical music. It got a bit stupid. You would have these total thrash bands going around praising the virtues of Bach, only because (it seemed to me, anyway) it was a trendy thing to say. You could draw a parallel for some of the music, but that doesn't mean that the bands were studying Bach.
>
> Sometimes it's really popular to be into one thing and you grasp that style or that genre of playing and make it your own. But then, all of a sudden, people are like, "Oh, you're playing *that*? Don't you know it's really cooler to just play three chords?"

You see? Everything you know is wrong. As much as you try to excel in one thing, someone is going to arbitrarily say something to the contrary. Whatever the prevailing trend, someone has to take the counterpoint and say "that's wrong." Whether that's a good thing or a bad thing, I can't say; it's just what happens. What you should do is play from the heart and play what you're interested in, because you'll find that you enjoy it more. Screw trends. Screw metal, screw alternative, screw grunge, screw blues, screw jazz, screw techno . . . screw all of it. Everyone thinks everything is crap anyway. What matters to you? Answer that question and make the right choice for yourself.

APPENDIX I
METALLICA DISCOGRAPHY

Obviously, as Metallica is such an enormous international entity, to list each and every release ever made in the band's name all over the world (CD, vinyl, cassette, L.P., E.P., single, promo, video, DVD, special editions, limited editions, etc.) over the past 24 years would literally be some kinda monster! To give you an idea of how ridiculously long such a discography would be, a pretty exhaustive one was printed in the 1994 issue of the Metallica club magazine *So What!* in 1994. I stopped counting when I got to 200 . . . and that was 13 years ago, amigo! So, the below contains just the regular USA releases that were readily available to one and all—and not weird and wonderful stuff like a 1993 release of a numbered picture CD single of "Sad but True" in the Netherlands that came with tattoos plus an entry card for "Snakepit" passes to an upcoming show!

Albums

Kill 'Em All
(Megaforce, July 1983)
1. Hit the Lights
2. The Four Horsemen
3. Motorbreath
4. Jump in the Fire
5. (Anesthesia)—Pulling Teeth
6. Whiplash
7. Phantom Lord
8. No Remorse
9. Seek & Destroy
10. Metal Militia

Note: Re-released by Elektra in 1986 and 1991 as above, and also in 1988 with covers of Diamondhead's "Am I Evil' and Blitzkrieg's "Blitzkrieg."

Ride the Lightning
(Elektra, August 1984)
1. Fight Fire with Fire
2. Ride the Lightning
3. For Whom the Bell Tolls
4. Fade to Black
5. Trapped Under Ice
6. Escape
7. Creeping Death
8. The Call of Ktulu

Garage Days Revisited '84
1. Am I Evil?
2. Blitzkrieg

Master of Puppets
(Elektra, February 1986)
1. Battery
2. Master of Puppets
3. The Thing That Should Not Be
4. Welcome Home (Sanitarium)
5. Disposable Heroes
6. Leper Messiah
7. Orion
8. Damage, Inc.

. . . And Justice for All
(Elektra, August 1988)
1. Blackened
2. . . . And Justice for All
3. Eye of the Beholder
4. One
5. The Shortest Straw
6. Harvester of Sorrow
7. The Frayed Ends of Sanity
8. To Live Is to Die
9. Dyers Eve

B-Sides & One-Offs '88–'91
1. Breadfan
2. The Prince
3. Stone Cold Crazy
4. So What
5. Killing Time

Metallica
(Elektra, August 1991)
1. Enter Sandman
2. Sad but True
3. Holier than Thou
4. The Unforgiven
5. Wherever I May Roam
6. Don't Tread on Me
7. Through the Never
8. Nothing Else Matters
9. Of Wolf and Man
10. That God That Failed
11. My Friend of Misery
12. The Struggle Within

Motörheadache '95
1. Overkill
2. Damage Case
3. Stone Dead Forever
4. Too Late Too Late

Load
(Elektra, June 1996)
1. Ain't My Bitch
2. 2 x 4
3. The House That Jack Built
4. Until It Sleeps
5. King Nothing
6. Hero of the Day
7. Bleeding Me
8. Cure
9. Poor Twisted Me
10. Wasting My Hate
11. Mama Said
12. Thorn Within
13. Ronnie
14. The Outlaw Torn

ReLoad
(Elektra, November 1997)
1. Fuel
2. The Memory Remains
3. Devil's Dance
4. The Unforgiven II
5. Better than You
6. Slither
7. Carpe Diem Baby
8. Bad Seed
9. Where the Wild Things Are
10. Prince Charming
11. Low Man's Lyric
12. Attitude
13. Fixxxer

Garage Inc.
(Elektra, November 1998)

Disc I—New Recordings '98
1. Free Speech for the Dumb
2. It's Electric
3. Sabbra Caddabra
4. Turn the Page
5. Die, Die My Darling
6. Loverman
7. Mercyful Fate
8. Astronomy
9. Whiskey in the Jar
10. Tuesday's Gone
11. The More I See

Disc II—Garage Days Re-Revisited '87
1. Helpless
2. The Small Hours
3. The Wait
4. Crash Course in Brain Surgery
5. Last Caress/Green Hell

S&M
(Elektra, November 1998)

Disc I
1. The Ecstasy of Gold
2. The Call of the Ktulu
3. Master of Puppets
4. Of Wolf and Man
5. The Thing That Should Not Be
6. Fuel
7. The Memory Remains
8. No Leaf Clover
9. Hero of the Day
10. Devil's Dance
11. Bleeding Me

Disc II
1. Nothing Else Matters
2. Until It Sleeps
3. For Whom the Bell tolls
4. – Human
5. Wherever I May Roam
6. Outlaw Torn
7. Sad but True
8. One
9. Enter Sandman
10. Battery

St. Anger
(Universal Distribution, June 2003)
1. Frantic
2. St. Anger
3. Some Kind of Monster
4. Dirty Window
5. Invisible Kid
6. My World
7. Shoot Me Again
8. Sweet Amber
9. The Unnamed Feeling
10. Purify
11. All Within My Hands

Death Magnetic
(Elektra, September 2008)
1. This Was Just Your Life
2. The End of the Line
3. Broken, Beat & Scarred
4. The Day That Never Comes
5. All Nightmare Long
6. Cyanide
7. The Unforgiven III
8. The Judas Kiss
9. Suicide & Redemption
10. My Apocalypse

E.P.s . . . Actually, Make That "E.P."!

The $9.98 E.P. Garage Days Re-Revisited
(Elektra, 1987)
1. Helpless
2. The Small Hours
3. The Wait
4. Crash Course in Brain Surgery
5. Last Caress/Green Hell

Videos/DVDs

Cliff 'Em All
(Elektra, 1987)
A home video–type affair released as a tribute to the late, great Cliff Burton. Includes some stunning bootleg performance footage that proves just how lethal the band was live in the mid-1980s with the inimitable Mr. Burton on bass.

2 of One
(Elektra, 1989)
To celebrate the success of Metallica's first-ever music video, both versions were released. It's available on VHS only, but it can also be found on *Metallica: the Videos 1989–2004*.

A Year and a Half in the Life of Metallica
(Elektra, 1992)
A fascinating glimpse into the world of Metallica. Part 1 shows the "black album" being meticulously recorded. Part 2 shows the band on the road, and includes their co-headlining US summer run with Guns N' Roses and their appearance at the Freddy Mercury tribute concert at Wembley Stadium in London, England. It's a must-have item for any serious fan of the band.

Cunning Stunts
(Elektra, 1998)
Two DVDs packed full of over 140 minutes of footage both onstage and offstage. Filmed at a two-night-stand in 1997 in Fort Worth, Texas.

S&M
(Elektra, 2000)
If you thought the *S&M* album was good, wait until you see the footage of Metallica playing toe-to-toe with the San Francisco Symphony Orchestra while acclaimed conductor Michael Kaman waves his baton, and the crowd at the otherwise-civilized Berkley Community Center goes nuts!

Some Kind of Monster
(Paramount, 2004)
A "warts and all" documentary filmed during the making of *St. Anger* from 2001 to 2003. "Compelling," "confusing," "heartwarming," "heartbreaking," and "delightful" are just a few of the words that critics and fans alike have used to describe this lengthy offering that digs deep. Kirk comes out of it looking like a champ, but this revealing exposé is definitely not for everyone.

Metallica: The Videos 1989–2004
(Warner Bros, 2006)
A compilation of every Metallica music video ever made—21 in all. It includes the 1989 release of *2 of One*, previously available only on VHS.

Metallica: Français Pour Une Nuit (i.e., French for One Night)
(101 Distribution, 2009)
This was recorded on July 7, 2009, at Arènes De Nîmes, the historic Roman amphitheatre in Nîmes, France—one of the most spectacular venues on the planet. Also, not only was it filmed in France, but every aspect of the project is French, all the way down to the credits. Featuring 18 classic Metallica tunes from old (e.g., "Seek & Destroy") to new (e.g., "All Nightmare Long"), this is a must have for diehard fans. As is . . .

Orgullo, Pasión y Gloria: Tres Noches en la Ciudad de México (i.e., Three Nights in Mexico City)
(Universal International, 2009)
This is comprised of 18 tracks culled from three World Magnetic Tour shows in Mexico City on June 4, 6, and 7, 2009. It was filmed by long-time collaborator Wayne Isham. The credits and liner notes are in Spanish. Unless you live in Latin America, this bad boy is hard to find, so click to *www.metallica.com* if you wanna buy a copy. I've seen it—it rocks!

Box Sets

Live Shit: Binge and Purge
(Elektra, 1993)
Expensive, but essential for any die-hard fan: three CDs & 2 DVDs (or 3 videos) featuring eight hours of music from seven shows.
- CDs: 23 songs from Mexico City, February 25th, 26th, and 27th, 1993.
- DVDs: San Diego, January 13th and 14th, 1992; plus Seattle, August 29th and 30th, 1989.

Honorable Mentions

There are a few compilation CDs lurking out there that contain Metallica material, but those aren't included here. A comprehensive listing can be found on the band's excellent site, *www.metallica.com*. Here are a couple of compilations well worth checking out, though.

Spawn: The Album
(Sony, 1997)
This techno-meets-rock movie soundtrack features a remix of "For Whom the Bell Tolls" by DJ Spooky, plus Kirk Hammett teaming up with Orbital on their song "Satan."

M:I-2 (Mission: Impossible 2 Soundtrack)
(Hollywood Records, 2000)
This Tom Cruise hit movie marks the first time Metallica wrote and contributed a song specifically for a soundtrack. The resulting "I Disappear" is definitely a highlight of this release.

APPENDIX II
THE USUAL STUFF ABOUT KIRK'S CO-AUTHOR, PLUS THE OBLIGATORY "SPECIAL THANKS" LIST

About Kirk's Co-Author, Nick Bowcott

Born and bred in good, ol' England, Nick Bowcott was the founder, guitarist, and riff writer of the 1980s cult heavy metal band, Grim Reaper. The band released three albums on RCA America—*See You in Hell* (1984), *Fear No Evil* (1985), and *Rock You to Hell* (1987)—all of which grazed the Top 100 of the *Billboard* Album Chart. The highpoint of Reaper's run was performing in front of 83,000 people at the 1985 Texxas Jam at the Cotton Bowl in Dallas.

By the time Reaper's reign came grinding to a premature halt, Bowcott had already established himself as a journalist specializing in "analyzing heavy metal/hard rock guitar playing." His popular monthly "Guitar Clinic" for *Circus* magazine clocked up a staggering 100 articles, and he also penned over 40 major pieces for the English monthly, *Guitarist*, including nine front-cover feature stories. In 1990, he joined the staff of *Guitar World*, principally doing "private lessons" with guitar heroes—a task he still carries out on a monthly basis with much enjoyment and pride. Nick has had major articles printed in several other publications including *RIP*, *Guitar*, and *Metal Hammer*. Add to that a six-hour teaching course for Hot Licks entitled *The Heavy Metalist*, and a Hal Leonard teaching video called *Crash Course in Brutality*. He also has two books out: *Hell Bent for Lead Licks: A Guitarist's Guide to Judas Priest*, and *Guitar World Presents Riffer Madness*, which he had the privilege and honor to co-author with the much-missed Dimebag Darrell.

In addition to his journalistic work, Nick has a "real job" working for Fender as Director of Artist Relations for Jackson, Charvel, EVH, SWR, and Gretsch. Prior to that, he worked for Korg USA as "Marshall Amplification's Man in America" for a staggering 17 years.

Kirk's co-author performing the solo in Pantera's "A New Level" at the 2008 Ozzfest in Dallas, Texas

At the time of this going to press, Nick was proud to rejoin his beloved Marshall Amplification as the Director of Marketing and Artist Relations of the newly-formed Marshall USA Division.

Special Thanks—The "I Owe You Big Time" Roll Call of Honor

First and foremost, the one and only John Stix of Cherry Lane who, with Job-like patience, stuck with me, kept smiling, and gave me numerous chances when others would've fired my sorry ass (trust me, dear reader, this book took me a long, looooooooong time) and ran for the hills. John, you rule!

Susan Poliniak at Cherry Lane for a supervising the layout and proofing of this tome, being a superb audio-cop, and also putting up with countless emails and calls from me as we whipped this thing into shape! Susan—it was a pleasure. Thanks a million!

Brad Tolinski, Jeff Kitts, and Jimmy Brown at *Guitar World* for giving me the chance to work with Kirk on his column in the first place and sticking with me for 20 years and countin'. Gents (and, boy, am I using that term loosely!), I can't thank you enough.

Arlen Roth at Hot Licks for giving me the teaching course gig that ultimately got me my first writing gig, and Paul Gallotta at *Circus* magazine for giving me my first shot as a writer. Paul, if you read this—please get in touch!

Matt "LA" Masciandaro at ESP for the lefty axe Kirk used in all the pictures (and then flipped via Photoshop to appear righty!), and also for the other ESP Kirk Signature guitar photos used in the book.

Scott Uchida of Dunlop for the Signature Kirk Wah photo, and also for taking the amazing shot used on the front cover—nice one!

John Conley at Sam Ash for the killer deal on the BOSS BR-600 digital recorder used to do the disc. Also a big thank you to Shane Nicholas at Fender for lending me the prototype Mustang III combo used on all examples.

Zakk Harmon at Metallica HQ for being "the man."

Extra special thanks have to go to my unbelievably patient and understanding wife, Tara, and our four kids: Paige, Jarod, Aiden, and Amber—for putting up with me trashing the house for months on end while I wrote and researched this friggin' tome. Without you guys I'd be nothing, and I love you all to bits.

The ultimate thanks, however, have to go to the man who is the sole reason this book exists in the first place—the one and only Mr. Kirk Hammett! Hey, bro, sincere thanks for your talent, patience, enthusiasm, attention to detail, self-effacing humor, and dedication to making your column such an incredibly informative, popular, and long-running success. I sincerely hope that this book does you proud. I had a blast doing it, and I'm honored you consider me a friend!

GUITAR NOTATION LEGEND

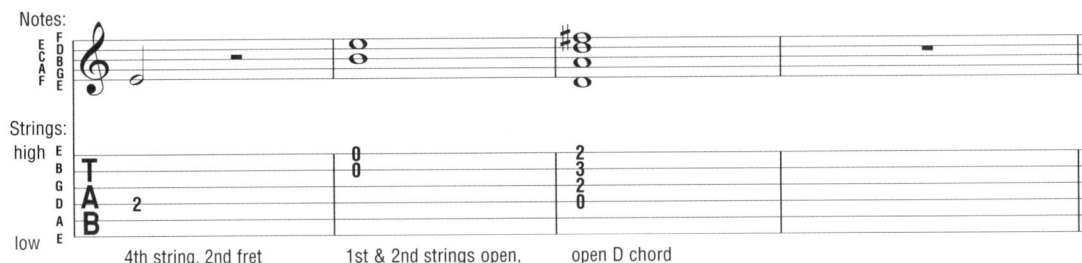

THE MUSICAL STAFF shows pitches and rhythms and is divided by bar lines into measures. Pitches are named after the first seven letters of the alphabet.

TABLATURE graphically represents the guitar fingerboard. Each horizontal line represents a string, and each number represents a fret.

HALF-STEP BEND: Strike the note and bend up 1/2 step.

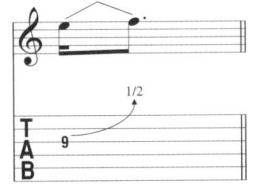

WHOLE-STEP BEND: Strike the note and bend up one step.

GRACE NOTE BEND: Strike the note and immediately bend up as indicated.

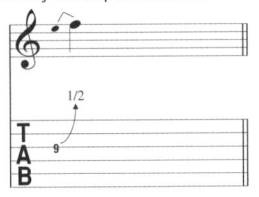

SLIGHT (MICROTONE) BEND: Strike the note and bend up 1/4 step.

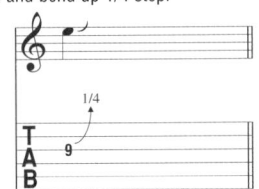

BEND AND RELEASE: Strike the note and bend up as indicated, then release back to the original note. Only the first note is struck.

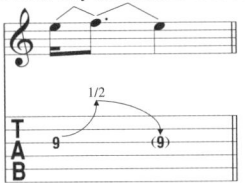

PRE-BEND: Bend the note as indicated, then strike it.

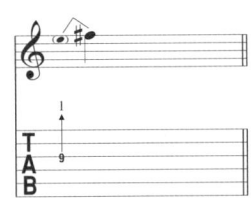

VIBRATO: The string is vibrated by rapidly bending and releasing the note with the fretting hand.

PALM MUTING: The note is partially muted by the pick hand lightly touching the string(s) just before the bridge.

HAMMER-ON: Strike the first (lower) note with one finger, then sound the higher note (on the same string) with another finger by fretting it without picking.

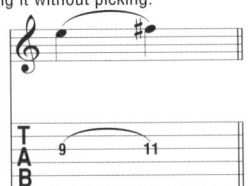

PULL-OFF: Place both fingers on the notes to be sounded. Strike the first note and without picking, pull the finger off to sound the second (lower) note.

LEGATO SLIDE: Strike the first note and then slide the same fret-hand finger up or down to the second note. The second note is not struck.

SHIFT SLIDE: Same as legato slide, except the second note is struck.

TRILL: Very rapidly alternate between the notes indicated by continuously hammering on and pulling off.

TAPPING: Hammer ("tap") the fret indicated with the pick-hand index or middle finger and pull off to the note fretted by the fret hand.

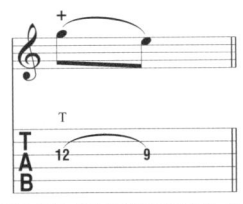

NATURAL HARMONIC: Strike the note while the fret-hand lightly touches the string directly over the fret indicated.

PINCH HARMONIC: The note is fretted normally and a harmonic is produced by adding the edge of the thumb or the tip of the index finger of the pick hand to the normal pick attack.

TREMOLO PICKING: The note is picked as rapidly and continuously as possible.

VIBRATO BAR DIVE AND RETURN: The pitch of the note or chord is dropped a specified number of steps (in rhythm), then returned to the original pitch.

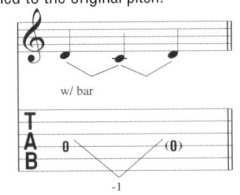

VIBRATO BAR SCOOP: Depress the bar just before striking the note, then quickly release the bar.

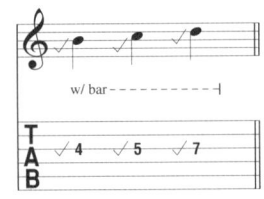

VIBRATO BAR DIP: Strike the note and then immediately drop a specified number of steps, then release back to the original pitch.

Additional Musical Definitions

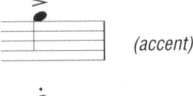 *(accent)* • Accentuate note (play it louder).

 *(staccato)* • Play the note short.

D.S. al Coda • Go back to the sign (𝄋), then play until the measure marked "***To Coda***," then skip to the section labelled "**Coda**."

D.C. al Fine • Go back to the beginning of the song and play until the measure marked "***Fine***" (end).

Fill • Label used to identify a brief melodic figure which is to be inserted into the arrangement.

N.C. • Harmony is implied.

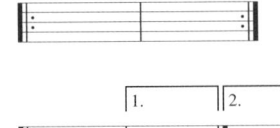 • Repeat measures between signs.

• When a repeated section has different endings, play the first ending only the first time and the second ending only the second time.

METALLICA

  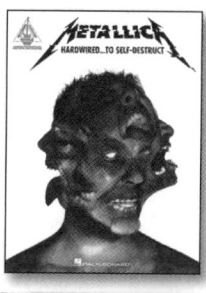

MATCHING FOLIOS

...AND JUSTICE FOR ALL
- 02506965 Play-It-Like-It-Is Guitar $22.99
- 02506982 Play-It-Like-It-Is Bass $19.95
- 02506856 Easy Guitar $14.99
- 02503504 Drums $19.99

DEATH MAGNETIC
- 02501267 Play-It-Like-It-Is Guitar $24.99
- 02501312 Play-It-Like-It-Is Bass $22.95
- 02501316 Easy Guitar $19.99

GARAGE INC.
- 02500076 Easy Guitar $14.95

HARDWIRED...TO SELF-DESTRUCT
- 00209876 Guitar Recorded Versions $22.99

KILL 'EM ALL
- 02507018 Play-It-Like-It-Is Guitar $19.99
- 02507039 Play-It-Like-It-Is Bass $19.99

LOAD
- 02501275 Play-It-Like-It-Is-Guitar $27.50

MASTER OF PUPPETS
- 02501220 Play-It-Like-It-Is Guitar $19.95
- 02501261 Play-It-Like-It-Is Bass $19.95
- 02503502 Drums $18.95

METALLICA
- 02501195 Play-It-Like-It-Is Guitar $22.99
- 02505911 Play-It-Like-It-Is Bass $19.99
- 02506869 Easy Guitar $15.99
- 02503509 Drums $19.99

RE-LOAD
- 02501297 Play-It-Like-It-Is Guitar $27.99

RIDE THE LIGHTNING
- 02507019 Play-It-Like-It-Is Guitar $22.99
- 02507040 Play-It-Like-It-Is Bass $19.99
- 02506861 Easy Guitar $15.99
- 02503507 Drums $17.95

S&M HIGHLIGHTS
- 02500279 Play-It-Like-It-Is Guitar $24.95

COLLECTIONS

BEST OF METALLICA
- 02500424 Transcribed Full Scores $24.95
- 02502204 P/V/G $19.99
- 02502449 Ukulele $16.99

METALLICA: CLASSIC SONGS
NOTE-FOR-NOTE TRANSCRIPTIONS WITH DVD
Book/DVD Packs
- 02501626 Guitar $19.99
- 02501627 Bass $19.99
- 02501625 Drum $19.99

5 OF THE BEST
- 02506210 Play-It-Like-It-Is Guitar – Vol. 1 .... $12.95
- 02506235 Play-It-Like-It-Is Guitar – Vol. 2 .... $12.95

LEGENDARY LICKS
AN INSIDE LOOK AT THE STYLES OF METALLICA
Book/Audio
- 02500181 Guitar 1983-1988 .... $22.99
- 02500182 Guitar 1988-1996 .... $22.95
- 02500180 Bass Legendary Licks $19.95
- 02500172 Drum Legendary Licks $19.95

LEGENDARY LICKS DVDS
A STEP-BY-STEP BREAKDOWN OF
METALLICA'S STYLES AND TECHNIQUES
- 02500479 Guitar $16.99

PLAY-ALONG
- 00234291 Guitar $19.99
- 00234292 Guitar $19.99
- 00234338 Bass $19.99
- 00234339 Bass $19.99
- 00234340 Drum $19.99
- 00234341 Drum $19.99
- 00242929 Violin $14.99

RIFF BY RIFF
- 02506313 Guitar $19.99

INSTRUCTION

METALLICA – EASY GUITAR WITH LESSONS
- 02506877 Volume 1 .... $15.99

LEARN TO PLAY WITH METALLICA
Book/CD Packs
- 02500138 Guitar Volume 1 .... $17.99
- 02500885 Guitar Volume 2 .... $17.99
- 02500886 Bass Volume 2 .... $15.95
- 02500190 Drums $14.99

PLAY LIKE METALLICA
THE ULTIMATE GUITAR LESSON
by Joe Charupakorn
Book/Online Audio
- 00248911 Guitar $24.99

REFERENCE

THE COMPLETE ILLUSTRATED HISTORY
by Martin Popoff
Voyageur Press
- 00122392 Hardcover $35.00

METALLICA – THE COMPLETE LYRICS – THIRD EDITION
- 00299371 Lyrics $12.99

7777 W. BLUEMOUND RD. P.O. BOX 13819 MILWAUKEE, WI 53213

www.halleonard.com

Prices, contents and availability subject to change without notice.

HAL•LEONARD GUITAR PLAY-ALONG

AUDIO ACCESS INCLUDED

This series will help you play your favorite songs quickly and easily. Just follow the tab and listen to the audio to the hear how the guitar should sound, and then play along using the separate backing tracks. Audio files also include software to slow down the tempo without changing pitch. The melody and lyrics are included in the book so that you can sing or simply follow along.

INCLUDES TAB

VOL. 1 – ROCK	00699570 / $16.99	VOL. 76 – COUNTRY HITS	00699884 / $16.99	VOL. 143 – SLASH	00702425 / $19.99
VOL. 2 – ACOUSTIC	00699569 / $16.99	VOL. 77 – BLUEGRASS	00699910 / $15.99	VOL. 144 – DJANGO REINHARDT	00702531 / $16.99
VOL. 3 – HARD ROCK	00699573 / $17.99	VOL. 78 – NIRVANA	00700132 / $16.99	VOL. 145 – DEF LEPPARD	00702532 / $17.99
VOL. 4 – POP/ROCK	00298615 / $16.99	VOL. 79 – NEIL YOUNG	00700133 / $24.99	VOL. 146 – ROBERT JOHNSON	00702533 / $16.99
VOL. 6 – '90S ROCK	00699572 / $16.99	VOL. 80 – ACOUSTIC ANTHOLOGY	00700175 / $19.95	VOL. 147 – SIMON & GARFUNKEL	14041591 / $16.99
VOL. 7 – BLUES	00699575 / $17.99	VOL. 81 – ROCK ANTHOLOGY	00700176 / $22.99	VOL. 148 – BOB DYLAN	14041592 / $16.99
VOL. 8 – ROCK	00699585 / $16.99	VOL. 82 – EASY SONGS	00700177 / $16.99	VOL. 149 – AC/DC HITS	14041593 / $17.99
VOL. 9 – EASY ACOUSTIC SONGS	00151708 / $16.99	VOL. 84 – STEELY DAN	00700200 / $17.99	VOL. 150 – ZAKK WYLDE	02501717 / $16.99
VOL. 10 – ACOUSTIC	00699586 / $16.95	VOL. 85 – THE POLICE	00700269 / $16.99	VOL. 151 – J.S. BACH	02501730 / $16.99
VOL. 13 – FOLK ROCK	00699581 / $16.99	VOL. 86 – BOSTON	00700465 / $16.99	VOL. 152 – JOE BONAMASSA	02501751 / $19.99
VOL. 14 – BLUES ROCK	00699582 / $16.99	VOL. 87 – ACOUSTIC WOMEN	00700763 / $14.99	VOL. 153 – RED HOT CHILI PEPPERS	00702990 / $19.99
VOL. 15 – R&B	00699583 / $16.99	VOL. 89 – REGGAE	00700468 / $15.99	VOL. 155 – ERIC CLAPTON – FROM THE ALBUM UNPLUGGED	00703085 / $16.99
VOL. 16 – JAZZ	00699584 / $15.95	VOL. 90 – CLASSICAL POP	00700469 / $14.99	VOL. 156 – SLAYER	00703770 / $17.99
VOL. 17 – COUNTRY	00699588 / $16.99	VOL. 91 – BLUES INSTRUMENTALS	00700505 / $17.99	VOL. 157 – FLEETWOOD MAC	00101382 / $16.99
VOL. 18 – ACOUSTIC ROCK	00699577 / $15.95	VOL. 92 – EARLY ROCK INSTRUMENTALS	00700506 / $15.99	VOL. 159 – WES MONTGOMERY	00102593 / $19.99
VOL. 20 – ROCKABILLY	00699580 / $16.99	VOL. 93 – ROCK INSTRUMENTALS	00700507 / $16.99	VOL. 160 – T-BONE WALKER	00102641 / $17.99
VOL. 21 – SANTANA	00174525 / $17.99	VOL. 94 – SLOW BLUES	00700508 / $16.99	VOL. 161 – THE EAGLES – ACOUSTIC	00102659 / $17.99
VOL. 22 – CHRISTMAS	00699600 / $15.99	VOL. 95 – BLUES CLASSICS	00700509 / $15.99	VOL. 162 – THE EAGLES HITS	00102667 / $17.99
VOL. 23 – SURF	00699635 / $15.99	VOL. 96 – BEST COUNTRY HITS	00211615 / $16.99	VOL. 163 – PANTERA	00103036 / $17.99
VOL. 24 – ERIC CLAPTON	00699649 / $17.99	VOL. 97 – CHRISTMAS CLASSICS	00236542 / $14.99	VOL. 164 – VAN HALEN 1986-1995	00110270 / $17.99
VOL. 25 – THE BEATLES	00198265 / $17.99	VOL. 99 – ZZ TOP	00700762 / $16.99	VOL. 165 – GREEN DAY	00210343 / $17.99
VOL. 26 – ELVIS PRESLEY	00699643 / $16.99	VOL. 100 – B.B. KING	00700466 / $16.99	VOL. 166 – MODERN BLUES	00700764 / $16.99
VOL. 27 – DAVID LEE ROTH	00699645 / $16.95	VOL. 101 – SONGS FOR BEGINNERS	00701917 / $14.99	VOL. 167 – DREAM THEATER	00111938 / $24.99
VOL. 28 – GREG KOCH	00699646 / $17.99	VOL. 102 – CLASSIC PUNK	00700769 / $14.99	VOL. 168 – KISS	00113421 / $17.99
VOL. 29 – BOB SEGER	00699647 / $16.99	VOL. 103 – SWITCHFOOT	00700773 / $16.99	VOL. 169 – TAYLOR SWIFT	00115982 / $16.99
VOL. 30 – KISS	00699644 / $16.99	VOL. 104 – DUANE ALLMAN	00700846 / $16.99	VOL. 170 – THREE DAYS GRACE	00117337 / $16.99
VOL. 32 – THE OFFSPRING	00699653 / $14.95	VOL. 105 – LATIN	00700939 / $16.99	VOL. 171 – JAMES BROWN	00117420 / $16.99
VOL. 33 – ACOUSTIC CLASSICS	00699656 / $17.99	VOL. 106 – WEEZER	00700958 / $14.99	VOL. 172 – THE DOOBIE BROTHERS	00119670 / $16.99
VOL. 34 – CLASSIC ROCK	00699658 / $17.99	VOL. 107 – CREAM	00701069 / $16.99	VOL. 173 – TRANS-SIBERIAN ORCHESTRA	00119907 / $19.99
VOL. 35 – HAIR METAL	00699660 / $17.99	VOL. 108 – THE WHO	00701053 / $16.99	VOL. 174 – SCORPIONS	00122119 / $16.99
VOL. 36 – SOUTHERN ROCK	00699661 / $17.99	VOL. 109 – STEVE MILLER	00701054 / $19.99	VOL. 175 – MICHAEL SCHENKER	00122127 / $17.99
VOL. 37 – ACOUSTIC UNPLUGGED	00699662 / $22.99	VOL. 110 – SLIDE GUITAR HITS	00701055 / $16.99	VOL. 176 – BLUES BREAKERS WITH JOHN MAYALL & ERIC CLAPTON	00122132 / $19.99
VOL. 38 – BLUES	00699663 / $16.95	VOL. 111 – JOHN MELLENCAMP	00701056 / $14.99	VOL. 177 – ALBERT KING	00123271 / $16.99
VOL. 39 – '80S METAL	00699664 / $16.99	VOL. 112 – QUEEN	00701052 / $16.99	VOL. 178 – JASON MRAZ	00124165 / $17.99
VOL. 40 – INCUBUS	00699668 / $17.95	VOL. 113 – JIM CROCE	00701058 / $17.99	VOL. 179 – RAMONES	00127073 / $16.99
VOL. 41 – ERIC CLAPTON	00699669 / $17.99	VOL. 114 – BON JOVI	00701060 / $16.99	VOL. 180 – BRUNO MARS	00129706 / $16.99
VOL. 42 – COVER BAND HITS	00211597 / $16.99	VOL. 115 – JOHNNY CASH	00701070 / $16.99	VOL. 181 – JACK JOHNSON	00129854 / $16.99
VOL. 43 – LYNYRD SKYNYRD	00699681 / $17.99	VOL. 116 – THE VENTURES	00701124 / $16.99	VOL. 182 – SOUNDGARDEN	00138161 / $17.99
VOL. 44 – JAZZ	00699689 / $16.99	VOL. 117 – BRAD PAISLEY	00701224 / $16.99	VOL. 183 – BUDDY GUY	00138240 / $17.99
VOL. 45 – TV THEMES	00699718 / $14.95	VOL. 118 – ERIC JOHNSON	00701353 / $16.99	VOL. 184 – KENNY WAYNE SHEPHERD	00138258 / $17.99
VOL. 46 – MAINSTREAM ROCK	00699722 / $16.95	VOL. 119 – AC/DC CLASSICS	00701356 / $17.99	VOL. 185 – JOE SATRIANI	00139457 / $17.99
VOL. 47 – HENDRIX SMASH HITS	00699723 / $19.99	VOL. 120 – PROGRESSIVE ROCK	00701457 / $14.99	VOL. 186 – GRATEFUL DEAD	00139459 / $17.99
VOL. 48 – AEROSMITH CLASSICS	00699724 / $17.99	VOL. 121 – U2	00701508 / $16.99	VOL. 187 – JOHN DENVER	00140839 / $17.99
VOL. 49 – STEVIE RAY VAUGHAN	00699725 / $17.99	VOL. 122 – CROSBY, STILLS & NASH	00701610 / $16.99	VOL. 188 – MÖTLEY CRUE	00141145 / $17.99
VOL. 50 – VAN HALEN 1978-1984	00110269 / $17.99	VOL. 123 – LENNON & MCCARTNEY ACOUSTIC	00701614 / $16.99	VOL. 189 – JOHN MAYER	00144350 / $17.99
VOL. 51 – ALTERNATIVE '90S	00699727 / $14.99	VOL. 125 – JEFF BECK	00701687 / $16.99	VOL. 190 – DEEP PURPLE	00146152 / $17.99
VOL. 52 – FUNK	00699728 / $15.99	VOL. 126 – BOB MARLEY	00701701 / $16.99	VOL. 191 – PINK FLOYD CLASSICS	00146164 / $17.99
VOL. 53 – DISCO	00699729 / $14.99	VOL. 127 – 1970S ROCK	00701739 / $16.99	VOL. 192 – JUDAS PRIEST	00151352 / $19.99
VOL. 54 – HEAVY METAL	00699730 / $16.99	VOL. 128 – 1960S ROCK	00701740 / $14.99	VOL. 193 – STEVE VAI	00156028 / $19.99
VOL. 55 – POP METAL	00699731 / $14.95	VOL. 129 – MEGADETH	00701741 / $17.99	VOL. 195 – METALLICA: 1983-1988	00234291 / $19.99
VOL. 56 – FOO FIGHTERS	00699749 / $17.99	VOL. 130 – IRON MAIDEN	00701742 / $17.99	VOL. 196 – METALLICA: 1991-2016	00234292 / $19.99
VOL. 59 – CHET ATKINS	00702347 / $16.99	VOL. 131 – 1990S ROCK	00701743 / $14.99		
VOL. 62 – CHRISTMAS CAROLS	00699798 / $12.95	VOL. 132 – COUNTRY ROCK	00701757 / $15.99		
VOL. 63 – CREEDENCE CLEARWATER REVIVAL	00699802 / $16.99	VOL. 133 – TAYLOR SWIFT	00701894 / $16.99		
VOL. 64 – THE ULTIMATE OZZY OSBOURNE	00699803 / $17.99	VOL. 134 – AVENGED SEVENFOLD	00701906 / $16.99		
VOL. 66 – THE ROLLING STONES	00699807 / $17.99	VOL. 135 – MINOR BLUES	00151350 / $17.99		
VOL. 67 – BLACK SABBATH	00699808 / $16.99	VOL. 136 – GUITAR THEMES	00701922 / $14.99		
VOL. 68 – PINK FLOYD – DARK SIDE OF THE MOON	00699809 / $16.99	VOL. 137 – IRISH TUNES	00701966 / $15.99		
VOL. 73 – BLUESY ROCK	00699829 / $16.99	VOL. 138 – BLUEGRASS CLASSICS	00701967 / $16.99		
VOL. 74 – SIMPLE STRUMMING SONGS	00151706 / $19.99	VOL. 139 – GARY MOORE	00702370 / $16.99		
VOL. 75 – TOM PETTY	00699882 / $16.99	VOL. 140 – MORE STEVIE RAY VAUGHAN	00702396 / $17.99		
		VOL. 141 – ACOUSTIC HITS	00702401 / $16.99		
		VOL. 142 – GEORGE HARRISON	00237697 / $17.99		

Prices, contents, and availability subject to change without notice.

Complete song lists available online.

www.halleonard.com

0719
173